No Parachute
Required

No Parachute Required

Translating Your Passion into a Paycheck—and a Career

Jeff Gunhus

New York

LIBRARY OF CONGRESS CATALOGING-IN-PUBLICATION DATA

Gunhus, Jeff
        No parachute required: translating your passion into
a paycheck—and a career / Jeff Gunhus. —1st ed.
        p.   cm.
        ISBN 0-7868-8551-3
        1. Job hunting—Handbooks, manuals, etc.   I. Title.
HF5382.7 .G86 2001
650.14—dc21   00-035060

Book design by Richard Oriolo

FIRST EDITION

10 9 8 7 6 5 4 3 2 1

For Nicole

Contents

Section Five:
Job Offers, Negotiation, and Other Fun

Section Six:
Unconventional Options

Acknowledgments

Jill Maverick, agent extraordinaire, a straight talker and a sharp mind. Your insights helped tremendously, your wit kept me amused, and your hard work made all this happen. Thank you. Thanks also to all the folks at Manus and Associates, especially Jillian Manus for first hearing me out at the San Diego Writer's Conference.

Diane Dunaway, for your class on getting published that started it all and for your hard work on the San Diego Writer's Conference each year. It is a must-attend event for every aspiring writer.

Jennifer Morgan, you made my first publishing experience something I would have never expected—painless. Your work on the book gave me several "why didn't I think of that" moments and improved the quality of the book tremendously. You have a true gift and passion for publishing. I was honored to work with you and all the other fine people at Hyperion. Thank you especially to Natalie Kaire, who brought this project through its last stages.

My business partners, Jason Reid, Spencer Pepe, Matthew Kennedy Stewart, and Tracy Meneses, who turned a blind eye to a slightly distracted first-time author and encouraged me each step of the way. I have learned more from each of you than I can express. Thank you for your friendship and your confidence.

There were people who helped me with drafts of the book and with some of the ideas found in it. Aunt Gloria, always an inspiration through your accomplishments and your dedication to family, thank you for your help with content and style. Joan Profant, thank you for your careful insights and quotes. They helped me overcome a tremendous hurdle in writing this book. Susan Block, one of the unwitting inspirations for this book, thank you for being one of the finest professors in my college career. Your end-of-the-year lecture on job-hunting influenced many parts of this book. Deborah J. McCoy, thank you for your honesty about the world of campus career centers. You cleared some misconceptions and represented your fellow directors well. Mrs. Harvey, Mr. McCauley, Mr. Phillips (grudgingly), Mrs. Hippie, and Professor Gordon, all teachers who encouraged and impacted my writing. Thank you Jeffrey Gitomer, Stacy Kravetz, Brian Krueger, Bruce Tulgan, Cynthia Kersey, Anthony Robbins, Meredith Bagby, Bill Shore, and Richard Nelson Bolles for teaching me so that I might teach others.

The content and themes of this book were made better by your insights.

Thanks to my friends who helped me through their encouragement, and sometimes simply through their presence—Jason Waybright (freedom dance), Mike Douty (shaved heads), and Jamie Speirs (ear falling off)—people who make me laugh and think the human race is worth saving. Thanks to my other partners, Michael Profant, Matt Landauer, Jim Bailey, all of whom share my passion for our business and for life.

Thanks also to the thousands of students who have completed our internship program. You are the heroes of this book because you not only had the passion for your future but you took the rare step of doing something about it. Whatever I was able to teach you, you taught me much, much more. Thank you.

Dad, you were always my hero as a child because that's how little boys always look at their dads. Now that I am a man and better understand who you are and what you have done for your family, you are more my hero than ever. Thank you for your love, your sacrifice, and for your example.

Mom, God ought to have provided you with a larger frame because the one you have can hardly contain the heart that He gave you. You are my model for so many things: optimism, sincerity, ambition, compassion, style, grace, love. I never knew your mother, but the person you are tells me about her every day. She would be proud, as I am.

Eric, given a choice to start from scratch and choose my own big brother, I'd choose you. Thanks for your lessons of courage, passion for your career, and creativity. And now you've made it to Broadway! I always believed that your passion would yield the excellence you worked so hard to achieve. Charles, you are a happy addition to our family. Thank you for keeping us all sane.

Grandpa Joe, you taught me humor, strength, and that with leadership comes great responsibility. Grandma Gwen, thank you for teaching me the art of the possible. You are an inspiring example of the result of passion converging with career. Grandpa Jim, I never knew you well, but still enough to know that you would wish me the best. Grandma Tuck, I still miss you terribly, but I know you probably have them in stitches in Heaven. Thank you for teaching me to laugh with life and not to take myself too seriously.

Joy, JR, and all my new family. Thank you for taking care of Nicole for me until I found her. Also, thanks for the words of encouragement throughout the writing of this book. They were much appreciated.

Nicole Gunhus. My favorite parts about myself are only there because of you. Thank you for your patience and understanding, your encouragement and your counsel. Thank you for kicking me out of bed at five each morning telling me to go write. You are a beautiful person, inside and out. I love you.

The end goal is not only to have a great career. It's to have a great life.

The young do not know
enough to be prudent,
and therefore they attempt the
impossible and achieve it
generation after generation.

—PEARL S. BUCK

No Parachute
Required

Section One:
How to Decide on a Direction

> **Universities are full of knowledge; the fresh-
> men bring a little in and the seniors take
> none away, and the knowledge accumulates.**
> —GLENN R. BERNHARDT

Neil Winters drives a taxi cab.

I realize this revelation probably has very limited shock value since you have never heard of Neil Winters, but trust me, it's big news.

Neil Winters was the guy in college every other guy wanted to be. He was a couple of years older than I and ruled the Santa Barbara social scene. Although not exactly a model student, he was always the life of the party, a big fraternity guy, incredibly popular with the ladies, and the absolute center of attention wherever he went. It seemed like Neil knew everyone and everyone knew Neil. Neil Winters, Master of the College Universe.

I only knew Neil as an acquaintance, so when he graduated I completely lost touch with him. I was sure he went on to great success because everyone knew he had "connections." His dad, Neil Winters Sr., was some kind of big businessman and had a handful of strings ready to be pulled to pave the way for his son's success. Neil made it a point to let everyone know he would be rolling in money right after graduation.

A couple of years later, at the beginning of my senior year, I went out for a night on the town with some friends. Several hours and more than a few adult beverages later, we decided to call a cab for the ride home. As we piled into the backseat of the taxi, I thought the driver looked vaguely familiar. You guessed it, an incredibly flustered Neil Winters slouched in front of the wheel.

I couldn't believe it! He was supposed to be a corporate raider, an investment banker, a lawyer, something . . . but a taxi driver? I mean, there's nothing wrong with driving a cab, but you have to admit that it's not exactly the pinnacle of achievement for a recent college grad.

As you can imagine, the conversation was a little uncomfortable. He explained how the job was just temporary until he found something else but that he had been making good money at it for the last six months. Six months! My jaw dropped again. We tried to make him feel comfortable, but the entire ride was awkward and weird. Even worse was the end of the ride . . . I mean, how much do you tip the guy?

That experience really put things into perspective for me. The fact that Neil Winters, a college graduate with formidable social skills, had been driving a cab for six months scared me. It made me realize that maybe this whole career thing wasn't as easy as I thought it would be. I never found out what chain of events put Neil behind the wheel, but that cab ride jump-started my prelife crisis and made me appreciate the urgency of developing a career strategy.

It is very possible that a story similar to the sad tale of Neil Winters scared you into getting some help. Your wake-up call might have been a recently graduated friend whose latest promotion was from busboy to waiter, or an older brother or sister who moved back in with your parents after graduation. Or maybe you *are* Neil Winters, or someone like him, and find yourself struggling in a dead-end job instead of pursuing a career you care about. Regardless of how you reached this point, the fact that this book is in your hands means your prelife crisis has officially started.

Welcome.

Whether you are in college, about to graduate, or already in the workforce, you are obviously concerned enough about your future to look for advice. You might not believe this, but the simple act of picking up this book has placed you in an elite group.

The prelife crisis can be an incredibly difficult time. It is full of uncertainty, inner conflicts, and difficult choices. Unfortunately, most people spend all of their energy stressing about their future instead of focusing on action that can create the future they want. They worry about it, talk about it, have anxiety attacks about it, but don't focus on how they can make themselves happy. You have decided to confront your prelife crisis head-on, and that puts you way ahead of the game.

It makes sense to do your soul-searching now, at the beginning of your career, and start on the right path the first time out of the gate. This will generate a positive life philosophy early on and enable you to build on your success and grow confident through your accomplishments. You have the energy and the spirit to do the work necessary to make the right decisions. You can always change direction, but if you choose a path based on your passions, you will always maintain your spirit to control and define your life.

You have worked hard to get to this point in your life, and now you deserve to get on to the good stuff.

The real world.

This is what you have been waiting for since you first started to dislike school. Remember all those early-morning classes when you first thought to yourself: *I can't wait until I get out of here and start making some money. I can't wait to get my own place. I can't wait to get out into the world and start living!*

Your twenty-some years on the planet have been spent in preparation for this one moment . . . your big debut into the real world. But now that the day is here, you might find yourself doing battle with a few unexpected emotions. The excitement is definitely there, but it's probably mixed with a little hesitation and uncertainty. As you gaze out expectantly over the void before you, the infinite choices and possibilities may fill you not only with excitement but also with an intense desire to crawl under a blanket and go back to bed.

Join the crowd.

The first thing you should know is that it is OK not to know exactly what you want to do. Contrary to popular belief (especially among parents), a diploma does not mean that you have all the answers. In fact, it usually means you have more questions. *What do I want to do with my life? What will make me happy? How do I get there?* The trick is not to ignore the questions but to examine them and use the answers to pick a course of action.

It is very easy to be lured into a false sense of confidence about your future. In a recent poll, 96 percent of twenty-somethings stated "I am very sure that one day I will get to where I want to be in life." As a college graduate, your optimism is likely even stronger, especially when you can pick up any major newspaper and read about the record lows in unemployment. You may not be sure of where you want to go, but you're probably sure you are going to get there. College is the infallible stepping-stone to success, so why worry, right? I hate to be the bearer of bad news, but while college is a great start, your work has just begun.

> *A college education isn't essential. Just being a graduate sometimes will do.*
> —GLENN R. BERNHARDT

Reality Check

For many in our parents' generation, a college degree meant instant success. Eager recruiters combed America's universities, and it seemed like college diplomas were handed out with job offers stapled to the back. Graduates signed up with a name-brand company, promised to serve their forty years, and planned to retire with a nice pension and the proverbial gold watch.

Times have changed.

In the words of Eric Michaels, 1997 graduate from California State University at Fullerton, "College just kind of happened. I chose a major for a reason I can't even remember, I had some fun, and then suddenly I found myself in a showdown with a diploma-wielding administrator who was telling me I was done. *Great!* I thought. *Now what?"*

"Now what?" is the plaintive cry heard across the country every spring as 1.2 million new college graduates prepare to enter the workforce. Everyone confronts the prelife crisis differently. Some choose quiet contemplation about their future, others hand-wringing angst, and some hate the decision so much that they simply decide not to make one. Unfortunately, instead of the big splash they hoped to make, most graduates create a dull, unpleasant *thud* when they make their career debut.

One year after graduation:

- **20 percent of recent college graduates have not found full-time employment.[1]**

- **50 percent hold a full-time job that they believe has no career potential.**

- **40 percent who hold a full-time job report that a college degree was *not* required to get their job.**

- **30 percent of people in their twenties live with their parents.[2]**

[1]U.S. Department of Education, *The Condition of Education*, 1997, Indicator 31.
[2]Margaret Hornblower, "Great Xpectations," *Time Magazine*, June 9, 1997.

These numbers are fairly depressing, but there is happier news. Graduates today face greater possibilities for personal success than any generation in history. The best economy in postwar America, one of the lowest unemployment rates on record, a technological revolution in the workplace and wide access to higher education have created incredible conditions for success. But, if things are so great, why are there college graduates restocking merchandise at the Gap?

The frustration people feel early in their careers is not due to a lack of opportunity. The dissatisfaction results from a lack of ability to identify and capture the *right* opportunity.

Here's the good part—it's not your fault.

The traditional career counseling that you have received since you could first say "I wanna be a . . ." has steered you in the wrong direction. Most career books, career counselors, and well-meaning parents give you career guidance based on which job areas are most in demand or which offer the highest salaries. These are terrible criteria on which to base your career choice!

Think about it. Just because there is a need for computer programmers shouldn't make it any more or less attractive to you as an option. It seems Orwellian to choose a career based on the "needs" of the economy. It's like Big Brother placed an order to the worker factory and you are the mass-merchandised product. As an economics major in college, I enjoy a nice labor supply-and-demand matrix as much as the next guy, but in a spate of economist blasphemy, I recommend that you ignore the market and pursue whatever your passion drives you toward.

Think of it this way. Traditional counseling asks you to choose a career based on what will be easiest to get and what will pay you the most money. It's like an arranged marriage where match is made for practical and economic reasons, but the two people really don't care for each other. While these marriages sometimes work out, they often result in unhappy, mismatched couples. If you choose a career path based completely on pay scale and job availability, it might all work out in the end, but there is a good chance that you will be mismatched in your career.

Also, the trendy careers of today could quickly fall out of fashion. You might think you are doing the smart thing by chasing after the fastest-growing career listed by some career magazine, only to find yourself in a shrinking field that you might not even like. It was only a few short years ago that manufacturing was a growth industry in America, and now it's a career graveyard.

Bottom line: The growth rates or the starting salaries of a particular career should have little bearing on your decision to enter it. This book will help you to choose a career path based on criteria that make sense, criteria that reflect your interests, skills, and priorities in life. It will guide you to discover your personal goals and give you concrete methods to achieve those goals.

The best way to avoid a midlife crisis in your future is to navigate the prelife crisis properly and to choose the right career from the start.

> *Do not allow yourself to be defined or confined by the choices you make. You always have options if you have the courage to act.*

Why Your Prelife Crisis Feels Like a Crisis

This is supposed to be one of the most exciting times of your life, so where did all of this stress come from? Actually, the pressure you feel is perfectly natural. In fact, it's a good sign because it shows that you care about your future. If you don't feel any pressure or stress, you might want to find some. People who end up "settling" for a dead-end job are often the same people who seem ambivalent and "above it all" during the prelife crisis. Don't get so uptight that you freeze in place, but be concerned enough to take the actions necessary to capture the future you deserve.

Here are the greatest stress centers during the prelife crisis. Once you identify these sources of stress in your life, you can minimize their negative impact and allow yourself to focus on the important decisions ahead of you.

■ **Expectations are high for you to be a "success."** Society puts an incredible premium on being "successful." Pressure from our parents and peers, not to mention from ourselves, can be relentless. Few people start their lives thinking *Now that I'm out of school, I can't wait to fail miserably*. The expectation is that you are going to be successful, and the pressure to perform can be intense.

■ **The choices you make can affect you for a lifetime.** Are you sick of people asking "What do you want to do with the rest of your life?" The prelife crisis can feel like this is the question you *have* to answer. While the decisions you make now will impact your life, *they will not condemn you to one path for the rest of your days*. You may decide to be an accountant but ultimately end up as a sports announcer. You can always change your direction.

■ **Parents apply a lot of pressure for you to make a decision.** After supporting you for twenty-some years, your parents are ready for some payoff. Their generation had very different attitudes about work than ours, and they can get impatient with all of this but-I-want-to-be-happy soul-searching. I own one of the largest student internship programs in the country, but it took my parents a few years to stop asking me when I was going to get a real job. Ultimately, most parents are just eager for their kids to have easier, better lives than they had. They are anxious to see you happy and successful. Just as important, parents have an unending need to brag about your accomplishments. They need some new material to give their friends, so the pressure is on for you to perform. Fast.

■ **You need to support yourself.** Unless you and your parents are comfortable with the terms "leech" and "slacker," you need to find a way to pay some bills.

If you are like the majority of people, these bills include car payments, insurance, rent, food, and very healthy credit card payments. The goal to find the "perfect job" can quickly be replaced with the more desperate goal to "find any job" once the bills start to pile up around the house. If you are in a job right now that you "settled for," you have an obligation to continue a serious career search until you find your passion. Don't wait until later; do it now.

- **You want to be happy.** This sounds like a good idea, but what makes you happy? You may already have friends in dead-end careers. Even though their jobs excited them at first, maybe because of the promise of money or prestige, they now find themselves part of the unhappy working masses. Every unhappy person you know started out with the intention to be happy, but each somehow lost his way. What are you prepared to do to avoid the same fate?

- **You don't want to make the "wrong" decision.** Somehow, the idea of making *the* right decision after graduation has taken root. This can be stressful because what if you really screw things up and make the wrong decision? Game over? Rest assured, there are many *right* decisions you can make about your future. Just make decisions based on your beliefs, your objectives, and your values, and pursue every course you take with passion and intensity. If you develop a pattern of excellence in your life, you will always have interesting opportunities to chase if you decide you need a change of direction.

- **You may have already made some "wrong" decisions.** The first few years in the job market will reveal a lot about your career choice. You might be in a career right now that you already know is the wrong direction. However, it is difficult to admit the mistake and change course, especially when your mom is so proud of your new job. Giving up on a career can feel like failure, but trust me, remaining trapped in the wrong career is a much worse fate. The right opportunity is out there. You just have to possess the courage to go find it. Remember, you only have one shot at enjoying life, so don't waste valuable time somewhere you're miserable. Find your passion and chase it!

If we are facing in the right direction, all we have to do is keep on walking.
—BUDDHIST PROVERB

Which Way Is the Right Way?

It's not difficult to figure out that you are not the first person to go through all of this soul-searching. It is a rite of passage that everyone passes through (albeit with varied levels of success). As with every rite of passage, certain clichés hover around just begging to be used. Here's one of my favorites:

The beginning of your career puts you in the middle of an enormous intersection. Radiating from this intersection are thousands of paths, each a different opportunity for your future. Some of these roads are smooth paved highways, others are overgrown dirt trails, but most are just normal roads. Very Robert Frost.

You turn in a circle and look down every road to try and see where it will to take you. But all the roads have an abrupt curve, making it impossible to see beyond the first bend. You can see where the road will start to take you, but the destination is out of sight.

You can choose any path you want. Nothing stands in your way and the power of personal choice is absolute. The problem is that each road seems to have fewer options branching off of it. Every time you choose a road, some of the paths seem to disappear. This can be a little disgruntling. Choose not to work for a great GPA in college, good-bye Ivy League graduate program. Choose a degree in business, good-bye medical school.

This fatalism can drive you crazy. What if you make the wrong choice? What if you would had been a great doctor, but you had a lousy biology teacher your freshman year so you decided to major in accounting instead? What if you miss out on what you were *meant* to do?

> **The world steps aside for those who know where they are going.**
> **—ANONYMOUS**

The Good News

The good news is that the options you face never really disappear. The road back to the intersection of options may be difficult once you travel for any distance, but the road is always there. You can be a sales executive for ten years and then go back to school and become a psychologist. You can go to medical school and eventually go into advertising.

The limiting factor that makes roads disappear is not the choices you make but rather how time changes your values and your priorities. While your options do not change, your willingness to take those options will definitely evolve. As you get older and more established in your life, you may find yourself less willing to take big chances. It sounds like a great adventure right now to go trekking in the Himalayas for a year, but try that idea on for size when you have two kids and a house payment.

You will find that the intersections you face have far fewer roads branching from them, but only because your priorities will change. You control your priorities and your values, so you control the options you face in your life and career.

Many self-help books agree on this point and emphasize that it is never too late to make radical personal changes. However, these books target people who are unhappy with their lives and where they have taken themselves. They need someone to show them how to change because they have lost the spirit to change themselves. Why wait until you have lost your way before you start actively looking for the right path?

> *Choose a job you love, and you will never have to work a day in your life.*
> —CONFUCIUS

Why Is a Career So Important Anyway?

We spend so much of our time working that we can't help but be influenced by our work in other aspects of our lives. It does not matter what you do. There is no inherent value assigned to one career versus another. Obviously, doctors are not better people than janitors simply because of their occupation. However, the character traits that you demonstrate in the pursuit of an occupation do have a value and a direct impact on your life.

A career represents a large part of the time you spend on the planet. It will strongly affect every aspect of your life. Express passion through your work, and life will be equally passionate. But spend a lifetime doing a mindless function that you hate, and the negativity from your job will eat away at the better parts of your life.

Every experience forms our character and our individuality. You decide the types of experiences and environments that will surround your career. More important, you control how you will react to these experiences. I have met doctors who respond to the enormous pressure and stress of their profession by becoming withdrawn and detached. Others use the intensity of their careers to drive them to be better doctors and to find ways to give back more to their patients, community, and family. You control your response to your environment.

Given that your career will be such a large part of your life, why choose anything except what intrigues and excites you? Why spend a lifetime doing something mundane in which you have only a passing interest? Why settle for mediocrity when you can choose to excel and innovate? Imagine fifty years from now looking back on a lifetime of effort in your job and not feeling proud or excited by your accomplishments. There is too much to get excited about in this world to allow you to accept an unexceptional career.

Consider the sheer volume of time you spend working on your career. Follow the math. Each week has 168 hours. The average person sleeps 8 hours a night. That is 56 hours a week, leaving a balance of 112 waking hours. Once you take out some of the daily routines of life (commuting, showers, brushing your teeth, laundry, etc.), you are left with approximately 98 hours. Career professionals work at least 45 hours a week, approximately one-half of the time they are awake each week!

One week	**= 168** HOURS
Average sleep per week (8 hours a night)	**= 56** HOURS
Average commute to work per week	**= 4** HOURS
Average time on routine (showers, brushing teeth, laundry)	**= 10** HOURS
Average work week for career professional	**= 45** HOURS
Free time left	**= 53** HOURS[1]

[1] *USA Today* reports that watching TV is by far the number-1 American pastime for this free time.

Over the next forty years, you will dedicate one-half of your conscious life to a career. Doesn't it seem insane that most people choose a career on little more than a whim? Take the time and spend the energy necessary to discover a field that excites and motivates you. There is nothing wrong with a simplistic job where you trade hours for a paycheck, but why not pursue high achievement? Why not do something exceptional that you will point to with pride because it represents your best effort and reflects your passion for life?

Why not make the term "my life's work" mean something?

Career satisfaction will improve every aspect of your life.

1. **Positive outlook.** If you are intellectually challenged and stimulated by your career, your outlook on life will be positive and optimistic.

2. **Character traits.** When you accomplish your goals through intense commitment and drive, you maintain those traits in other aspects of your life.

3. **Intensity.** People who are intense and passionate in their careers usually approach life with the same intensity. Life is best lived with vivid intensity.

4. **Confidence.** You create confidence through accomplishment.

5. **Integrity.** If you maintain a high sense of integrity in your career, your reputation will carry over into your personal relationships as well. When people know that your word is your bond, there is not much that you cannot achieve.

A man is what he thinks about all day long.
—RALPH WALDO EMERSON

Living for the Weekends

There are too many people who hate their jobs. Their stomachs turn at the thought of the 6 A.M. alarm, the slow, anguished walk to the shower, the commute through rush-hour traffic to get to an office where they pretend to look busy all day in front of other bleary-eyed people. Eight hours later, they face the same commute back through traffic, then flop on the couch to watch TV for a few hours or head to the local happy hour to whine about their boss with other people who hate their jobs.

What a way to live!

How can people be unhappy for half of their waking hours and expect to be happy during the other half? A bad career creates a bad personal life, no matter how well you can compartmentalize your emotions. Regardless of how hard you try, it is impossible to completely block out negative feelings from a job immediately after you get home.

We are given only so much time on this Earth, and

that time is too short to be unhappy. Spend your life in a career that creates a positive influence in your life, and that will carry over to success in other parts of your life as well.

Every day is a day spent living, or it's a day spent dying. Choose to live.

> **The sum of a man's toil is not what he gets for it, but what he becomes by it.**
> —ALEX RUTKIN

How Do You Define Success?

Webster's Collegiate Dictionary defines success as "the attainment of wealth, favor, or eminence."

My goal with this book is to give practical advice on just that, attaining wealth, favor, or eminence through the application of your skills and talents. The value attached to each of those goals varies dramatically depending on whom you ask. The challenge with any attempt to define success is that everyone is allowed to define it for him- or herself.

One of my favorite sayings is that success is a journey, not a destination. And as with most great truisms, we nod our heads knowingly when we hear it, but then promptly dismiss its message in our lives. Instead, we tend to think of success as an event.

"I'm going to be successful one day."

"Some day I'm going to make it."

It's hard to imagine the day that successful people "made it." They wake up one day, look in the mirror, do a double-take, and say "Wow, would you look at that! I'm a success!"

I don't think so.

The most successful people I know are the ones who possess a true love for their work and recognize the need for constant self-improvement. They know they are successful in their field, but it is a gradual realization. They constantly strive to grow into their successful roles and continue to seek ways to be better at their jobs, affect their community in a more positive way, and more devoutly commit themselves to their family, friends, and associates.

You have to decide on a definition of success for yourself. The challenge is to separate the messages society gives us about success and what success truly means to us. Society (or, more accurately, advertisers) says success equals a big house, expensive car, fame, and fortune. But it's amazing how many people have those things and are still miserable human beings.

If you can personally define success to reflect your values, priorities, and goals, you are halfway to achieving it. We are going to work on this definition together in the "Six Steps on Purpose" exercise in Chapter 3 and then give you the tools throughout this book to make it a reality. Remember, only you can choose your definition. Make it personal and make it a goal that makes you proud.

> *The definition of success has as many variations as it does people trying to achieve it.*

A Quick Word About Money

Let's be real. There is nothing wrong with wanting money. I am an entrepreneur. That makes me an old-fashioned, money-grubbing capitalist, and I'm proud of it. Money is a great motivator. It motivates me and it probably motivates you. In fact, money has motivated people (for better or worse) since the first conch shell was used as currency. However, money creates an interesting trap when you use it as the main criterion in your career search.

The more you chase money, the more elusive it becomes.

People who excel in our society are rewarded. Whether it is an innovator who brings a new product to the market, a doctor who pioneers a new surgery, or an athlete who is the best at his sport, excellence is rewarded, and the reward is often money. So, if you want money, the question that needs answering is not "How do I make money?" it's "How do I create excellence?"

Excellence comes from incredible determination and work ethic, and these both come from intense personal passion for what you are doing. If you pursue money only for the sake of money, you are running a race you can't win. You might be able to fake passion for a career in the short term, but you will burn out in the end. You might be able to make money in the short term by being unethical and unscrupulous, but your choices will come back to haunt you.

If your goal is to be wealthy, start by finding out what you are best at and most passionate about and make that the vehicle to acquire your wealth. Don't fall into the trap of trading joy in your life for the pursuit of money. It is easy for money to become a controlling desire. When that happens, people become very small and petty. Don't allow money to hold you back from your aspirations. If you want to get rich, why not get rich doing something you love? Whatever you choose, focus on excellence and you will receive the rewards you deserve.

*I get work satisfaction of three kinds. One is
creating something, one is being paid for it,
and one is the feeling that I haven't just been
sitting on my ass all afternoon.*

—WILLIAM F. BUCKLEY

What Will Make You Happy?

Happiness, at its simplest level, is getting what you want.
But determining what you want can be tricky.

What do you want from life?

Is it money? Challenge? Time with your family? Success for the people around you? Is it wealth or prestige that appeals to you? Which goal holds a higher priority for you?

The simplest answer is "all the above," and that is not a bad goal to have. But what will get you there?

These are not simple questions to answer. The inability to create a strong personal definition of success is one of the most frustrating parts of the prelife crisis. When I graduated, I knew there was *something* that was perfect for me. I could see a fuzzy outline, but I could not fill in the details. It drove me crazy.

We all have vague ideas about happiness and fulfillment, but we can't always put our finger on what it means to us personally. This indecisiveness about what we want from life can increase our sense of trepidation and personal frustration. We all know we want something, but what?

Trust me, you are not alone. Everyone goes through periods of self-doubt and dissatisfaction. Sometimes it's difficult to keep your eye on the prize because the definition of the prize changes as your priorities change. You might wake up one day and realize that all of your actions have been in the pursuit of a result that you don't even want anymore. You might be a fourth-year pre-med student who subconsciously knows that science is not your passion. Admitting that fact and changing your life in midstep takes incredible courage.

Even though it is difficult to change, the ability to do so is one of the greatest qualities we possess as human beings. In a split second, we can make a decision and take an action that completely shifts our behavior toward a entirely new objective. That power is exciting and our changing priorities make that power possible and necessary. Always remember that you retain the ability to change directions in life to capture your definition of personal success.

The definition of happiness is one of the most challenging issues in life. If there were some magical rite of passage, a moment when we suddenly hit ourselves on the side of the head and thought to ourselves, *Oh, that's what I want out of life*, then the term "midlife crisis" would not exist. No matter how much you prepare, life will always come up with the unexpected and the unannounced. However, if your sights are set on excellence and the pursuit of passion, you will always be well ahead of the game.

The best advice often comes from the unlikeliest of places. Not long after I decided to write this book, I met an older man during a layover in Denver. We started a conversation about the things travelers often talk about: our homes, our families, our eagerness to get back to each. He was a nice old man, with deep wrinkles, thin hair that barely covered his liver-spotted scalp, and a halting, trembling voice.

He was the first person I told about this book. I explained to him that I wanted to write a book that would help people choose the right path in life. I wanted to encourage them to pursue their passions and ignite their imaginations about the possibilities in front of them.

When I finished, he stared at me for a few seconds, shook his head, and stared at the floor. He didn't say a word. The silence stretched out between us, and I started to get uncomfortable. I thought that either I had offended him somehow or my book idea really stunk. Finally, he raised his eyes to meet mine and said, "Do you want some advice for those young people that has the benefit of a few years of experience?"

"Sure," I said. I took out a pad of paper and waited.

He gathered his thoughts, ran his tongue across the front of his teeth, and, with a strong and somehow younger voice, gave me some of the best advice I've ever heard.

- **Do what you love, otherwise you will have regret. Nothing is more distracting from the important things of life than regret.**

- **Happiness is the easiest thing in the world to find, because you create it with your own hands . . . and there it is. Don't look for happiness. *Make* happiness.**

I can't say it any better.

Where Do We Go from Here?

We're just getting started.

This book is designed to give you tangible, concrete results that you can use immediately in your career search. However, in order to get these tangible results, it's going to take some effort on your part. The next few chapters revolve around interactive exercises that will ask you to think seriously about your future and about your skills and interests.

Some of the worksheets are pretty intense and will require that you do some heavy-duty introspection. Others are more lighthearted and often will get you laughing at yourself. I can't stress how important it is to complete each of the worksheets in the book. Only by taking the time to work through them completely can you expect to get the best results from the information I provide.

In the pages ahead you will find out:

■ **How your parents' career experiences have impacted your career decisions more than you might think and what that means to your career decision now.**

■ **What outside influences have directed (often wrongly) your career choices.**

■ **How the careers you liked when you were a kid may point you to the adult career you'll love.**

■ **How the choices you have already made in your career may be completely at odds with the priorities you want to have in your life.**

■ **What unrealized strengths you possess that may dramatically change your intended career path.**

■ **How to define your career choice by the passion you have for the work involved and how to escape the traps that society has set for you.**

Each of these insights has the potential to fundamentally change both the direction and intent of your life. These are eye-opening results that come at a very cheap price. Think about it. If you spend a few hours working through some simple exercises, you *might* learn something about yourself that will completely alter your perspective and dramatically change the direction you take in your life. I say *might* because you *might* not learn a damn thing and reading this book might not impact your life whatsoever. I seriously doubt that would happen, but for the sake of argument, let's suppose that it does. What have you lost, a few hours? A few uncomfortable questions answered on some worksheets? That's nothing compared to the *possibility* that you will learn something significant that will completely change the way you approach your career.

So don't just use this book as a prop for when your parents visit your apartment. ("Yeah, I'm looking for a job. See, I even bought this book about careers and stuff.") Let's keep going and solve some of the problems you're facing right now.

> **The quality of a person's life is in direct proportion to their commitment to excellence, regardless of their chosen field of endeavor.**
> **—VINCE LOMBARDI**

The Last Word

- Everyone goes through a prelife crisis, a combination of excitement about the future, frustration from not having a clear direction to follow, and anxiety about making the wrong choices. It's normal. This book will help you solve the problems you are facing.

- Times have changed since your parents entered the workforce, and a college diploma no longer guarantees you a good job. For many careers, it has become a *minimum* qualification. To compete in the new job market, you need to know all of the new tricks of the trade.

- Choosing a career is one of the most important decisions you will make. Almost half of your waking hours between graduation and retirement will be spent at your job. Because it is so important, commit yourself to choosing a career on purpose and not just by default.

■ There are as many definitions of success as there are people trying to achieve it. The key to deciding on a future is to decide what will make you happy.

Two:
Big Lies and
Fat Uncles

Choose your rut carefully; you'll be in it for the next ten miles.
—NEW YORK ROAD SIGN

I heard a rumor once that work sucks.

Most people put work right up there with bee stings and Barry Manilow music as a form of cruel and unusual punishment. They can't stand their bosses, dislike their coworkers, are bored with their responsibilities, feel unappreciated or stifled by ridiculous rules and regulations. People spend the weekdays counting down to the weekend, only to spend the weekend dreading the start of the workweek. The twin sports of Monday-Hating and Bitching-About-The-Boss long ago replaced baseball as the national pastime.

If work is so bad, why do people subject themselves to it on such a regular basis? You know, free country and all.

The answer is rather simple. Most people have bought into the biggest myth of the workplace. It's a sneaky myth, so pervasive and widely accepted as a fact of life that at first it's hard to realize that it's just a monumental lie, a lie so large that I cleverly labeled it the Big Lie. Everyone has heard the Big Lie before, but someone in each family always takes on the responsibility to formally pass it down to the new generation. For some unknown reason, an overweight uncle with a comb-over is usually the designated delivery-man. After a few good hours of drinking, he'll corner you at your graduation party or some family get-together. The conversation will go something like this:

> "You got yourself a job yet, or are you still 'researching your opportunities'?" he says with two fat fingers in the air to emphasize the quotes and to make it clear that he thinks you're a pansy.

> "Yeah, Uncle Chuck. I'm researching away. I want to find something I really like."

> "*Like*? What's there to *like* about work? You damn fool, work is work! Why don't you come on down to the car lot tomorrow and I'll set you to work selling some Ford Contours."

> "Gee, let me think about it Uncle Chuck. I'll get back to you."

> With a grunt, Uncle Chuck stumbles away to get his fifty-fourth drink, mumbling the whole way "Want to *like* my job. . . . I'll get back to you. . . . Work is work. . . . What a pansy."

"Work is work." "It doesn't need to be fun or exciting, it has to pay the bills." "When are you going to get a *real* job that makes real money?" Sound vaguely familiar? The essence of the Big Lie is that the majority of your waking hours should be dedicated to getting a big paycheck and whether you enjoy yourself is inconsequential. Just get the money! The Big Lie has been around since the first factory jobs during the Industrial Revolution and is unfortunately still a major influence in the way we think of work.

Our attitudes about the purpose of work have a huge impact on our career search. It's easy to buy into the Big Lie because it makes it simple to choose a job. All you have to do is find out who is willing to buy your time for the most money and off you go. According to classical economic theory (I warned you earlier that I was an *economics major*), worker drones will always chase money. As wages rise in an industry, more workers will enter the industry to meet the demand. Economists call this "rational behavior," because what rational person would want to work with inner-city youth for almost no money when he or she could work in a coal mine for the big bucks? Hmmm. . . .

Employment models have become more sophisticated over time because it seems some people act "irrationally" and write novels or work with disadvantaged children rather than work in a coal mine, even if it means less money. Some people refuse to accept the Big Lie and view work as an opportunity to do more than just pay the bills. The downside to adopting this view is that your job search becomes more challenging as you have more criteria to meet. The upside is you might actually enjoy what you do for the next forty years.

Most of us fall in the middle between the pragmatic "get a job, any job, as long as it pays well," and the idealistic "I want to love what I do." The difference between the two extremes is only in the attitude about work, not about money. Idealists can be just as money-motivated as pragmatists, but they feel that they can achieve their financial goals *and* love their jobs. Pragmatists don't want to hate their careers, but they're willing to *tolerate* their jobs in exchange for the paycheck. They will accept a job they dislike because that was their expectation about work to begin with; to tolerate the weekdays, live for the weekends. Remember, work is work.

If we understand our own attitudes about work and where those attitudes come from, we can exert more control over our career decisions. For example, suppose you do the exercise in this chapter and realize that you are a pragmatist. You think all this pursue-your-passion stuff I've been talking about is interesting, but you're not sold on it. Continuing the exercise, you realize that your attitude about work is exactly the same as that of your parents but that you don't want the same career outcome they experienced. Being conscious of your attitudes toward work will give you a helpful perspective as you sort through your career decisions.

None are so blind as those who will not see.
—ANONYMOUS

What's with the Attitude?

The following exercise is designed to explore your attitudes about work and seek out their source. Typically, the greatest influences on our attitudes come from our parents. Like most lessons we picked up from our childhood, these were less from what our parents said to us in words than what they said to us in actions.

Throughout our childhood, we were constantly bombarded with messages about work and its role in life. It might have been as subtle as overhearing our dad complain about his boss, or our mom talking about how much she looks forward to the weekends because she dislikes her job so much. The messages may have been louder, like our dad being laid off from work or our mom running a successful business. The messages were constant for the first eighteen years of our lives, so we couldn't help but be affected by them.

I have always found it interesting that families often have different generations in the same occupations. One of my friends is the fourth generation in her family to be a lawyer. Another of my friends works in construction right beside his brother, Dad, and two uncles. It's not just coincidence that we gravitate toward our parents' occupations. After all, we are more familiar with these careers because of our parents' experience, and it often makes them proud when their child "follows in their footsteps." The problem is that sometimes the footsteps that we follow can lead us in the wrong direction.

It's important to learn from your parents' work experiences, but it is also important to gain some perspective and separate the good advice from the other stuff. Once you analyze your parents' work experiences, you might be surprised about the connections you can make to your current attitudes about work. Once you understand the source of your attitudes, it's easier to decide if you want to hold these beliefs or replace them with new attitudes based on your own life experiences.

Without courage, all other virtues lose meaning.
—WINSTON CHURCHILL

Regardless of what career path your parents followed, it likely had a tremendous impact on you. Before you decide to follow in their footsteps, either by choosing a similar career or by choosing one based on similar attitudes about work, let's take a look at some of the lessons to be learned from their experience.

1. Write a brief description of each parent's career path. Write it out chronologically, and separate the different phases they have gone through. (Phases include going into different industries, getting promoted to new responsibilities, or moving to a new area.)

2. What lesson do you feel can be taken from that experience? For example, if they switched careers, what did they learn that made them no longer want their former job? Try to encapsulate that lesson into one or two sentences.

3. Next, ask your parents what lessons they feel they learned from that experience. Keep in mind that their answers are not necessarily the right ones, just one more perspective to help you understand your own ideas.

Let me give you an example of how this works.

My career decisions have been strongly influenced by my father's career and the conflicting messages I saw there.

When I was born, he was in his early twenties and owned a chain of men's clothing stores. In a bold move, he left the clothing business and transported the family overseas to Athens, Greece, to start an import-export business.

Lesson #1: Take chances and follow your dreams. Owning your own business is the best path to take.

Three years and one worldwide recession later, the

business went under and Dad had to scramble. Times were tough for the Gunhus family. I was still young, so it didn't seem odd to me that sometimes we would only have potatoes for dinner. It wasn't until years later that I understood the potato feasts were because we couldn't afford anything else. Dad eventually took a construction job in Saudi Arabia while the family moved to Cyprus pending our visas. That took nearly two years, during which time I saw my dad about once every four months.

Lesson #2: Being an entrepreneur can turn into a disaster and put your back up against a wall.

Later, back in the United States, he tried several different sales jobs, then ended up back in the construction industry. As a superintendent for a large paving company, he worked seventy to ninety hours a week and commuted one and a half hours to work each way. He was well paid and was providing all the material things that we wanted, but he was missing out on the opportunity to participate in the family. The job wore on him as he became more stressed out, less energetic, and generally miserable. After a few years of this craziness, he decided he had to make a change.

Lesson #3: Pursuit of money and being a workaholic can throw your life out of balance and detract from the more important things in life.

He became a construction inspector for the City of Los Angeles, working forty hours a week in a job he loves. As an outlet for his entrepreneurial skills, he and my mother started a successful bed and breakfast, a business they love so much that they want to "retire" to run a larger B&B in a few years. Between his regular job and the B&B, he still works seventy hours a week, but you'll not meet a happier, more positive guy.

Lesson #4: Happiness comes from balance, enjoying how you spend your time, and the strength of the relationships with people you care about.

Once I wrote out this chronology, it was easy to see how my parents' experiences impacted my own decisions. I chose to become an entrepreneur, in spite of the message that lesson #2 seemed to be sending me. I discounted the message because of the power in lesson #4. My passion and what I saw as my opportunity to control the balance in my life was provided by the entrepreneurial life I intended to lead. If my parents had worked run-of-the-mill jobs while they raised me, it would have been difficult for me to break free of that pattern. I shudder to think of what it would have been like to slave away at a desk job in corporate America.

Also, your parents may surprise you when you ask for their interpretation of their career paths. For example, given my dad's story, it seems likely that he would have warned me away from entrepreneurship. However, both of my parents have been my greatest supporters and have always encouraged me to take great risks.

UNDER-THE-INFLUENCE EXERCISE

This exercise continues to examine the role our parents play in developing our attitudes about work. Once again, if you can identify the source of your work attitudes, you can be more objective in deciding if you want to allow those attitudes to define your career decisions. Take the time to complete each step and remember to write your answers down!

1. Read the sentence on each end of the 1 to 10 scale and choose which best describes your attitude about work. The scale indicates how strongly you feel about your answer. The closer you are to the either end of the scale, the more strongly you feel on the issue. For example, a 10 indicates you agree completely with the statement on the right, while a 1 indicates that you agree completely with the

statement on the left. Hint: Usually your first reaction to the question is the most accurate.

Work is . . . work. It doesn't need to be fun, it just needs to pay well.	1 2 3 4 5 6 7 8 9 10	Work is a chance for self-expression and needs to be fun and stimulating.
A paycheck rep-resents paying my bills and sur-viving.	1 2 3 4 5 6 7 8 9 10	A paycheck is a way to create choices on how I will spend my life.
The best way to choose a career is to pick one from a list of the fastest-growing professions.	1 2 3 4 5 6 7 8 9 10	The best way to choose a career is to follow my interests and passions.
I'm willing to take a job I dis-like to get a larg-er paycheck.	1 2 3 4 5 6 7 8 9 10	I'm willing to accept a smaller check for a job that I love.
A good job is one that's tolerable and enables me to pay my bills.	1 2 3 4 5 6 7 8 9 10	A good job is one that I will be intensely proud of when I retire.

2. Next, answer the questions for your parents, marking their answers with an O. Try to anticipate where they would score on each of the questions. If your parents would have dramatically different answers from one another, use a different letter for each and score them separately.

3. After you have guessed what their answers might be, give them a call and get the real answers. Mark down their answers with a P. Make sure that you explain the 1

to 10 scale to them and get numbers from them, not just an either/or answer.

4. Add up the totals for each time the questions were answered. For example, if you answered 7 for each question, your total would be 35.

	Totals
X (you)	_____
O (your guess for your parents)	_____
P (your parents' actual answers)	_____

The more I want to get something done, the less I call it work.

—RICHARD BACH

What It All Means

First, let's look at how you scored on the exercise.

0–15 points: You are a pragmatist in your attitude toward work. The focus of your career search will likely be on the compensation package offered and on your job location. You may try to find a job you enjoy, but you will likely tire of the search quickly and take the first reasonable offer you receive. I challenge you to look at the source of your attitudes and to reconsider. Life is awfully short to spend too much time doing something you are not passionate about. Why not work a little harder on your career search and find a way to achieve your financial goals and enjoy your career?

16–34 points: You are caught in the middle. The dividing line between idealists and pragmatics is 25 points, so anything less than 25 means you are slightly more pragmatic, while anything higher than 25 means that you are slightly more idealistic, but this area extends into each zone. You may have difficulty focusing on your career search and feel like it's hard to know where to start. Your conflicted attitudes toward the purpose of work can be confusing as you try to decide what outcome you want from your career search. Your search will be easier if you think through your attitudes about work and decide what purpose you want your career to serve. Once you decide on a direction, you will find it easier to evaluate your opportunities.

35-50 points: You are an idealist in your attitude toward work and it shows. The focus of your career search will be for long-term opportunities that appeal to your passion and interests. You are likely to do extensive research and take the job of finding a job seriously. Remember, just deciding that you want a career relating to your passions is not enough. Make certain that you do the work necessary to find the career that meets your goals, but be careful not to miss great opportunities because you're looking for perfection.

Refer to the key below to see how your parents scored. The interesting part of this exercise is to compare your attitudes with how you thought your parents would score and how they actually scored.

1. Parents scored very differently from you.

a. You're idealistic and they're pragmatic. This is the most common outcome. Our parents' and grandparents' generations were part of a very pragmatic job market that emphasized getting a good job with a good paycheck. This means that you can expect some pressure from them to choose a serious career, especially something in the "professions" (lawyer, doctor, etc.). Keep in mind whose life we're talking about here and stick to your guns. Keep your idealism and work hard to make it a reality.

b. You're pragmatic and they're idealistic. Although this is not a very common outcome, it can happen. Try to discern how you developed your attitude about work. Do your friends have similar attitudes? Other family members? Are you comfortable with this attitude and the implications for your career decisions? Once again, why not spend the extra time to find a way to reach your financial goals and find a career that stimulates you? Life is short. Use it well.

2. Parents scored similar to you.

a. Both idealistic. This is a helpful scenario. It can come about either by your parents really enjoying their careers and recommending that you find the same type of life for yourself or because they dislike their careers and are guiding you from a don't-do-it-this-way perspective. Either way, you can expect to get a lot of help and support in your career search.

b. Both pragmatic. This is the second most common outcome. Pragmatic parents are usually very vocal about their kids making pragmatic career choices. We are so used to following our parents' advice, we sometimes forget that we've grown up and can make our own decisions. If you find yourself with this outcome, I challenge you to rethink the issue and decide if your attitude is of your own making or a reaction to your pragmatic parents. Give the exercises in this book a chance to uncover the aspirations you have for your career and see if your attitude about work changes.

3. Parents scored differently from how you thought they would.

a. You guessed idealistic, they scored pragmatic. This is a rare outcome as we often associate our parents with practicality and tend to err in that direction. It sometimes occurs because parents often place security (regular paycheck) as their first wish for their children, even above happiness. To many parents, safe and unhappy is better than happy and in danger.

b. You guessed pragmatic, they scored idealistic. This happens often because we associate our parents with practicality, but they surprise us with the wisdom of experience. Sometimes parents have labored in a job they disliked not because they were pragmatists about work but because they were sacrificing so that you could pursue your dreams. If so, do the work necessary to make their sacrifice pay off.

4. Parents scored how you thought they would.

a. They were idealistic. You can count on them for support through the difficult decisions ahead. Don't overlook them as a source of good advice.

b. They were pragmatic. Pragmatic parents want the best for their children and they tend to be very outspoken in their advice. The fact that you scored them as pragmatists means that they may have already given you advice a time or two. If you are an idealist, things can get touchy as they are likely to be impatient with a long, drawn-out decision process or with what they perceive to be frivolous pursuits. Stand firm by your convictions and your passions. It will pay off.

*Too many people overvalue what they are not
and undervalue what they are.*

—MALCOLM FORBES

The New Attitude

The exercise you just completed outlined your attitudes about work and their origins. It focused on your parents because parents have a huge impact on our attitudes about work. Their influence on our career choices can be as straightforward as constant unsolicited advice or as subtle as our perception of their career satisfaction. As kids, we were incredibly observant of our parents and were acutely aware of any difficulties they had. Our parents' experiences and some fundamental shifts in the job market have had a direct impact on twenty-something attitudes toward work and careers.

1. **Downsizing.** My dad is a sharp guy with an incredible work ethic. As an entrepreneur who reentered the workforce, he always took ownership of the responsibilities he was given and rose quickly in management positions. So when my dad came home early from work one day to let us know that he had been "downsized," my world was rocked. I watched as he circled the want ads, dusted off a résumé that he hadn't looked at in years, all the while remaining the pillar of certainty in uncertain times.

   Nearly 75 percent of the generation now entering the workforce had a friend, neighbor, or family member who lost a job due to downsizing since 1980. Unlike past economic downturns when workers were rehired when the economy improved, only 20 percent of downsized workers were rehired by their former employers. The message was clear: Nothing is certain in the working world. Loyalty and doing your job well, even for a "good company," doesn't ensure that your job is going to be there forever.

2. **High divorce rates and working moms.** Twenty-somethings grew up at a time of skyrocketing divorce rates, single-parent families, and Mom going to work as an equally important breadwinner for the family. Many female Generation Xers watched their moms struggle to reenter the workforce after a divorce. Thanks to these two trends, we developed a fierce independence that we have taken with us into the workplace. This independent thinking makes us unlikely to "follow the company line," blend into corporate cultures, or blindly accept that the company we work for will take care of us. We're used to taking care of ourselves, and we continue to do so in the way that we manage our own careers.

3. **Fast-evolving technology.** Technology has changed the world at a furious pace over the last two decades. While Boomers struggle to keep up in the whirlwind, the younger generation is creating the energy that makes the whirlwind spin faster. We stand at the cutting edge and are taking advantage of the opportunities that technology has provided younger workers.

4. **The end of jobs.** Bruce Tulgan, in *Work This Way*, describes that linear jobs have ceased to exist. A new college graduate used to have a clearly defined career path: Get a job with a good company, be on time, do your job well, listen to your boss, and pretty soon you start to climb the ladder. First, you get a few small raises, a promotion, a title, maybe your own office, and then you ride the coattails of the supervi-

sor immediately above you. When she gets a promotion, you might get her job. Not a bad way to spend thirty or forty years. At the end of the road you get a little party, a gold watch, and a pension, and then you move to Florida, wear loud shirts, and play bogey golf.

The definition of labor has changed as much for corporate America as it has for its employees. Temporary employees, independent contractors, employee leasing, and consultants have become a large part of the hire-'em-as-you-need-'em philosophy in business. In this philosophy, people are hired to tackle a specific problem or work on a specific project and are employed only as long as that problem or project continues. Support jobs, such as secretaries and clerks, are evolving to encompass broader duties or are eliminated by outsourcing. Classic "entry-level" positions from which to start your climb to greatness are quickly disappearing. Think about it. Why hire a mail clerk when everything is e-mailed?

God sells us all things at the price of labor.
—LEONARDO DA VINCI

The Birth of the Career Free Agent

These changes in the job market, the Generation X sense of independence, and record low unemployment have combined to create a new animal: the career free agent. It's hard to use the term "free agent" and not launch into a sports analogy, so I won't even try to resist.

Owners of professional sports teams used to "own" the players who played for them. Players couldn't change teams or negotiate a better deal unless the team allowed them to leave. A great deal for the owners, not so good for the players. Enter free agency. Now players are under contract for a certain number of years but then are free to sell their services on the open market to whatever team is willing to pay the most money.

Once free agency was introduced, a few things happened. First, teams experienced a lot of turnover as players hopped from team to team as better opportunities became available. Where it once was common for a player to spend a whole career with one or two teams, players now make the rounds to as many as a dozen or more. Second, wages for athletes went up as teams chased after talent. Third, athletes' performances were even more important because a strong season meant more marketability as a free agent.

Career free agency has created the same effects. First, workers tend to jump from company to company as better opportunities arise. Second, wages for top talent have risen as more companies chase after the elite. And third, job performance and skill acquisition are more important than ever because the better you perform at your job, the more marketable you become in the open market.

How were free agents born? The trends just discussed created the right environment for a dramatic shift in twenty-something work attitudes.

Cause: Downsizing.

Effect: Free agents understand and accept that they are not entitled to a job and that no job is guaranteed to last forever. Circumstances beyond their control could result in their losing their job at any time. Therefore, free agents always prepare for that possibility by constantly upgrading their skills and marketability. They keep their ears open for new opportunities and are not afraid of change. Free agents will work hard for a company that challenges them and creates opportunities for self-improvement but will not hesitate to leave for greener pastures when the job becomes stale.

Cause: High divorce rates and working moms

Effect: Free agents have a strong sense of independence. This independent thinking makes them unwilling to trust a company to look out for their best interests. Free agents take an active role in managing their careers. Where an entry-level candidate of yesteryear may have felt secure that hard work alone would ensure advancement, today's free agents value networking opportunities, company training programs, and mentoring relationships in their career decisions.

Cause: Fast-evolving technology

Effect: Technology has broken down seniority/age barriers that governed the business world for decades. Enough twenty-two-year-old computer hacks revolutionized their employers' businesses that it has become common and acceptable for young workers to be given tremendous amounts of responsibility and autonomy. Technology has made expertise more important than seniority, a trend that favors more technologically astute twenty-somethings.

Cause: End of jobs

Effect: Free agents approach each job as a stepping-stone to the next opportunity. They are loyal bunch, but have to be shown there is a good reason to be so. Loyalty to a company just for the sake of loyalty is a foreign idea to them. (Downsizing showed corporate America's lack of loyalty to many of their parents, so it's poetic justice) They gauge their opportunities by whether it teaches them a new skill, makes them more marketable, and fits into their lifestyle decisions. They are happy to look for that next opportunity within the company they work for, but don't hesitate to look outside it for a better deal.

> **Success is to be measured not by wealth, power, or fame, but by the ratio between what a man is and what he might be.**
>
> **—H. G. WELLS**

Free Agency Causes a Stir

Free agency has given birth to a million marketing gurus. Every job hunter has become his own marketing director, wrapping himself in the best possible package and going to market to find the best opportunity. The best free agents are continually refining their product, acquiring more skills, pursuing more education, and gaining more experience. It all becomes part of the new package, and then it's off to market once again.

This process is causing quite a stir in the workplace. At first, companies loved it. Young, technologically advanced employees who were striving to acquire more skills and were intent on creating strong careers sounded like a pretty good deal. Sure, they might be a little headstrong and independent thinking, but that would fade away, right?

Slowly, companies started to realize that they had a problem. Independent, goal-oriented free agents are not willing to wait around in unchallenging or stuffy rule-bound environments. Employee retention has become one of the greatest challenges in corporate America as free agents career-hop their way to more interesting and rewarding opportunities. High turnover and the training costs incurred each time companies rehire for a position has forced them to adopt new practices to maximize employee retention. The result has been some interesting changes in the workplace.

- **Quality of life.** Free agents are picking and choosing their next opportunity based on more than salary. Twenty-somethings, perhaps in reaction to their parents' high divorce rates, are looking at quality of life as a key aspect of any career decision. Hiring managers say that new candidates regularly voice concerns over vacation time, family leave policies, and geographic location. One hiring manager said, "A great salary used to be enough to get a recent college grad excited. Now they want to make sure they will have enough time for their family. It's great, but it's a different kind of sell."

Lifestyle Changes in Corporate America

- **Flextime**
- **Digital commuting**
- **Day-care facilities**
- **In-house gyms and sports facilities**
- **Remote offices**
- **In-house massages**
- **Concierge service for key employees**

Companies are reacting to quality-of-life issues by introducing programs like flextime (workers decide when they want to work during the week), digital commuting, remote offices (eliminating tedious commutes), and even in-house massages during office hours. Others have changed geography to compete for talent. A brokerage firm in New York City recently attracted top-notch candidates due to its decision to relocate in a family-friendly suburb. Andersen Consulting, where 100-hour workweeks are not uncommon, now provides associates with a concierge service to water houseplants, do laundry, or take care of pets during business trips.

■ **Incentive pay.** Employers are taking lessons from the incentive pay programs made popular by start-up companies. Stock options, once reserved for the big fish in the corporate food chain, have become a popular part of compensation for all levels of employees. Small technology start-ups used stock options as a way to keep initial costs low. What better way to pay people when you don't have any money than give them a little stock of a company that isn't worth anything? However, if that company happens to be the next Microsoft, then the stock options are suddenly worth a ton of cash. Wedged between the options of being worth nothing and a ton of cash are years of employee loyalty. Larger companies such as Coca-Cola, Procter & Gamble, and The Home Depot use aggressive employee stock plans to retain their best people.

■ **Relaxed work environments.** The idea of a "professional environment" has changed dramatically since the Baby Boomers entered the workforce. Rigid, stuffy, and conservative have long been the stereotype of the professional office, but things have changed.

Litronic Inc, a computer security products company in California, has management sanctioned Nerf gun wars during lunch. Younger workers run through the halls shooting foam darts at each other. Their Boomer coworkers tolerate the game but seldom join in.

Oakley Inc., makers of designer sunglasses, installed a full-sized basketball court and fitness center in the middle of its office space. Long, intense basketball games at lunch let employees blow off steam and actually have fun while they're at work.

PricewaterhouseCoopers, the consulting company, recently redesigned its office space to resemble the open, democratized spaces found in most Silicon Valley start-ups. Good-bye, corner offices. Hello, Nerf gun wars.

The key to all of these changes is that it's become acceptable to have some fun while you're at work. Relaxed dress codes and relaxed codes of conduct in the workplace are chipping away at the Big Lie that work is tough and is meant to be endured, not enjoyed.

■ **Entrepreneurship.** The latest generation to hit the workforce is an extremely entrepreneurial group. By starting their own businesses, twenty-sometings have found an outlet for their sense of independence, unwillingness to rely on traditional career paths, and self-confidence in technology. Entrepreneurial ventures, especially in computer-related industries, has been a modern-day gold rush for young innovators. The rise of the dot.com (shorthand for Internet start-up) coupled with an overheated initial public offering (IPO) market has created a whole crop of young millionaires. A recent example: Todd Krizelman and Stephan Paternot started theglobe.com in their Cornell dorm room in 1994. Five years and a successful IPO later, the twenty-five-year-olds own stock worth $35 million each.

Small start-ups are drawing top talent away

from large corporations and making millionaires out of mid-level employees through stock options. Investment banking companies are hard-pressed to compete against start-ups that hold out the promise of a big payoff with a successful IPO. Top MBAs are heading West, ditching New York's prestigious institutions of higher earning in favor of the opportunity to strike it rich with a dot.com. In 1999, 20 percent of Harvard MBAs paid their own airfare to interview with Silicon Valley companies. The incredible Internet riches may fade when the market slows down, but the entrepreneurial fever will continue. Nothing quite matches our aggressive, "damn the torpedoes" personality as well as being able to write our own rules and redefine the workplace to our own liking.

The purpose you assign to work dramatically changes your expectations of what work will add to your life. The Big Lie says that work doesn't need to be fun or exciting, it just needs to give you security and pay the bills. If you enter the job market with that expectation, you probably will not be disappointed because a *job* is fairly easy to find. There are positions open in every city in America where you can trade long hours for a decent paycheck if you don't care what kind of work you do. On the other hand, if you enter the job market with the expectation that a career should be a valuable part of your life and should reflect your interests and passions, then you have your work cut out for you.

If you want to change, you're the one who has to change. It's as simple as that, isn't it?
—KATHERINE HEPBURN

The trends described in this chapter showcased the incredible opportunities available to our generation. These opportunities exist largely because of an unparalleled sense of security created by the sacrifices of earlier generations. World War II challenged our grandparents in ways we might never appreciate. Vietnam and communism were the battles fought during our parents' formative years. Our generation has never had to read a list of thousands killed in battle, grow a "victory garden," or practice duck-and-cover drills to prepare for a nuclear blast. Our monumental challenges are saving the salmon and controlling the size of our SUVs. I don't mean to make light of the serious problems that still exist in society, but our challenges are about improvement, not survival.

Twenty-somethings are blessed to live in a time of great stability and prosperity. Every generation goes through phases and we are just now entering the time when GenXers can start to impact society. The opportunities are absolutely amazing—almost as amazing as the scrutiny we receive from the Boomer generation that wonders out loud whether we can handle it.

This scrutiny has led to some unfair appraisals of the twenty-something generation. The national media assigned words like "slacker," and "apathetic" to a generation just coming into its own. Much of this judgment had to do more with the frustrations experienced by an aging Boomer generation than with an honest appraisal of the generation following it.

Boomer frustrations arise in many different areas. The promises and expectations of the revolutionary 1960s lost some of their edge when our activist parents traded in their protest signs for three-piece suits and wing-tip shoes. The first president from the Boomer generation yielded more scandal than social reform, and the generation that coined the phrase "midlife crisis" is starting to enter its fifties. (Be on the lookout for the term "midcentury crisis.") As the Boomer generation ages, there will be increased scrutiny of the younger generation and more negative labels assigned to the young no-goodnicks. The result of this aging Boomer population will be a reflective mood and increasing scrutiny on the younger generation rising behind them.

Twenty-somethings have responded to all the negative press highlighting their slacker ways by letting their actions do the talking. Amazing accomplishments and achievements have painted a very different picture of this generation's character and intentions. The GenX profile has changed dramatically. It has become less identified with the grunge-rock slacker and more with the e-commerce millionaire. People your age are doing amazing things all over the country. They're not waiting. They are taking advantage of the opportunities out there because they exist right now. Use their example to raise the expectations of what you can do in this lifetime and make your career a centerpiece to those expectations. The potential of passionate human spirit is a terrible thing to waste on mundane, routine tasks done in the name of being a good little worker. Think big and spend the next forty years in the pursuit of your passions, not in the pursuit of a paycheck.

The person who says it cannot be done should not interrupt the person doing it.
—CHINESE PROVERB

- The Big Lie is that work is work and it doesn't need to be interesting or fun. It just needs to put food on the table.

- Our attitudes about the purpose of work are often shaped by our parents' experiences in the workforce. These attitudes can have a strong impact on the career choices we make.

- Twenty-somethings have become career free agents in response to new trends in the workplace. Job seekers now must be more hands-on in managing their careers and more proactive in seeking out new opportunities. The concept of forty years of good service and a gold watch at retirement has become extinct.

- Free agency and a tight labor market have improved working conditions with major companies trying to attract top talent by promising a higher quality of life, incentive pay packages, and relaxed work environments.

- We live in a time of amazing stability and economic prosperity. There are incredible opportunities for high achievement and excellence for anyone with the courage to pursue them.

Three:
The Path Meant for You

This above all: to thine ownself be true.
—WILLIAM SHAKESPEARE

What I Want to Be When I Grow Up . . .
Now That I've Grown Up

Try to think how many times in your life people have asked you what you want to do when you grow up. That was the cool thing to ask when you were a kid, and back then you had great answers: fireman, astronaut, policeman, doctor.

Throughout elementary school and junior high you updated your answer. I used to change mine formally with my parents. "I have changed my mind. I'm not going to be a movie star, I'm going to be a football player." They would congratulate me on my decision and wish me luck in my new career.

Then the question lost its sex appeal during the high school years, replaced by the much more interesting topic of true sex appeal. Questions like *What are you doing this weekend?* seemed much more important than what you wanted from your life. Then college happened, a major was chosen for a reason long forgotten, and now school is over and you're out on your own. Where are the easy answers now?

Everyone confronts the question differently. Some choose quiet contemplation, others hand-wringing angst, and some hate the decision so much that they simply decide not to make one. The most hated group is the people who know exactly what they want to do. How dare they!

I have some bad news for you. I can't tell you what you should do with your future. I haven't a clue. How could I since we have never met before? It drives me crazy when I hear from students that they have received strong advice from a career counselor to go into a particular career. After a little probing, it usually turns out that the student and the counselor spent very little time discussing the student's aspirations and goals. Usually the advice is based on a casual interest the student wrote on a profile sheet or, worse, based on a list of the most popular careers that year.

Listen, it took me twenty-two years to figure out what I wanted to do for a career, and I knew myself pretty well! Do not be lured in by easy advice from someone who barely knows you. Sometimes it is easy to abdicate the responsibility of a decision to a "professional," but this is your *life* we are talking about. Step up to the plate and make some decisions.

> **I try to learn from the past, but I plan for the future by focusing exclusively on the present.**
> **—DONALD TRUMP**

The Path Meant for You

Imagine that you are arrested for a serious crime that you didn't commit. The trial is long and drawn out, but lacking an alibi, you are found guilty. The judge, sympathetic to your cause, decides to hand down an unusual punishment. You are sentenced to forty years of hard labor in a professional career, and the court will choose the career based on the needs of the economy.

This might not be so bad, right? There are some good jobs out there. It might even be something you like. In fact, you might be able to start from the bottom and work your way up the ladder to fame, glory, and a corner office. Then again, you might also end up on a horrible, dead-end job that you hate, trapped in a lifetime of meaningless and mundane labor. You pray for the best and throw yourself on the mercy of the court. Your fate is sealed.

Can you imagine this ever happening? No way! Talk about cruel and unusual punishment. The ACLU would be all over the place squawking about civil liberties. You would be off the hook faster that you could say "Who's paying for all these lawyers?"

But here's the crazy thing: People punish themselves this way all the time.

Careers are often chosen completely by chance. Jobs are taken because "It was advertised on campus" or "My parents said that it was a good job for me to pursue." Many times careers are chosen by following the path of least resistance rather than through objective criteria and personal passion.

Just remember, what is easy and what is good are often at odds with one another.

If you are going to spend half of your waking hours over the next forty years at your job, doesn't it seem like a good idea to spend a little time deciding on a direction? I'm all for spontaneity, but reserve it for something like an unscheduled trip to Hawaii, not for your career decision.

Don't rely on luck. Choose your career on purpose. Make decisions, not reactions. Put yourself on a road to a destination, not into a holding pattern until you find something that excites you. Have purpose in your actions, and then act on purpose.

> **Nothing is really work unless you would rather be doing something else.**
> —JAMES BARRIE

Take Six Steps on Purpose

This chapter is divided into six steps that try to help you in that decision. These six steps are the most important part of this book, so don't skip them. They will walk you through a decision-making process that can give you valuable insight into your future career. Simple questionnaires and exercises will challenge you to get specific with your goals, passions, interests, and values. While holding a mirror up to yourself can be an uncomfortable experience, it is always revealing. Here are the steps.

■ **Step One: Cleanse the palate.** We need to start clean. Clean of all preconceptions. Clean of outside influences. Clean of negativity. This section will spell out some of the most common mistakes made when choosing a career. Try to find yourself in the examples, and then remove yourself from the trap it describes with a simple decision to be open-minded throughout the rest of the exercises. Do not allow anything outside of your own will and determination define you or your options.

■ **Step Two: Find your passion.** Life is meant to be lived with passion. What are your greatest interests? What would make you happiest? What did you want to do as a kid? No limits, no boundaries. If you can dream it, you can achieve it. If you have trouble identifying your passions, the Dead-Uncle method will help to get the creative juices flowing.

■ **Step Three: Determine your skills.** What skills have you developed over the past twenty-some years? What unique traits do you have to help you pursue your passion? Do your skills point to a hidden passion you don't even realize? Don't buy into the false belief that there are "work" skills and "play" skills. Maybe your incredible snowboarding skills should shape you career decision.

■ **Step Four: Set your priorities.** What is most important to you? What trade-offs are you willing to accept in your life? How do you balance your different passions? Simple exercises give you the tools to help make these decisions.

■ **Step Five: Dream a destination.** What does all this soul-searching mean? What career will allow you to realize your passions? What will it look like when you get there? Where do you start? This is the most challenging step because it requires you to creatively mix all of the ingredients you have identified in the previous steps. Don't worry, it's easier than it sounds.

■ **Step Six: Have faith in DBA.** What the heck is DBA? Dream It, Believe It, Achieve It, a philosophy of accomplishment that will actually make sense. Give it a chance because it may very well change the way you look at every part of your life.

These steps will give you the opportunity to explore your goals, your ambitions, and your passions. Unfortunately it's not as easy as throwing a few variables into an equation, doing a few calculations, and wham, here's what you should do for a career. It's not $A+B+C =$ be an investment banker! Use these tools to bring out all the raw materials you need to make your career decision. You still have to put it all together and make the logical leap from the results to a career choice that will reflect your goals and passion. I can't do the work for you, but I have given you the tools to make the work easier.

> *Arriving at one goal is the starting point to another.*
> —JOHN DEWEY

My Request of You

Before we start on these steps together, I need to ask you for something I do not have the right to ask for. But I'll ask anyway.

I need your trust.

I need your trust that these exercises can dramatically impact your future. I need your trust when I tell you that looking through them and thinking of answers in your mind is not enough. *You have to write the answers down.* Unless you believe me, unless you take the uncomfortable step of actually working through this chapter seriously, you and I are wasting our time. We are not going to impact your future.

Think of it this way. If you spend the next few hours working through these exercises, the worst thing that can happen is that you waste a little time. But the best thing that can happen to you—the *best* thing—well, the best thing would be to someday look through what you write here during the next few hours and say to yourself, "I did it. I achieved my passion. I reached the destination that I truly wanted and the journey started that day when I took a few hours to clearly define my passions." Isn't it worth the chance?

Commit yourself before you start. Do every exercise and write for the amount of time specified. If you finish early, keep writing because your best ideas are the ones beneath the surface. Your first answer is often the answer that your friends and family would predict from you. The answers that come after are the ones no one would expect, maybe not even yourself. Write the entire time. No one else has to read it, so let it flow.

Finally, it's a good idea to do the exercises over a period of a few days and to do the exercises more than once. Your answers will be influenced by your attitude at the time you do the exercises. You might not list writing as a passion the day after you receive a D on a creative writing paper, but a month later you might be ready to become the next Stephen King. Also, if you try to blast your way through all the exercises at one sitting, likely the ones toward the end (the most important ones) will not get as much attention as they need. Judge your own attention span and do the exercises at your own pace. Of course, once you stop for the day, there's always the chance that procrastination will postpone your next session indefinitely. Hint: Pick a definite time the next day when you will resume the exercises and then stick to your schedule.

Thank you for your trust and thank you for your willingness to pursue your passion. Good luck.

STEP ONE:
CLEANSE THE PALATE

Each person's work is a portrait of himself.
—SAMUEL BUTLER

Before we talk about some ways to find answers to the now-that-I'm-grown-up question, I want to issue some warnings about the common traps people fall into when making career choices. This section is a cleansing of the palate, a removal of all the preconditions and prejudices from your mind before we work together on some real answers.

Really Bad (and Very Common) Ways to Choose Your Future

The Major Mistake

Somehow, somewhere, it became common knowledge that you *have* to get a job that is related to your major. As in "So you are a political science major. Where are you going to law school?" Or "You're an English major? What the hell can you do with that?"

I can't believe the number of people who actually buy into this nonsense.

Try to remember the amazing amount of contemplation that went into choosing your major. If you are like most people, the biggest influences in the decision were that:

1. You liked your high school teacher in that subject.

2. You had a friend who was in the major.

3. You heard it was easy.

4. Your parents suggested it.

5. You just picked one with the intention of changing it once you had more time to analyze your options.

These are *not* the best criteria for choosing a career.

I interview students all the time who are resigned to their major. My personal favorites are the accounting majors. At least a few times a week, I interview an accounting student where the conversation goes something like this.

"What do you want to do after you graduate?"

"I want to be an accountant at a major firm and then go back to get my MBA."

"Then what?"

Blank stare.

"Why do you want to be an accountant?"

In a resigned voice: "That was my major."

Since I do not interview people for accounting positions, they can be little more open about their feelings with me than they would with a recruiter from an accounting firm. A little bit of probing usually turns up that they chose accounting because it seemed practical (a parental word). They often confess they do not really enjoy accounting; some even admit they hate working with numbers! But they are still dead set on a career in accounting.

What else can they do? That was their major!

The following point may seem completely obvious to you, or this may be an incredibly enlightening moment.

You are not required to pursue a career related to your major.

Do not allow anything as simple as a decision you made when you were eighteen years old, probably for all the wrong reasons, determine the options you will pursue. While this point seems so basic, it is the most common mistake made by recent college graduates in their career choice. Only by doing what you love and are passionate about will you achieve success. Regardless of your major, leave everything open as an option.

> *We have to settle for the elegant goal of becoming ourselves.*
> —WILLIAM STRYON

The Parent Trap

Parents, by and large, are usually pretty decent people. There are exceptions, of course, but most parents want their children to be happy and successful. The friction comes because of those two words, "successful" and "happy."

Parents tend to want you to have the things that would have made *them* happy when they were your age or what would make them happy right now; these things include security, money, less stress, and the like. They want you to be successful based on their definition of success. They have the best intentions at heart, but they may not understand that you could be happier as an inner-city youth counselor with a $24K/year salary than you would be as an investment banker making $100K+.

The problem is that too many people end up as unhappy investment bankers instead of happy inner-city youth counselors.

Parents exercise an incredible amount of influence

over our lives, and rightly so. They have, after all, done some things for us along the way! However, there is a time when children need to take parental commands and accept them as parental advice, *advice that they may or may not follow.*

My company, National Services Group, is the largest management internship program in the country. We teach college students leadership and management skills by having them run a small business for the summer. We are one of the most competitive programs to get into, so every year I interview people who very badly want to do my program. They recognize that it will be challenging and difficult, but feel it will be essential for their career. I want to hire them. They want to work. Then they come back and say that their parents will not let them.

These people are twenty-one years old!

Remember, this is *your* life we are talking about. Respect your parents, but make your own decisions. You are part of a different generation, have different values, and need to find your own path. Be true to yourself by following your passions. You will make your parents happy because in the end you will have found success.

Everything keeps its best nature only by being put to its best use.
—PHILLIPS BROOKS

The I-Know-What-I-Want-to-Do trap

Some people have been on a career path since birth.

They have always known they wanted to be a doctor, they love science, they excel in school, they love medical school, they become a great doctor, they have an incredible career, they retire happy and without a regret in the world.

A truly charmed life.

If you are one of these people, you have the battle half won. However, make sure it is you talking. Too often, the "I have wanted to be a_____since I was a kid" statement comes from outside pressure rather than a true passion.

Some warning signs:

1. **Your parents are in the same field you want to be in.** There is nothing wrong with family tradition, but make certain that you are passionate about the field as well. Do not become a lawyer simply because you would be the fourth generation to do so in your family.

2. **Your parents talk about your career far more than you do.** Do not become an actor in someone else's script. Write your own plot.

3. **When you are nervous about telling your parents you might pursue a different field.** Alarms should go off at this point. Whose goals are you trying to reach? Where did this "calling" come from?

4. **Family and friends assume you will pursue a particular career, even though you seldom bring it up.** Friends can create as much pressure as family.

5. **You do not really know what your career entails, only that you have "always wanted to do it."** Ignorance is bliss, until you get your first job. If you do not really know what's involved in the career, you should question why you are so committed to it.

6. **You do not particularly enjoy the classes related to your "calling."** When you hate finance, accounting, economics, and management classes, you might want to reconsider that career in investment banking.

Even if every one of these points apply, you still might be on the right track with your career and your "calling" might be the right one. This list is only meant to make you pause on your career sprint to make certain that *you* made the decision.

Life is too short to invest your time heavily in something that you are ambivalent about.

> **Money is better than poverty, if only for financial reasons.**
> **—WOODY ALLEN**

The Money Trap

There is nothing wrong with wanting money, and lots of it. However, I meet a lot of people who are ready to choose a career based only on money.

Lawyers make a lot of money. I think I'll be a lawyer.

Never mind that you hate school, hate research, hate writing, hate public speaking, and do not like to be under pressure. Good lawyers make a lot of money, but you probably would not be one of them if you pursued a law career merely to chase money. While money can motivate you in the short term, only passion and genuine interest will make your truly brilliant in your career. Without these two things, you will burn out and be ineffective.

Money *does* motivate. It motivates me and it probably motivates you. Very few people are lining up to take a vow of poverty, but the singular pursuit of money will not lead to a successful career or happiness.

Money chases excellence and excellence comes from passion. You can fake passion and work hard for success in any field. But in the long run, you will lose the battle and you will burn out.

There exists a constant battle between the altruism of pursuing your dreams and the bothersome reality of paying your bills. Money is a very real consideration, but there are so many incredible opportunities open to you that you can afford to have more selective criteria than money alone. Pursue your goals, but pursue them with an intensity that will elevate you to the top of your field. Keep in mind that excellence is always rewarded and that money finds people who are the best at what they do.

Make this statement yours: "I get paid a lot of money to do something I love!"

> ### Great spirits have always encountered violent opposition from mediocre minds.
> **—ALBERT EINSTEIN**

The Stereotype Trap

Every job and every field is open to you. Do not allow a preconceived notion of a career limit you in any way. People will give you all kinds of unsolicited advice: "That is a male-dominated industry." "For a woman to succeed, she has to basically become a man." "You need to have an Ivy League degree to work there." "That company only hires athletes." Do *not* accept the advice.

Stereotypes are manufactured labels that serve as convenient excuses. Granted, in certain fields women and minorities are underrepresented and have a more difficult challenges to face. However, there are countless examples of people who overcome these obstacles to have brilliant careers in every field you can imagine. Do not restrict yourself. Give yourself credit for your strengths and pursue your interests despite the stereotypes that might hold you back.

If you have to support yourself, you had bloody well better find some way that is going to be interesting.

—KATHERINE HEPBURN

The Charmed-Life Trap

Some people have great success through school, and it seems like they never work at all. Their natural ability makes them successful in sports, they get great grades in school, and they are the life of the party in their social circle. Everything comes pretty easy to these people, and they lead their charmed lives.

I have known a number of these people and have seen this kind of ability become a trap. Several of my friends who lived the charmed life throughout college now have horrible, dead-end careers. (Remember good ol' Neil Winters?) They did not prepare themselves for graduation or for the job market and just assumed that everything would turn out right in the end. It always had.

If you have strong natural ability, do not allow yourself to become complacent. You have an obligation to refine and strengthen your ability. While you can "wing it" in school and do pretty well, the real world will not respond the same way. If you build a strong work ethic as the vehicle to drive your ability, you can continue to lead the charmed life.

In the middle of difficulty lies opportunity.

—ALBERT EINSTEIN

Make Yourself a Promise

There is a good chance that you recognized yourself in one of these traps. If so, just decide to remove yourself from the trap and let's move on. It really is that easy. Simply decide not to have your career dictated by your major, your parents, the pursuit of money, or whatever category you fall in. The next five steps are tremendously more effective once you clear your mind of these preconceptions.

Old habits die hard, so if you can't let go easily after all those years of conditioning, at least make a promise to yourself: Promise to at least suspend your preconditions long enough to complete the next five steps. Even if you think you know what you want to do, test yourself through this process. Keep an open mind about your future and find out if the six steps have anything to offer. You can always go back to the career path you have right now. I'm only asking for a two- to three-hour time investment that could change the direction you take in your life! Isn't it worth taking the chance that it has something to offer?

Have an open mind. Answer the questions honestly and completely **and write your answers down.** Don't fall into a career by chance or freak consequence. Live a life that you created. Do it on purpose.

STEP TWO:
DISCOVER YOUR PASSION

> *Is life not a thousand times too short for us to bore ourselves?*
> —FRIEDRICH NIETZCHE

The purpose of this exercise is not to find out what you might *want* to do with your future. It's to figure out what you are dying to do in your future. A true passion is something that burns in your chest every day and empowers you to endure even the most impossible conditions that lie in your way. A true passion catches in your throat when you talk about it. It stings your eyes when you think of your life without it.

But wait. If your passion is so powerful, so insistent, why do we even need an exercise to talk about it? It should be so obvious, right in your face every day, right? Unfortunately, we often bury our passions for one sad reason. We grow up. We stop thinking so irrationally about our future and start to confine our dreams to the neat little boxes supplied to us by society and by our circumstances. It is easier to let self-doubt and insecurity guide us toward safe actions than to take the bold path required of our passions. Sometimes our true passion gets buried so deeply in the name of "maturity" and "reality" that it takes a little work to find it again.

> **High aims form high characters, and great objectives bring out great minds.**
> **—ANONYMOUS**

The Dead-Uncle Method

Uncle Charlie is dead. You are sad to hear the news, but you know that he had a rich and full life. "No regrets!" was his favorite saying, and you're sure that old Uncle Charlie had none of his own.

You were always Uncle Charlie's favorite. He had spent long hours talking to you about the joys and beauty of life. Charlie had collected experiences the way other people collect stamps, and, like a stamp collector, Uncle Charlie liked to display the best parts of his collection. Hours and hours of stories over the years have left you in awe of the intensity and magnitude of Charlie's life. He was an exceptional person.

After the funeral, all of the family members gather in the study of Uncle Charlie's mansion. There is an enormous estate left behind, and Charlie has no direct heir. Some of the family sits casually, comforting each other. Others hover expectantly, overeager vultures ready to rush in and feed.

Uncle Charlie's lawyer, an ancient man in a three-piece suit, enters the room with the will. The moment of truth. The lawyer starts to list off the family members and the small sum of money that has been bequeathed to each. Everyone is accounted for except for you. Then it happens.

The rest of the inheritance, most of the estate, has been left to you! But the ever-tricky Uncle Charlie has one catch. In order for you to receive the inheritance, you are required to have a career. The will states that you can choose any career as long as you are applying yourself completely to it and that you love it. No other external factors exist . . . no family pressure, no peer pressure, no societal pressure. Just you, your inheritance, and your dream career.

Writing as quickly as possible, come up with five careers you would pursue. (5 minutes)

		Ranking	Rerank
1.	_____	_____	_____
2.	_____	_____	_____
3.	_____	_____	_____
4.	_____	_____	_____
5.	_____	_____	_____

Good. Now use the space at the end of each line to rank the careers 1 to 5 (1 being the career that excites you most). Starting with #1, answer the following questions for each answer. (Spend at least 15 minutes on your first two careers and 5 minutes on the others.)

1. Briefly describe what you imagine your life would be like if you had this career.

2. What is it about this career that appeals to you? Specifically, why would you be proud to do this career?

3. If you are not already pursuing this career, why not? What specific obstacles stand in your way?

4. How could you defeat the obstacles in your way?

5. Is pursuing what you love worth the work necessary to defeat these obstacles?

A few interesting things can happen when you answer these questions. Now that you have finished the exercise, let's work with your answers a little. These are philosophical issues we are talking about, but feel free to write down your thoughts to the next few questions in the margins next to your original answers.

1. Rerank the careers now that you have completely answered the questions. Does the ranking stay the same? Or do the rankings change once you spend time defining them more thoroughly? The perceived value of a career can change if you ask the right questions.

2. Do the obstacles you listed seem as significant once you write them down? Or do some of these "dream" careers seem more realistic now? If you can dream it, you can achieve it, so why let anything stand in your way? People achieve the impossible every day. Look at the obstacles in your way as opportunities to move a step closer to your goal.

3. If money or risk is the main deterrent, are you willing to let that stop you? Don't you think that it is worth the risk to capture your dream? Listen to me. You're young, you're full of ambition and energy. There will be no other point in your life where you will be better able to

accept risk and bounce back from possible setbacks. Risking it all when you are young is great because you usually don't have that much to lose and you have plenty of time to recover. When you are a little older and have responsibilities to your family and to your bills, your propensity to take the big risks will diminish. If you don't pursue your dreams now, you will always have to wonder "what if." If you pursue what you are passionate about, don't you think that the money will follow because of the excellence you will achieve? More important, don't you think that the happiness will follow, making the money seem inconsequential? Thirty years of joy as an underpaid schoolteacher beats a big house and nice cars after thirty years of hating your job as a financial analyst. Something to think about.

4. Is there a strong difference between this career list and the "realistic" career list you have been working with? If so, why? The end goal is to have a great life, not a great career. Success in a career that you are not passionate about will be an empty victory. Apply yourself to something you can succeed at and be proud of. Don't sacrifice your passion in the name of practicality. Make your uncle Charlie proud.

> *I'd rather be a failure at something I enjoy than a success at something I hate.*
> **—GEORGE BURNS**

The I-Wanna-Be-A   Method

The dictionary definition of the word "passion" is "the emotions as distinguished from reason." Given that, let's indulge in a little unreasonable thinking. The most unreasonable time of all is childhood. (Or is it the most reasonable?) Everything is possible, and every emotion we have is worn on our sleeve. These formative years strongly affect our attitudes and our perspective throughout our entire lives. All of those cute answers to "So, what do you want to be when you grow up?" can turn up some very interesting results.

Use the following worksheet to look back at some of your early career choices. There is often a lot of wisdom in those early decisions. Try to remember them all, no matter how silly they seem today. For example, I went through an archeology phase when I was ten. I read everything about Egypt, wrote letters to the *National Geographic*, even did my own "excavations" in my backyard. Even though I was a serious little archeologist at the time, I can look back now and clearly see the link between my "passion" and my favorite movie, *Raiders of the Lost Ark,* and my boyhood hero, Indiana Jones.

Archeology didn't hold my interest after I discovered that archeologists use more microscopes than bullwhips, but that "I'm gonna be Indiana Jones" phase still impacts my life. It made me pay attention to my early history classes, which in turn encouraged me to take history courses in college. Even now, I have a broad interest in world affairs and read history books for enjoyment. It's a stretch to say that it all comes from that movie, but it was definitely a starting point.

While these childhood goals can be insightful, don't read too much into them. I wanted to be a bus driver at one point because my bus driver was nice to me. That doesn't mean I have a buried passion for public transportation. Have fun with the exercise, but don't go overboard. Use this worksheet for each of the childhood careers that you can remember. If you have problems, give your parents a call because they probably remember the phases you went through better than you.

Childhood Dreams Worksheet

Complete entire sheet for each childhood dream you can remember.
Make additional copies of the sheet if needed.

Childhood Dream #1

I wanted to be a:

Age that I started to want the job:

Why it was cool:

Age that I stopped wanting to be it:

Why? Be specific.

Is this something you could be passionate about?

How can you involve it in your life or your career?

Childhood Dream #2

I wanted to be a:

Age that I started to want the job:

Why it was cool:

Age that I stopped wanting to be it:

Why? Be specific.

Is this something you could be passionate about?

How can you involve it in your life or your career?

Childhood Dream #3

I wanted to be a:

Age that I started to want the job:

Why it was cool:

Age that I stopped wanting to be it:

Why? Be specific.

Is this something you could be passionate about?

How can you involve it in your life or your career?

Once you complete the exercise, look for trends to develop.

■   Is there a common theme throughout the occupations you listed? For example, did all the jobs have a sense of adventure, revolve around helping others, or focus on money?

■   Is there an old occupation that you enjoyed thinking about, maybe because you haven't thought about it for a while? Did the reasons you don't want to do it any-more still make sense? Or are they merely obstacles you could overcome if you chose to?

■   Is there an old occupation that you felt embarrassed to put down because it was so "unreasonable"? If so, whose definition of "unreasonable" are you using? If it truly is off the wall, that's fine. But is there a message here? Could it still be incorporated into your life?

It's amazing how kidlike we all stay. We still want approval and acceptance from people around us. So much so that we might even be willing to pursue a career different from our true passions just to "fit in." Take a lesson from the younger you and look at the world with irrational and unre-alistic eyes. Sometimes that view can give you the courage to pursue your true goals in spite of doubt and uncertainty.

Theresa Newsome was born in 1931. As a child she loved dolls. She loved dolls so much that all she dreamed of was one day making dolls for a living. As she became older, dolls still excited her, but they did not excite her friends. After incessant teasing from her teenage friends and from her parents, she "grew up." Theresa put away her dolls and put her passion away with them. More than fifty years later, at the age of sixty-two, she opened a doll store in Westlake, California. She made dolls until she was sixty-six, when her eyesight failed. She told her friends that her four years making dolls were some of the happiest she had in her life.

The only tragedy in life is regret. Make a decision now to do what you love, and accept no obstacle in your path. Dedicate yourself to fulfilling your passion. It is the greatest gift you can give to yourself and to the world.

STEP THREE: BUILD ON YOUR SKILLS, INTERESTS, AND STRENGTHS

> *Follow your bliss. Find where it is and don't be afraid to follow it.*
>
> —JOSEPH CAMPBELL

Everyone would like to believe she has something unique and interesting to offer the world. You no doubt do. But what is it exactly? The following worksheet asks you to describe some of your strengths and weaknesses. It is important for you to be honest with yourself and to make an accurate assessment of your skills. You might be able to convince yourself that you have strong skills in a particular area, but if you really don't, the job market will point that fact out to you very quickly.

> *The secret of joy in work is contained in one word—excellence. To know how to do something well is to enjoy it.*
>
> —PEARL BUCK

Play Skills and Work Skills

When I do this skills exercise with students, they always list off their "serious" skills—accounting, spreadsheet manipulation, constructing web-based solutions, managing group dynamics, and the like.

My response is "Can you ski?"

This always brings a smile to whomever I'm talking to. For some reason, they weren't smiling when they were telling me about Microsoft Excel and programming in HTML. Why? Because we are trained to think of "work" skills and "play" skills. Work is . . . well, work. It's serious stuff. I don't know about you, but I would rather have a little fun.

When you consider the skills you want to incorporate into your career plan, remember that play skills are as important as work skills. Do you throw great parties? Maybe you should go into event planning. Are you a great skier who wants to go into marketing? Be a marketing analyst for a ski resort or a ski manufacturer. As you answer the questions in this step, don't forget about all of that fun stuff that you love to do. Usually the things you enjoy doing the most showcase your greatest interests and skills. These are central criteria to your career choice. Wouldn't it be great to get paid to do it for a living?

> **Discontent is the first step in the progress of a man or a nation.**
> —OSCAR WILDE

Questions, Questions, Questions

OK. Same deal. Commit yourself to writing down answers to these questions. Take the amount of time specified (or more) and be creative. It's hard to hold up a mirror and take a look at yourself, but remember your goal—to find a great career that will help you create a great life. Answering a few questions is a small price to pay!

Personal Assessment Worksheet

Tangible Skills

List every tangible skill you possess. These are physical skills that you can demonstrate, such as speaking Spanish, writing computer programs, balance a general ledger, or riding a horse. List them all. (5 minutes)

Intangible Skills

List every intangible skill you possess. These skills are character traits that you possess that are reflected through your actions. For example, are you a good listener? Highly organized? A leader? (5 minutes)

Interests

What interests you the most? The passions you listed in Step Two reflect some of your interests, but what else gets you excited? What subjects in school did you enjoy the most? What do you do in your spare time? What do you read about for fun? What part of the newspaper do you read first? What type of magazines do you buy? List everything that appeals to you. (5 minutes)

Likes

What types of situations do you enjoy? Do you like a fast-paced, intense environment, or something more laid back? Do you like change or consistency? Do you like being in charge? Working alone? If you had a day off work and no other plans, what would you do all day? List the things that you enjoy the most. (5 minutes)

Dislikes

Knowing what you don't like can be as instructive as what you like. What kind of environment would drive you crazy? What kind of people? What activities? Does sitting in front of a computer for hours make you a little nuts? Vent for 5 minutes.

Strengths That Others See in You

This exercise, which requires some feedback from friends and family, can be very surprising. Your friends and family may also point out strengths you have never considered. Sometimes we are insecure about how other people view us and reluctant to view our strengths for what they are. For example, you might hate public speaking and feel like a fool every time you have to talk in front of a group. During your feedback, you might find that all of your friends consider you to be a polished and articulate speaker. Take the praise and evaluate if you need to incorporate this strength into your career choice.

Write down the results from your feedback.

Weaknesses Others See in You

This is a much harder task than asking your friends about your strengths. Ask your family and friends to take this seriously and to help you identify your weaknesses. Promise that you will not argue with them or hold a grudge for anything they say. The minute you try to argue why their feedback is unfair or incorrect, they'll hold back on the rest of their input. The first time I asked my office staff for feedback, I was shocked to find out that every single one thought that I was an organizational nightmare. And I thought my organizational ability was one of my strengths! After their feedback, I realized that they were right, and I worked hard to improve in that area.

If everyone you know is too chicken to give it to you straight, go ask someone who doesn't like you. Ask an old boyfriend or girlfriend whom you dumped and watch the "constructive criticism" flow.

If you are not getting enough feedback, try using a few questions to prompt a response. "How do you think I react under authority?" "How do you feel I react under stress?" The point of this exercise is not to talk you out of doing something if everyone thinks you are terrible at it. But if you are serious about doing something and the people who know you best point out some important weaknesses, you need to take action to improve in that area.

Write down the results from your research.

Using Your Results

If you have done your job properly, there should be scribbles all over this book. The most important part was to write for as long as possible on each question. Some of your best answers will come out in the last thirty seconds of the five minutes. If you did not spend the full amount of time, I strongly recommend that you go back and do so. The results will be more effective if you do.

The last step is to figure out which part of all your scribblings is the most important. While it is important to surround ourselves with the things we like, avoid the things we don't, and utilize the skills we enjoy, some of these criteria are more useful than others. For example, I hate sitting in front of a computer screen but I love writing. So, guess where I am sitting right now while I write this sentence. Get the point?

To distill all of the information contained in your scribblings into something usable, now go through the exercises and select four keywords from each section or category. These four keywords are the four answers that are most important to you. A keyword can be either a phrase or a single word that conveys an idea. Start by choosing them instinctively, whatever you gravitate toward naturally. Then screen them again by thinking through them a little more thoroughly.

For example, suppose you instinctively circle *sports, football, basketball,* and *baseball* as your keywords under "Interests." Next, you have to decide whether they are equally important to you or if one stands out. Perhaps your interest is just in professional sports and you don't really care what the sport is; if so, your keyword would be "professional sports." Perhaps the other sports are interesting to you but you would do anything in the world to be around professional basketball; if so, obviously your keyword would be "basketball."

Go through all of your answers and decide on four keywords in each section. These are your power answers, the most essential components that you want to include in your life. (If there is a tie for fourth place, you can include a fifth item.)

The following worksheet, entitled "Power Answers," will be useful throughout your career search. It is a good reference tool to use when analyzing a possible career or a particular position. There are so many great opportunities out there that it is possible to include most of your criteria in your future career. Don't bang your head against a wall trying to tie together watching old movies, playing solitaire, and reading Agatha Christie novels into a career. Some of your interests are not going to be represented in your job, but if you use your power answers as a reference point, you have a better chance of creating the job you love.

Power Answers

Tangible Skills

1. _____   3. _____

2. _____   4. _____

Intangible Skills

1. _____   3. _____

2. _____   4. _____

Likes

1. _____   3. _____

2. _____   4. _____

Dislikes

1. _____   3. _____

2. _____   4. _____

Interests

1. _____   3. _____

2. _____   4. _____

Strengths Others See in You

1. _____   3. _____

2. _____   4. _____

Weaknesses to Work On

1. _____   3. _____

2. _____   4. _____

STEP FOUR:
DEFINE YOUR PRIORITIES

We either make ourselves miserable, or we make ourselves strong. The amount of work is the same.

—CARLOS CASTANEDA

Any decision about your future should hinge on your priorities. Although the questions in the following worksheet make you choose between two options, your life does not need to be so restrictive. For example, there is no reason why you can't have both a high income and a career that challenges you. However, priorities are best discovered when they are put in contrast to one another. Answer the questions as quickly as you can. Do not spend time analyzing what the trade-offs mean, but choose your answers based on your instinct. By doing so you will get a much clearer picture of your true priorities.

Instructions: Compare the priority in the left column with that in the right. If you had to decide to pursue one over the other, which would you choose? Mark the circle that is closest to your selection. Once you complete the exercise, count the number of marks you made in each vertical column and write that number in the box at the bottom of the page. Hint: Don't ponder your answers to these questions. Go with your first instinct of how you feel, not how you think you "should" answer.

Personal Priority Worksheet

	A	B	C	D	E	F	
High income	○	○					Challenge in career
Challenge in career		○	○				Respect from peers and prestige in career
Respect from peers and prestige in career			○	○			Time with family and friends
High income	○		○				Respect from peers and prestige in career
Respect from peers and prestige in career			○		○		Personal growth and learning
Personal growth and learning					○	○	Fun and recreation
High income	○			○			Time with family and friends
Respect from peers and prestige in career			○			○	Fun and recreation
Challenge in career		○		○			Personal growth and learning
High income	○					○	Fun and recreation
Time with family and friends				○		○	Fun and recreation
High income	○			○			Personal growth and learning
Challenge in career		○				○	Fun and recreation
Time with family and friends				○	○		Personal growth and learning
Challenge in career		○		○			Time with family and friends

TOTALS:

A B C D E F

The numbers at the base of each column represent the importance of that priority in your life. The higher the number, the less willing you will be to give it up for the other priorities on the list. Here is the key for the priorities you just worked with.

A. High income

B. Challenge in career

C. Respect from peers and prestige in career

D. Time with family and friends

E. Personal growth and learning

F. Fun and recreation

How did you do? Were there any surprises? Take a look at the numbers and ask yourself a few questions. Remember, change and positive development come through action, not quiet contemplation. If you are serious about making an impact on your future, take the time to write the answers down to these questions.

Personal Priority Analysis

1. What are my most important priorities? Why?

2. What are my least important priorities? Why?

3. Does my life currently reflect these priorities? How?

4. What will I do to ensure that these priorities are met?

Deciding on and sticking to your priorities are two of the most difficult parts of personal development. It is easier to choose priorities than it is to stick with them as you make your choices through life. The knowledge of what our priorities *should be* is useful, but that knowledge is useless if it is not followed with actions that demonstrate what our priorities *are*.

Also, remember that these priorities are not mutually exclusive. You have the power to have your life reflect every priority listed in the exercise. You do not have to decide between high achievement in your career and time with your family. The exercise points out where your priorities are to make you recognize the value you place on each area. They are presented as trade-offs, but do not accept them that way in your life. Pursue a balance that enables you to achieve all of your goals and priorities.

> *Life is either a daring adventure or it is nothing.*
> **—HELEN KELLER**

INDIVIDUAL PRIORITIES

Every individual has a different set of priorities to choose from in her life. The preceding exercise uses some of the most common trade-offs and decisions that have to be made at this point of the prelife crisis. However, you can make this exercise much more meaningful by creating your own chart.

Select and write down what you feel are six competing priorities in your life. Take some time with this because it can be very revealing. What trade-offs are you afraid to make in your life? What issues do you think you will face as you balance your career with the rest of your life?

A. _____   B. _____

C. _____   D. _____

E. _____   F. _____

Here are common priority issues that others have used:

Further education	Have children
Care for parents	Big house
Free time	Expensive lifestyle
Write a novel	Travel
Fame	Be a role model
Pursue a hobby	Get married
Compete in a sport	Be rich
Religious adherence	Financial security
Run for office	Impact community
Learn a certain skill	Be happy
Give to charity	Proud of occupation
Leave a legacy	Physical fitness

You should now have listed your six priorities. Each line has a letter, A to F, in front of it. Using the letter that corresponds to each priority, fill out the following worksheet writing the priority next to the letter in either the left or right column. When you get done, it should look like the exercise you just completed, but with your own priorities listed as the choices. Complete the exercise by checking off the box closest to the priority you choose on each line and then answer the questions at the end of the worksheet.

Personal Priority Worksheet—Part II

A. _____		B. _____
B. _____		C. _____
C. _____		D. _____
A. _____		C. _____
C. _____		E. _____
E. _____		F. _____
A. _____		D. _____
C. _____		F. _____
B. _____		E. _____
A. _____		F. _____
D. _____		F. _____
A. _____		E. _____
B. _____		F. _____
D. _____		E. _____
B. _____		D. _____

TOTALS:

A B C D E F

Use the same method as you did in the priority exercise earlier. Take the time to seriously consider the answers to these questions. Sometimes the "obvious answers" are what we feel is expected of us instead of what we believe. Spend at least five minutes on each question.

1.   *What are my most important priorities? Why?*

2.   *What are my least important priorities? Why?*

3.   *Does my life currently reflect these priorities? How?*

4.   *What will I do to ensure that these priorities are met?*

This tool will be useful as you move through your career and through your life. The priorities in this exercise will likely change over time and as the circumstances in your life change. For example, having kids and financial security seem more important after you find out that you are about to have twins.

I want to reemphasize that life is not an either/or proposition. This exercise uses that approach only to help discover priorities. In fact, a successful life balances different priorities and enables you to enjoy the best of several areas: great family life, successful career, financial security, world travel, whatever you choose. You can have all of those things. Just remember that you can't walk through life and expect to stumble across happiness and fulfillment. You live what you create, so create something spectacular!

STEP FIVE:
DREAM YOUR DESTINATION

> *If you cry "Forward," you must make plain in what direction to go.*
> —ANTON CHEKOV

The steps so far have given you tools to explore your passions, identify your skills, and prioritize the important issues in your life. The challenge is to blend the results from these exercises into a tangible career objective. As you can imagine, this is the tricky part.

No specific rules govern how to mix these three steps together to create a career goal. Doing so will vary dramatically depending on how extensively you answered the questions and how clearly defined your objectives have become since you started. You might find that the path is crystal clear. You have a strong idea what field you want to pursue, and these exercises have been an affirmation that you are indeed following your passion. Or you may be more confused than ever because the exercises shook up the way you thought of a career and changed your whole decision-making process. That's fine. Either way, the exercises in this step will help you to solidify your career ideas.

You have to use your creativity in this step. Open your mind to every possibility and commit yourself to exploring every option. You will be challenged to draw together all of the information you have created in the last three steps and put it together in the context of a future career. Read through all of your notes from the previous exercises before you start to remind yourself of your results and to pick out any recurring themes. Also, read Step One again to clear your mind of any preconceptions that could interfere with your conclusions.

Let me listen to me and not to them.
—GERTRUDE STEIN

Line Up the Ingredients
Before You Start Cooking

Imagine you are in an enormous kitchen and are about to prepare a meal. The kitchen is fully stocked. Every ingredient you could possibly want to use is available. Before you start cooking, you have to decide what you want to create. Are you going to fix a sandwich and some chips, or are you going for the five-course extravaganza? There are pros and cons to each. The sandwich is kind of plain and not very exciting, but it would be the easy way to go. The five-course meal sounds like a lot of work, but it would be a great dining experience. You get to decide how many ingredients will be used and the meal you eat will reflect your choices.

Steps Two to Four have shown the ingredients available to create your career choice. You can take your passions, skills, interests, and priorities and decide to be a janitor. Like a plain sandwich, it would be easy to do, but it may not be very fulfilling. Or you can choose to create a complicated blend of your ingredients and determine a career that will allow maximum use of your talents.

Let me give you an example. Keith Frye was an excellent intern in my program several years ago. After college, he bounced around a few different sales jobs, selling Internet advertising, human resource tools, and a few other things. Keith was an English major with a passion for literature, art history, and film, and his sales jobs satisfied none of his passions . . . but they paid the rent.

When I talked to Keith about his life goals, he was very dissatisfied with his progress since college. It was time for a change. We spent a few hours walking through the "Six Steps on Purpose" exercise and came up with some ideas for him to pursue. Three weeks later, he had quit his job and was transcribing a diary of a Civil War soldier that he had located through a historical society. He was excited and he loved what he was doing.

Problem. He wasn't making any money doing it. While money can't solely guide your career decisions, a paycheck helps if you are in the habit of eating. Keith worked on the book in the evenings and continued his job search until he found the perfect position. He is now the assistant to one of the most acclaimed art appraisers in the country who evaluates private art collections for film industry celebrities. Keith is learning the ropes, acquiring his appraiser's certification, and being trained to be the firm's specialist in appraising historical documents.

What a great job!

Keith translated three of his passions into a career that he loves: art, literature, and the film industry. It was not easy. He spent weeks looking for the right opportunity and trying to find a way to tie everything together. People can't believe how lucky Keith was to find an opportunity that reflected so many of his interests. Obviously, it wasn't luck but rather the result of a dedicated search with a specific goal in mind.

Use Step Five to create a destination that excites you. Don't allow yourself to settle for something because it is easy and uncomplicated. I know that peanut-butter-and-jelly sandwiches are good, but you'll get tired of them after a while. Be a gourmet. Challenge yourself to combine as many ingredients as possible to fix a masterpiece of a meal.

> **Some aspects of success seem rather silly as death approaches.**
> —DONALD MILLER

Dream a Destination

Use the ingredients you have listed to create the ideal job. Idealism is highly underrated. Dreaming about the perfect job can give you insights into your aspirations and goals when they are unfettered by bothersome reality. Make your destination a reflection of Steps Two to Four. Your ideal job can be concrete—"CEO of an education software company," or broad—"I want to impact people's lives in a positive way." Spend a creative ten minutes to create the future you want.

> **The method of the enterprising is to plan with audacity and execute with vigor.**
> —W. W. ZIEGE

The First Job Evaluation Method

It's interesting to evaluate something you do not yet have. Doing so is an effective tool for you to start painting the details of your future career position. This is not your destination job; it is the first step in your path to your destination job. Answer the following questions based on what you discovered in the previous exercises. Be creative and try to be as detailed as possible. Also, don't feel like you have to limit yourself to one job description. If you are undecided between several paths, this worksheet will be very effective in helping you to figure out which is best for your future. Sometimes your most dramatic insights about your future will come to you out of the blue when you least expect it. It's a good idea to create a notebook that contains all of your ideas and musings about your future career. When you meet interesting people, work hard to engage them in a conversation where you can learn as much as possible about their careers. Collect business cards like they're money and start a card file. A trick of the trade is to fill up the back of every business card that you file with as much information about the contact as possible. Your notebook and your file will become two great resources to keep track of all the information you acquire during your search.

First Job Evaluation

Job description:

What do I want to learn in the first two years?

What type of responsibilities do I want to have?

What kind of people do I want to meet?

What advancement opportunities are important to me?

What attracts me to this field?

Is this a field/industry that I can be passionate about? Why or why not?

How does this position fit into my overall goals for my career?

Is there another career I would rather pursue? If so, what is stopping me, and is it a good enough reason?

> **Our plans miscarry because they have no aim. When a man does not know what harbor he is making for, no wind is the right wind.**
> **—CHIEF SENECA**

The Write-Your-Own-Ad Method

Imagine that you are the recruiter responsible for filling the position you want. You have tried to source candidates from inside the company, professional contacts, and your friends, but nothing has worked. You have decided you need to place an ad in the newspaper. Write a descriptive ad for your position, leaving out any skills or background required by the candidate. Include:

- **List of responsibilities**
- **Work environment**
- **Geographic location**

- **Travel opportunities/requirements**
- **Opportunities for advancement**
- **Learning opportunities**
- **Salary range**
- **Benefits**

Remember, the position you describe should reflect your answers in all of the previous steps. Try to be as specific as possible, but generalities will do if you get stuck on the details. This exercise should condense the information that you wrote in the "First Job Evaluation" worksheet and give you a good model to work with in your job search.

Next, write an ad for the job you hope to have at the end of your career. Include all of the areas just listed. Again, try to be specific. If you are unsure of an area, try to be as descriptive as possible. Instead of "Run a division of Xerox," your general description might be "Be in a position to influence others and give them opportunity for achievement." Both are long-term goals, but the second leaves open the vehicle you intend to use to accomplish your goal. Describe the intangible parts of your future position. How will it make you feel? Why do you want to be in that position?

These two ads will flex your job-hunting muscles. If you spend enough time on writing them, you will have a very useful tool in your job search. The second ad gives you the ultimate goal to shoot for. As you move along in your career, remember the goals you listed in this exercise. Make decisions that move you closer toward that objective and strive to fulfill every part of the description you created.

Ad for your ideal first job

Ad for your ideal first job at the end of your career

Live your own life, for you will die your own death.

Die a Little

Combining your skills, passions, and priorities into a career choice is a challenging exercise. It requires creativity, patience, and the investment of a lot of time. However, the payoff is tremendous when you choose a destination for the right reasons and get your life off to a great start because of it.

This last exercise is designed to fine-tune the choices you made in the previous exercise and help you evaluate the destination you think you want to pursue. The exercise is fun, but in a macabre way. It asks the question that we young people hate to consider: "What if I died tomorrow?"

No warning, no long good-byes, you just die. Have you ever stopped to wonder what people would say at your funeral? It's hard even to imagine, but if you seriously take the time to figure out what people would say, you often find insights that can teach you how to live better. The overall message in this exercise is "Die a little . . . you'll live better."

At your funeral:

1. What would your friends say about your character?

2. *What would your family say about your commitment to them?*

3. *What would people list as your strongest character traits and accomplishments?*

4. *Complete this sentence and write a short speech you hope would be delivered at your funeral. "The person we honor today had an incredible impact on . . ."*

5. *Complete this sentence and write a short speech you hope would be delivered at your funeral. "The person we honor today lived life to its fullest. This is evident because . . ."*

Try this same exercise and write the speech at your funeral if you died five years from now, fifteen years from now, and fifty years from now. Where will your life take you and how will you affect your surroundings?

Don't forget to die a little every now and then. You'll live better.

STEP SIX:
HAVE FAITH IN DBA

> *Great minds have purposes; others have wishes.*
> —WASHINGTON IRVING

Whatever career you decide to pursue, start the chase. Soul-searching is not recognized as valid work experience on a résumé and employers will not be impressed with long "I'm finding myself" sabbaticals.

Right now, you face incredible opportunity. You have absolute control over the direction and intensity of your journey through life. There is so much to do, to experience, to feel. Don't hesitate. Explode into your life by choosing the most aggressive path to your future.

I know that "explode into your life" sounds like a high-minded platitude, but early on in this book I promised you that we would create a concrete plan for goal achievement, and that's exactly what this step will do. Over the last few years I have spent a lot of time interviewing and reading about successful people, covertly trying to steal their "secrets." Instead of secrets, I have found an excess of clear planning, hard work, and intense dedication to goals. (Surprise, surprise.)

There was a common theme behind all of the stories I read and conversations I had. Each of these individuals started his journey with a dream, had a constant and iron-clad belief in himself and the outcome he would produce, and then launched into goal-oriented action. The lessons I learned have been distilled into an achievement program called DBA: Dream It, Believe It, Achieve It.

Dream It

Aim at heaven and you get Earth thrown in; aim at Earth and you get neither.
—C. S. LEWIS

Dreams are wonderful. They have no limits, no boundaries. You can dream about anything. Unfortunately, many people dream less as they get older. They start to "mature" when they enter the real world and leave all of that foolish dream-stuff behind.

Remember when you used to dream about being president, traveling to the moon, starting a business, or joining the Peace Corps to save the world? Those were great dreams. Now, confronted with the daily grind of life, your dreams may have a more realistic slant. Instead of traveling to the moon, you would settle for a few days off work to travel to a local ski resort. Instead of wanting to be president, you would settle for being made shift supervisor at work. What happened?

Some argue that the naïve dreams of youth change because we acquire a better understanding of how the world works. How boring!

The greatest innovators in the history of humankind reached beyond the accepted "way the world works" and dared to dream unimagined possibilities. Creators, artists, leaders, great thinkers, and theorists are all united by a retained ability to dream outcomes that others could not. They are daring, bold, risky, and responsible for changing the world. Be a dreamer and you are in good company.

A dream is a completely intangible phenomenon. Something strangely terrific in the human mind enables us to create scenarios and outcomes completely beyond our immediate experience. I can dream about being a pioneer in science before I do anything significant in the field. Use this lack of limits to explore every possibility. Remove all inhibitions and let your mind wander into the impossible.

This step can be a very difficult one. Some people have been raised in an environment that constantly limits dreams instead of encouraging them. Without a supportive environment, it can be hard to consider high achievement as a possibility. But it can be done.

Veronica Sanchez came from a very traditional family. The role of women had been clearly dictated to her from a young age. According to her parents, high school was *OK* for women, but college was out of the question. Childbearing and running a household were expected to be Veronica's roles in life. This attitude was inconsistent with the dreams Veronica had for herself, but she was reminded daily that her place in life had already been chosen for her, "so she had better learn to accept it."

Veronica refused. During her senior year of high school, she forged her parents' signatures to apply to college and for financial aid. She was accepted at UCLA and received a complete financial aid package. After high school graduation, she attended UCLA and earned great grades. Fearful of her parents, she told them she was going to her department store job every day, when actually she was attending one of the premier universities in the country! Finally, she mustered the courage to tell her parents.

Instead of being proud of their daughter, they were furious. She was told to drop out immediately or she would be thrown out of the house. It didn't take Veronica long to decide. She moved into her own apartment that week. When I interviewed her for my company, she was in her third year at UCLA, still getting great grades, and still working two jobs to support herself.

Although she had accomplished so much, her confidence and her willingness to dream big were still hampered by all of the years of being told she could not have a successful career. She wanted to become an accountant. When I challenged her to think ten or fifteen years into the future, her goal was still to be a staff accountant. When I pressed her to see if she had ambitions for management or entrepreneurship, she replied with a nervous laugh, "I couldn't do that!"

Here was a bright woman who had demonstrated

more work ethic and drive than 99 percent of her peers, and still she doubted her ability to excel. Her upbringing had confined her and limited her so much that even dreaming about certain outcomes seemed impossible. By the end of our conversation, we were talking about possibilities she had never considered before and a future that energized her. She had the talent and the drive; all she needed was someone to tell her it was OK to dream big. I'm not sure what happened to Veronica (my internship didn't fit in with her schedule), but I pray that she is happy and fully in pursuit of her passions.

Veronica's story points out that dreaming is not always simple. It is important to remove all of the mental limitations that block the most creative dreams. You have to dream big to accomplish big things. Time is a fleeting thing. Use yours to achieve your dreams.

Believe It

> *Think you can, think you can't; either way, you'll be right.*
> —HENRY FORD

Creating the dream is just the first step. Unless you buy into it, unless you truly believe your dreams are attainable, they are likely to remain unfulfilled. Dreams put a name on your greatest potential, and it is a tragedy to waste that potential.

So how do you create a personal belief in your dreams?

First, it starts with a simple decision to start believing. Too simple? Well, true belief can be as simple as a decision.

Think of what the word "decision" means. It comes

from the Latin *decidere*, which means "to cut off." So, the root definition of the word "decide" is "to cut off all other options." Isn't that what true belief represents? Belief is the absolute rejection of any other alternatives. If you believe in God, you reject the possibility that God does not exist. If you truly believe in your dreams, you reject the possibility that you might not achieve them.

Before you become fully committed to your beliefs, you have to choose to be open to those beliefs. Once you decide—cut off all other options—to believe in your goals, you will open the door to true commitment to your dream.

Second, it's important that your mind can logically connect your dream to a plausible reality. What I mean is, if your dream is to sprout wings and fly, your mind knows that the dream is not plausible, so it will stand in the way of true belief. Once you decide on a dream destination, take steps to convince yourself logically that your goal is attainable.

Let me give you an example from when I was a kid. I remember when I was very young, standing by a stream. My friends and I wanted to get to the other side of the stream, but it was too far to jump. We soon found a tree trunk that was lying across the stream, creating a natural bridge. We were all excited to find a way across, but we were also scared to try it. What if we fell off? What if the tree broke? Oh, the horrors that would befall us in that swift-flowing three feet of water!

Finally, Kirk Patterson was brave enough to go first. He slid across the tree trunk on his butt, white-knuckling it the whole way across, but he made it to safety. One by one the older kids crossed the trunk, getting braver and braver each time. Tom Stevens even *walked* across! The younger kids, my group, were still hesitant, but we were starting to believe we could do it. Then, out of nowhere, little Chris Stevens walked across! Chris Stevens was a runt of a kid who was usually scared of everything—bugs, shadows, everything. Once he crossed the trunk, it was open season. Within a few days, that trunk was kid highway and no one thought twice about walking, running, or even skipping across it.

This little story says a lot about human behavior. When we faced the unknown, we were scared and unwilling to take a risk. A leader had to come out of the group to be the first to try it. Once the older kids had walked across the tree trunk, we younger kids figured that it was safe, but we weren't certain if we could do it. Our minds still weren't sure that it was plausible. *Sure, the trunk was safe, but maybe you needed to be an older kid to do it.* Once Chris Stevens went across, our minds had all the proof they needed and we knew that we could do it. This belief hadn't changed the size, length, or width of the tree trunk, but it sure made it easier to walk across.

Your mind demands the same proof of your dreams before it will allow you to become a true believer. Go out and show your brain example after example of people who have achieved the goal you have set for yourself. Interview people who have done what you want to do and find out what makes them special. You'll be surprised to find out that they are probably very much like you, only they are on the journey that you are deciding now whether to begin. Don't allow your mind to doubt that you can become a high-powered lawyer or a world-renowned artist. Prove to yourself that it has been done before, and your mind will allow you to truly believe in your goal. Watch the older kids cross the stream, get the confidence that it can be done, and then do it better.

All that stands between the graduate and the top of the ladder is the ladder.

—ANONYMOUS

Everyone has goals. Some people just seem better at achieving them. You probably have some pretty big goals for your life, both personal and career-related. They might be general, as in *I want to raise a family*, or specific, such as *I want to run a software business*. Either way, you undoubtedly hope for the best when you look ahead to your future.

Put it this way: I doubt you are walking around thinking "I can't wait until I graduate so I can go out and get a really dead-end job, have a horrible marriage, and be hopelessly depressed."

You stand at a definitive point in your life, and opportunities call to you from every direction. You should be full of incredible enthusiasm and optimism. This is your chance to capture the future you want for yourself.

The question is: *How serious are you about your goals?*

■   **Do they represent something far off, distant, even unattainable?**

■   **Or are you committed and driven enough to make them a reality?**

Life moves along so quickly and seamlessly that we forget to ask that simple question "How serious am I about realizing my dreams?"

Try this exercise. Imagine that I came to your campus, stood in front of the largest class, and said: "Raise your hand if you think you will be incredibly successful in the career you plan to enter."

Most likely, every hand in the room will go up.

Now imagine that we have a fifteen- or twenty-year reunion of that same class. I stand up and ask those who achieved the level of success in their career that they thought they would to come to the front of the room.

A few people would be able to come up, but not many.

So, what happened? What happened to all the great plans and aspirations? What happened to all the goals that people were so intent on? Everyone had the same opportunity, the same education, the same job market to enter.

Write down an answer to each of the following questions.

- **What was it about the people in the front of the room that made them different?**

- **What character traits do you think they possess?**

Now evaluate your personal goals by spending at least five minutes writing answers to these questions.

- **Have you made decisions that indicate that you are completely committed to your goals?**

- **Have you put off actions that could have helped you to reach your goals? What are they?**

- **Why did you put them off?**

- **What character traits would you demonstrate if you took these actions today?**

- **Is there anything out of your control that would prevent you from taking these actions?**

This last question is probably the most difficult. Everyone faces obstacles that have the potential to limit her success, but people respond to these obstacles in different ways.

The easiest thing to do is to allow these obstacles to camouflage a lack of determination. Excuses are infinitely less satisfying than achievement, but they certainly require a lot less effort. It is human nature to pursue the easiest and least painful path. Using an excuse is always easier than working for success.

> **The world stands aside to let anyone pass who knows where he is going.**
> —DAVID STAR JORDAN

Whining, Whimpering, and Other Bad Habits

1. **I don't have enough time.** Everyone is given the same number of hours each day, only some people accomplish more in that time than do others. Think of all the time in your day you waste on activities that do not add to your life. I'm not talking about time spent having fun with your friends, because that is one of the best parts of life. But what if you cut out things like watching TV and playing video games?

   People who have accomplished what they wanted to do with their lives had as much time as you do right now. Some had a lot less time (single mothers, people who paid for their own school) and much more difficult circumstances (overcoming a disability, coming from a disadvantaged background). These people were able to find time and get the success you say you want.

   You have time. You just have to choose to make the time for your future.

2. **I'm too young.** The following people were in their early twenties when they started their businesses; Bill

Gates, Microsoft; Jeff Bezos, Amazon.com; Sky Dayton, Earthlink. Alexander the Great conquered the known world by the time he was twenty-three. Joan of Ark led the French army against the English at the age of seventeen. Einstein wrote his theory of relativity at the age of twenty-six. The president of the Sierra Club is twenty-five. A seventeen-year-old in California recently sold his Internet business for $1.2 million.

Any questions?

3. **I'm not ready to get serious. I want to be a kid for a few more years.** Your success depends on only two things: skill and ambition. You can learn skills, but no one can teach you ambition and work ethic. That's something you need to bring to the table. Ambition tends to manifest itself early. If you think your ambition is sleeping until that magical day when you are suddenly "grown-up," you might find it hard to wake it up at all.

4. **My chances of success are so slight that I might as well not even try.** You are right in one respect. If you never try, you are guaranteed never to fail. If your primary goal is to protect yourself from disappointment, then you should stay in bed all day. Unfortunately, a one-in-a-million chance becomes a zero-in-a-million chance if you never get up and try for your goals. Why do we have the capacity to dream big things unless we were meant to achieve them?

Imagine a world where no one tried to accomplish the impossible. The greatest achievements in history were made against incredible odds. I'm not saying that you have to cure cancer in order to be a success, but do not allow yourself to be limited because society tells you that you probably will fail. The people who will doubt you the most are the people who lack the ambition to try the task you have set for yourself.

It is easy to sit back and comfortably predict failure. It is bravery to pursue something in spite of difficulty. If you fail, you will have the pride that at least you tried your best.

5. **But my parents want me to be a . . .** Give me a break! Start to live your own life. Trust me: If you do not do what your parents have always dreamed for you, they will recover. If you pursue a career you hate because of your parents, it might take you years to come to your senses. Don't waste the time. Take control of your future. You are the one who has to live in it every day.

6. **It's too late.** I love it when someone in his early twenties tells me that it's too late to change directions in his life. Think about it! For example, suppose you graduate with a degree in business and you desperately wish you had gone into medicine. You have two choices:

- **Pursue a nonmedical career and regret your decision for fifty years as you always wonder what it would have been like to be a doctor, or**

- **Go back to college for two years to complete the science requirements that would allow you to apply to medical school.**

I know, I know. Two whole years! How could you possibly spare the time?

You always have options open to you, and you can exercise those options at any time. Do not be held hostage by all the things in your life that can hold you back and limit you. It is never too late or too early for you to take action that will advance your life goals. Don't be afraid that you will "fall behind" if you take longer to finish school or to prepare for your career.

It is better to take the time to reach the right destination than it is to be the fastest person to get lost.

If it has been done before, it can be done again. If it has never been done, be the first to accomplish it.

Foolproof Goal Achievement

If you can work your way past these self-limiting and defeatist excuses, your chance to achieve your goals are much improved. There are a few things you can do to further increase your success of attaining your goals.

1. **Write down your goals.** Abstract ideas about your goals can pop up throughout the day, only to be swallowed up by the daily grind and forgotten forever. Take the time to make these goals concrete. Get specific. Pull out a huge piece of paper and write down your goals in big block letters. Write down a series of big goals, such as start a business before the age of twenty-five, buy a new car, and so on. Also write down smaller goals—anything that you want to accomplish or possess.

2. **Stare your goals in the face, literally.** Post your goals anywhere that you will be forced to see them every day. Stick a piece of paper on your bathroom mirror, on the visor in your car, or, my favorite, in the middle of your TV screen. Don't write your goals down and stuff them into a dark drawer. You'll never see them again!

3. **Get a taste for success.** Find out what it will feel like when you achieve your goals. If you want to be a

doctor, go spend a day with one. If you want a BMW, go take a test-drive. The more concrete your goals feel, the easier it will be to stay focused on them.

4. **Take small bites.** I encourage you to have big goals. Without big goals, you will never achieve big things. However, large goals can be discouraging if they seem too far away and too unattainable. Plan a strategy of smaller goals that will result in achieving your overall objective. This way you can see tangible results and measure your progress. As long as every day is a small progress toward your overall goal, you will achieve the end you want.

5. **Share your goals with people.** Some of us carry goals and dreams hidden deep inside. It's safer that way. If you keep your goals to yourself, no one can judge them and no one will know if you do not achieve your goal. It is risky to tell your friends and family your dreams. You might actually feel the need to do something about them!

6. **Celebrate success.** Reward yourself when you achieve one of your goals. Share the celebration with others and let them know why you are celebrating. A reward makes the goal more tangible and will make it easy for you to take on the new challenges ahead of you.

You must have long-range goals to keep you from being frustrated by short-range failures.
—CHARLES C. NOBLE

Grow The Roots of Your Success

Dedication and commitment are the roots to any success. Goal setting will do absolutely nothing unless you commit yourself. If you do not commit yourself, you are just wasting your breath when you talk about the incredible things you want from your future. If you feel you have commitment, you should have every confidence that you can achieve your goals. However, there is an important difference between confidence in your future and arrogance about your future.

Confidence comes from accomplishment. Accomplishment comes from a conscious decision to act. The key word is "decision." Only you hold the power to make such a decision. Arrogance is ambition spelled out in words instead of action. You will not talk your way into accomplishment. You have to act. Set goals, act on your passion, and create your future.

The six excuses listed earlier comprise the greatest enemy that stands between you and your achievement. Be aware of the negative influences that will rise up to derail you from your goal. There is always an easy way out of any challenge you face. Decide ahead of time whether you will allow these cop-outs to get in the way of your future.

Once you commit, stand firm and you will achieve your goals. You have an incredible power within you if only you have the courage to release it. I have such incredible faith in you, and I don't even know you! What I do know is that the human spirit has an awesome capacity to accomplish the impossible. You just have to want it badly enough and you have to be willing to do the hard work. Whatever your goal, people have done it before. What made them any better than you? Nothing, only the application of incredible focus and desire to one specific goal. You can do it too.

Section Two:
How to Prepare for Your Job Search

Four: Make Yourself a Better Product

Are You Ready to Be in the Career Market? ■ Build Your Experience Base . . . Fast ■ Intern Your Way to the Top ■ Understanding Internships ■ What Qualifies as a Good Internship? ■ How to Find the Right Internship ■ Character-Building Internships ■ Cop-outs: Why I Can't Do a Challenging Internship ■ Top Reasons Why Good People Do Bad Internships ■ Grad School, Anyone? ■ The Last Word

Five: Strut Your Stuff

How to Write the Best Résumé in the World ■ The Seven Résumé Rules ■ The Format ■ Write an Incredible Objective Statement ■ Beware of the Thesaurus ■ Do I Really Need an Objective? ■ Summary—the Most Important Part of the Résumé You'll Forget to Do ■ Education ■ Work Experience ■ Activities and Interests ■ Skills ■ Reference Power ■ Final Résumé Tips ■ How to Write the Best Cover Letter in the World ■ Creative Options ■ Final Cover Letter Tips ■ Prepare for the Response ■ The Final Word

Four

Make Yourself a Better Product

The poor man is not he who is without a cent but he who is without a dream.
—HARRY KEMP

Are You Ready to Be in the Career Market?

Now that you have decided on the type of career you want to pursue, you need to assess what you have to offer an employer. A few chapters from now we will do some work on how to market yourself to employers, but let's make certain that you are prepared for your introduction into the working world.

Assess for yourself:

		YES	NO

1. Are you nervous that you do not have enough work experience? ☐ ☐

2. Does your résumé stretch your work experience to sound more impressive than it really is? (Pizza delivery = responsible for Just-In-Time delivery of high-quality food merchandise directly to the end user.) ☐ ☐

3. Can you illustrate your work ethic, tenacity, and ingenuity with tangible examples that will be different from other recent college graduates? ☐ ☐

4. Do you think your résumé truly stands out and does not blend in with those of other candidates? ☐ ☐

5. If you have a lot of self-confidence, will a recruiter be able to understand why once she has read your résumé? ☐ ☐

6. If you have exceptional plans for your career, have you shown a pattern of exceptional behavior? ☐ ☐

Some of these questions can be difficult to answer honestly. All people like to believe that they are exceptional. It can be hard to admit that you may not yet have tangibly demonstrated the character traits that you feel best describe you. It does not mean that you do not possess these traits, it only means that you can't prove them. If you already have the accomplishments to back up the claims about your character, you are to be congratulated. If not, we have some work to do.

Some students argue to me that these questions are unfair. They give me a variety of reasons why they are different and why the questions are not necessarily an indication of their readiness for the job market. Here are some of the common complaints and common employer answers.

■ **If the recruiter only knew the real me, I'd have the job.** If the real you hasn't done anything exceptional so far, why should I believe the *new* real you will be any different?

■ **I haven't had the opportunity to prove myself.** I stare at a stack of résumés all day of people who have done exceptional things. They have the same opportunities as you, but they chose to pursue challenge while you only did enough to get by. Nothing stopped you from paying for your own school or getting solid work experience during the summers.

■ **Good grades are not the best indication of talent.** I understand that. The only problem is that the best candidates for the best jobs have great grades, were active in extracurriculars, have strong leadership skills, *and* have significant work experience. I want to consider you seriously for this job. Can you give me a good reason why I should?

If it weren't for the last minute, a lot of things wouldn't get done.
—MICHAEL TRAYLOR

All types of great advice are out there to tell you what you should have done over the last four years to prepare for your career. Learn three languages, take computer classes, intern as a freshman, and other not-at-all-helpful bits of wisdom. But there are four things that you can do right now to help yourself and be more appealing to employers.

1. **Be a joiner.** Everyone joins everything on campus. The only time club associations are a point of interest on a résumé is when they are absent. A recruiter wants to know that you are active and social. If you are out of school, join professional groups in your industry of interest.

2. **Be a leader.** Once you join everything, volunteer for any leadership role that is available. Leadership skills are always in demand, and active leadership roles are tangible proof. Even if your "leadership" role is to type the minutes from the meetings, it looks better than a blank space on a résumé.

3. **Organize an event.** It can be anything—a charity, a speaker for a group, a newsletter. Whatever it is, make it something you can point to with pride during an interview to show initiative and innovation.

4. **Do a meaningful internship.** *The* best way to help yourself.

> **The tragedy of life doesn't lie in not reaching your goal. The tragedy lies in having no goal to reach.**
> **—BENJAMIN MAYS**

A great internship will change your life.

Obviously, I am a great believer in internship programs, since my business is one of the largest student internship programs in the country. I cannot overstate the importance of gaining experience and concrete skills during college. You have a choice of where your starting point in your career will be.

- **Your résumé will be either another one in the stack or a standout.**

- **You will go into your job as a novice and go through the learning curve with everyone else, or you will have acquired skills and experiences before your first job that will allow you to excel beyond your employer's expectations.**

- **You will interview with a low-level recruiter, or you will be asked to interview with someone who has already been impressed by your skills and experiences.**

- **You will talk abstractly in an interview about your character traits, or you will point to your accomplishments as concrete proof of your ability.**

As you ponder the way you will spend your next summer (even if it is the summer after your graduation), consider this: the 1.2 million people who graduate from college each year have two things in common: (1) They have a diploma, and (2) they need a job.

Like it or not, you are one of the masses, a very small part of a very large labor pool. I'm sure that you are special and unique, but how are you going to make other people understand the intangible talents that you believe you possess?

Attention, Working Stiffs

If you are already a few years into the workforce, don't skip this chapter. Internships are not limited to people still in school or people who do not have other jobs. Interning is a viable option at any age and at any point in a career. There is no better way to explore new options if you are dissatisfied with your current career or even just curious about a different one. Interning part time while you work somewhere else can give you a safe preview of a possible career change and give you options to choose from if your current career stagnates. If the word "intern" bothers you, think of yourself as someone simply auditing a career just as you might audit a class at a graduate school to decide if you want to enroll. Better to lose the ego than miss out on the opportunity to find your calling!

Everything's in the mind. That's where it all starts. Knowing what you want is the first step toward getting it.

—MAE WEST

Understanding Internships

There are a variety of internships out there from which to choose. You have to decide what type of position best fits your personality and your objective. An internship is an introductory experience to a possible future career. Before you start on your internship search, it is helpful to understand what an internship represents, both for you and for your employer.

Internship Objectives—
The Student Perspective

1.   **Acquire skills.** This has to be the overriding goal of the internship. Positions that provide you with exposure to an industry without creating skills are not a good investment.

2.   **Career taste test.** This is the "test drive" for your career. You may have an idea of the career you want to pursue, but you really are unsure what it is all about. The internship is your chance to see what your job would be like after graduation but also what it could be like years down the line.

3.   **Make connections.** This is a popular reason for interning—and it works. According to *What Color Is Your Parachute?* by Richard Nelson Bolles, "85% of the employers in San Francisco did not hire any employees through the want ads." This shows that there is a huge hidden job market where good positions are not even advertised. If you perform well in an internship, you will tap into the hidden job market where some of the best opportunities exist. Even if you do not work for the company you intern with, chances are pretty good that you will cross paths with the people you meet there. Keep in touch with everyone you talk to because you never know when the connection might come in handy.

4.   **Build your résumé.** Most résumés look very sparse right after college. It is difficult to keep a straight face as you try to explain to a recruiter that pizza delivery created a strong sense of responsibility and work ethic. Everyone stretches past jobs to look just a little better than they were, but there is a limit. An intern-

ship finally puts some solid work experience on your résumé and gets you ready to land *the* job.

If you are confused about the difference between a job and an internship, think of it this way. Pouring coffee at Starbucks for six dollars an hour is a job. Pouring coffee for your stockbroker boss who has "allowed" you to work for free in exchange for exposing you to the business is an internship.

5. **Get school credit.** Many colleges will give you class credit for internships. Some of the procedures involve more red tape than the immigration department, but it is definitely worth the effort.

6. **Do something challenging.** Some people feel a need to differentiate themselves from their peers through their accomplishments. Internships can provide that opportunity.

Internship Objectives— The Employer Perspective

1. **Source of cheap labor.** Many intern positions are low- or nonpaying positions. As a rule, the more glamorous the industry, the less pay. Classic supply and demand.

2. **Find future superstars.** The get-them-young strategy enables companies to capture the brightest new talent in each graduating class.

3. **Reduce hiring risk.** When a company hires a new college graduate for a career position, it takes a large financial risk. Training and career development will cost thousands of dollars, an investment often lost when the college grad suddenly decides the job is "just

not for me." Internship programs enable the company to have a "trial run" for future employees.

4. **Help train current employees.** Internship programs often serve as a low-risk training ground for up-and-coming managers.

> *Perseverance is not a long race; it is many short races one after the other.*
>
> **—WALTER ELLIOTT**

What This Means to You

Lucky for you, your objectives and the company objectives are a perfect match. They provide something you need, real-life skills and exposure to an industry, and you provide them with what they need, cheap labor and a chance to discover strong talent with very little risk.

> *Whether or not our efforts are favored by life, let us be able to say, when we near the great goal, "I have done what I could."*
>
> **—LOUIS PASTEUR**

What Qualifies as a Good Internship?

1. **A foot in the door versus getting the skills to keep you in the room.** While an internship for a prestigious firm looks great on a résumé, the fact that you served coffee and made photocopies will quickly become apparent in your interview. This is especially true if you intend to apply for a career job at the same company where you just interned. They know exactly what responsibilities their interns have. This

fact makes it difficult to "strengthen" (exaggerate) the internship job description in the interview. Internships should truly create strong skills and character traits that you feel will be important for your career.

A great company name on your résumé may open a few doors or raise a few eyebrows, but if you have not invested the time to build strong skills, the door will close just as quickly. Also, keep in mind that smaller companies often provide the best opportunities for strong internships. Sometimes they are less structured, and you are more likely to be placed on meaningful projects.

2. **Your responsibilities include more than secretarial/gopher work.** If you do not choose a character-building internship, you can expect to get all of the tasks and responsibilities that no one else wants to do. You probably will be expected to answer phones, file papers, cold-call customers, make photocopies, and even pour coffee. It's hard to argue that these are life-changing, skill-building experiences. While you can expect to do some of these things, if they are more than 25 percent of your day, go find a different internship. Make certain that you have defined projects outside of secretarial/gopher duties.

Since most internships are exactly what you do not want to do, be prepared to be an activist in defining your duties. This means that you must have the initiative to go to your internship supervisor and suggest how you can add more value to the company. Can you do a special project? Can you play a significant role in a presentation? Is there an inefficiency or a problem that no one has been able to solve because they can't afford to spend the extra time? Bring your supervisor answers to these questions and a concrete proposal on how you would spend your time with your new duties. If you get resistance, offer to do these duties in addition to the other work you are already doing. Even offer to work for free! Sound crazy? I know that most people like to get paid for work because of that little issue of *survival,* but I'm not suggesting that you work the next six months for free or necessarily work that many extra hours. If you need to work a second job on the weekend to make up the extra cash, but the extra fifteen hours a week at your internship creates an opportunity for you in the career of your dreams, I think you're getting a pretty good deal. Also, most people who have tried this tactic usually end up getting paid for their time anyway. Even executives feel guilty getting something for free.

3. **You have exposure to your destination job, not just the one you would have right out of college.** An internship is not only to find out what the industry is all about but to find out what your career might be like. It is hoped that your career will not stop at the first job you get.

   The best way to see into your future is to expose yourself to as many different stages of your possible career as you can. Talk to people who started their careers one, two, five, and ten years ago. Find out what advances they have made and what positives and negatives they can share with you. As an intern, you will have far better access to people up the food chain than you would as an employee.

   If you were Joe Schmo employee in the accounting department of a major corporation and you sent a memo to the CEO requesting an informational interview "just to talk about the industry in general," the response would be lukewarm at best. Your peers would think you were sucking up to the boss, and you have to work with those people every day. But CEOs often view the same request from an intern as a chance to influence a young person's life, and it is often successful. Other interns will still think you are a suck-up, but who cares? They're just interns. Not only that, but if you're destined for rising stardom, there will always be a cadre of wannabes who will think you're a suck-up. Once again, who cares? Some day you can transfer them to the branch office in Fargo, North Dakota.

4. **It is a career or industry that you are seriously considering for your future.** I have interviewed hundreds of students who have interned in fields far removed from their interests. While it is nice to expand your horizons and explore new fields, your career choice is right around the corner. Why not spend the time to find out if your interests translate into a good career?

Think of it this way. When you buy a car, you probably test-drive the one you want to buy. Doing an internship way outside of your interests is like a test-drive in a Dodge when you want to buy a BMW. Go drive the BMW and see if you like it.

The exception to this rule is if an internship outside your field provides the character traits necessary for your future. For example, my program teaches students leadership and business skills by having them run a small house-painting business for the summer. No one who does my program wants to be a house painter. Their destination jobs are CEOs, chiefs of surgery, entrepreneurs, and other leadership roles. My program gives them the skills to excel in their field. To extend the BMW analogy, make sure that you have learned how to drive before you test drive a high-performance career.

5. **You spend significant time on it.** I have interviewed applicants who spend more time explaining their internship to me than they spent doing the internship. A ten- to fifteen-hour-per-week commitment will not give you a clear understanding about the career you are trying to test-drive. If you are still in school or working full time to support yourself, ten to fifteen hours is better than sitting at home and just wondering what the inside of a hospital or a law office looks like. If you can, however, spend serious time with your internship. If you want to see what a career in the field is like, then work at your internship as if you were in the career. Arrive early and work late. It's the best way to get noticed and achieve your objectives.

6. **It is for a company that you may want to apply to in the future.** Do your research. Find companies that offer the type of opportunity and environment you want for your career. Internships often lead to your first job, so be picky about where you go.

    WARNING: Make certain that you have built strong skills before you do this internship, either through a character-building internship or work experience. (Character-building internships are described later in this chapter. These internships are not designed to give you insight into any particular career but are designed to develop character traits such as leadership, work ethic, and perseverance that can be used in any career.) The worst-case scenario is to get an internship with the company of your dreams and then prove your incompetence!

None of my inventions came by accident. They came by work.

—THOMAS EDISON

How to Find the Right Internship

The process of choosing a good internship is similar to choosing which jobs to apply for, only there is less at stake. While your first job is a jump off the high-dive, an internship is still in the shallow end of the pool.

Use the tools in Chapter 3 to decide on a field of interest and then follow the next five steps.

1. **Take out a sheet of paper and a pen and answer these questions.**

   a. What are my goals for an internship? Try to make them as specific as possible. If you want to become a journalist, perhaps a goal would be to get published. If you want to go into medicine, your goal might be to get exposure to an emergency room setting.

   b. What type of environment do I want to be in? Be honest with yourself. Do you work well in high-pressure environments, or do you need something more subdued? If you are intent on a career that is high-pressure and have never experienced that kind of environment, now is the time to try it out.

c. How serious am I about my future? What is more important to me, comfort or challenge? As you do your research, you will find some challenging opportunities as well as some that you could do in your sleep. Are you ready for a challenge? If you are not, what does that say about your commitment to your goals?

d. Am I willing to work for free if the position gives me strong skills? We are a society built on immediate gratification, but trust me on this one. The skills you will acquire from a strong internship will pay you back over and over again throughout your career. If you support yourself, find out whether loans are an option for you. If not, figure out how much you "need" to make each month and either target paid internships or work a "regular" job in addition to the internship. Is the pursuit of your passion worth not being able to afford a new car this year?

2. **Find out what opportunities exist. Armed with your wish list for the perfect internship, use every resource available to you to find the best match.**

a. Internship review publications. These giant books do a good job of listing major internship programs. While they can be a little overwhelming, each has its own system of breaking down the information for you. Although reasonably priced, they can also be easily accessed at your career center. Some of the best are *Princeton Review Internship Bible, Kaplan Internship Review,* and *Adams Intern Review.*

b. Websites. Everything is on the Internet these days. Company home pages will often have an employment section that will include internship opportunities. If you have a company in mind, try its Website first.

c. Career center. Your college career center staff are a helpful bunch. They make it their goal to know all the opportunities that are available to you. They can point you in the right direction and save you from reinventing the wheel.

d. Professors. The first resource many recruiters use are the professors. They are asked to recommend any standouts in their classes for either career interviews or internship programs. Let your professors know that you want to be considered for any opportunities that come their way.

e. Alumni. This is the most underutilized and underestimated resource on campus. I never understood the power of alumni networks until I started doing interviews for my own company. If a résumé comes across my desk from UC Santa Barbara, I immediately give it attention. Strange and unfair, but I love to talk to applicants about my old school. Use your school alumni throughout your career, because they will help you.

3. Identify and research the opportunities that interest you.

a. Conduct the same research as in your job search. Find out everything you can about the company, its products, its customers, and its future.

b. Evaluate your options. Review your internship wish list. You probably are not going to find an internship that includes everything on your list, but you can get close. If you have difficulty deciding on what trade-offs to make, go back through your list and assign a value to each item. Once you prioritize your wish list, your choice will become easier.

4. Interview.

a. Follow the interview guidelines in Chapter 9. The interview process probably will be less strenuous than for a career position. However, every interview needs to be approached as if it were for your dream job.

5. Commit and shine. Don't spend too much time wringing your hands trying to decide which internship to do. If you are accepted into an internship that meets most of your objectives, jump in and start learning.

In the long run men hit only what they aim at. Therefore aim high.
—HENRY DAVID THOREAU

Your Responsibility

Once provided with an opportunity, it is up to you to stand out. An internship gets your foot in the door, but what is important is what you do once you are in the room. Take personal responsibility for your learning and for your access to the chain of command above you.

Try these tactics.

■ **Schedule an informational interview with as many people above you as possible.** Use the technique described in Chapter 10, Top-Down Job Hunting.

■ **Find mentors.** Offer to work extra hours for free on the condition that you can shadow a senior person during that time. Your eagerness to learn what some-one does gives that person a nice ego boost. It makes her excited to help you in your career.

■ **Find projects for yourself that demonstrate your skills and ingenuity.** If your internship does not give you anything challenging to do, create your own project!

■ **Industry-specific projects.** Some programs require that you do a formal project during your internship. If not, do your own. Use the project as an opportunity to interview everyone important in your company and industry. This can be a useful tool when you use top-down job-hunting tactics.

> *Striving for success without hard work is like trying to harvest where you haven't planted.*
> —DAVID BLY

Character-Building Internships

I reserved a separate section for a separate type of internship.

You can choose to learn anything at your own speed. For example, suppose your goal is to learn to speak fluent Spanish. You could take seven years of a foreign language through high school and college, or you could live in Spain for one year and completely immerse yourself in the language and the culture. The same skill is learned, but the time line is dramatically different.

You have the same choice about the skills and character traits you feel you will need to have in your career. Everything can be learned over time, but why not completely immerse yourself in the action of acquiring those skills in the shortest amount of time possible?

An exercise I have my interns do is to imagine their destination job and write down what skills the person in that role would have. Next, write down the character traits that person would need to rise to that position. Is it a strong work ethic? Leadership skills? The ability to rise to a challenge?

Each of the necessary character traits is impossible to learn out of a book or in a classroom. They are purely experience-based skills. You can attend every seminar in the world on leadership and still not have a clue what you are talking about if you have never been in a leadership role.

For those impatient people who are unwilling to wait to learn these skills and character traits incrementally, there are what I call "immersion" internships, programs designed to challenge you and push you to your limits. They create strong leadership skills and incredible self-confidence. They are not for the faint of heart, however, but rather for people who are serious and dedicated to their futures. Descriptions of just a few of these types of internships follow.

Student Works Painting/College Works Painting

Student Works Painting and College Works Painting are my favorite option for a character-building internship. (Both are the same concept but have different names in different states for trademark reasons.) I am a bit biased since I am a co-owner of National Services Group, the parent for these internship programs. However, I am not the original owner. I actually worked my way through the ranks of Student Works, starting as an intern my freshman year. Although I now own a company that operates in sixteen different states, I still look at my first year as a Student

Works intern as one of my most challenging business and leadership experiences in my life.

The program is designed to immerse you in a challenging and intense experience that pushes you to leave your comfort zone and create the skill set you need to compete for the career you want in the future. It gives you the experience of running your own business by allowing you to run your own house-painting business for the summer.

Interns design and implement a marketing program; conduct sales presentations; calculate estimates; recruit, hire, and train their own employees; and manage customer service, quality control, production management, and cost control. Program participants attend a thorough training program and work hand in hand with a mentor. It is a paid internship, with the average intern earning $6,700 over the summer. Top interns earn over $20,000.

Obviously, this program has nothing to do with painting houses. A painting business is simply the tool we use to teach our interns the character traits that are inherent in entrepreneurs and leaders. Many interns have no intention of pursuing a career in business but recognize the need to build strong leadership skills for the field they want to pursue.

Our interns do not want to go on to become middle managers, they want to be CEOs. They do not want to be surgeons, they want to be chiefs of surgery. They do not want to be stockbrokers, they want to be portfolio managers. They do not want to be engineers, they want to be project leaders. The Student Works program starts to instill the values and character traits necessary to achieve this kind of success.

The program is designed to give interns a realistic experience as an entrepreneur, but it's essentially the real world with a safety net. First-year participants are taken through extensive training and are provided a mentor to walk them through the learning curve. The Student Works program forces interns to deal with situations and problems that most people do not have to face until they are well into their careers. It is designed for people who are eager to get skills early so that they can set themselves apart from their peers. Past interns describe their experience as difficult, challenging, and one of the most important experiences that shaped their career success.

Connections: The people you meet through a character-building internship are just as important as the skills that you learn from the program. Everyone you meet is intent on achieving something great in his or her life, and all are impatient to do it. These are great people to know and to hang out with.

Although I had great friends in my social circle in college, their goals usually centered on beer consumption. In comparison, my Student Works summer introduced me to my four business partners as well as over ten other people who currently run multimillion-dollar businesses. I continue to meet exceptional talent every year that I run this program.

Student Works provides an extensive alumni network of young professionals and entrepreneurs to assist top interns in their careers after they complete the program. Our alumni understand what it takes to be successful at this program and are more than willing to recommend, and in many cases, hire Student Works interns.

The most successful interns will be invited to continue with the company as a career. There exist several opportunities within Student Works and the parent company, National Services Group. These opportunities range from management, finance, and accounting, to sales, marketing, and human relations. All senior management positions in my companies are held by past Student Works interns.

How to Apply: Student Works admissions run from the fall quarter/semester to the end of March. Current states include California, Colorado, Utah, Washington, Oregon, North Carolina, Arizona, Texas, Massachusettes, Maryland, Virginia, Florida, Illinois, Michigan, and Ohio. Admissions are very selective, only one in ten applicants is accepted to the program. The selection process includes an initial screening interview and two formal interviews with senior management. A résumé, application, and strong personal references are required.

Call or write to:

STUDENT WORKS PAINTING
1505 East 17th Street, Suite 210
Santa Ana, CA 92705
(888) 450-9675
(800) 394-6000
Web:www.nationalservicesgroup.com

Southwestern Books

Celebrating its 128th year of existence, Southwestern Books is the oldest and most renowned summer internship programs for college students in the United States. It is designed to foster leadership, independence, and confidence through a difficult sales-oriented program.

Students are hired at their respective universities during the school year and are walked through a very personalized and extensive mentorship program. This mentorship program prepares the student for a summer selling educational books in communities throughout the United States. New York students, for example, may find themselves selling books in Virginia for the summer.

Interns learn independence by living on their own

throughout the summer while maintaining the responsibilities for their sales volume. Southwestern offers exceptionally strong support and mentorship throughout the entire program. Successful participants are invited to work their way up in the organization and pursue a career path with the company.

Connections: Southwestern participants are a happy and positive group of people, and you will be well saturated with motivational techniques throughout the program. Participants tend to be very ambitious and adventurous. The shared experience of living through an intense program (and it is intense) makes for some very strong friendships. Also, Southwestern provides an extensive alumni network of past Southwesterners who can help you in your future job search.

How to Apply: Southwestern recruits throughout the first part of the school year. Any past participant will be able to start the interviewing process for you, so ask around. Information workshops are held at most major universities.

Call or write to:

SOUTHWESTERN BOOK COMPANY
P.O. Box 305140
Nashville, TN 37230
(615) 391-2500
Web:www.southwestern.com

Inroads, Inc.

Inroads is an organization dedicated to arming young minority men and women with the skills necessary to make it in corporate America. Founded in 1970, Inroads annually helps over 7,000 minority students train for future management positions. Participants in the Inroads program attend twenty hours of preparation during January and February, which qualifies them to enter the program's Talent Pool. Training includes preparation for interviews, writing a résumé, and workshops on how to excel in the workforce. Candidates apply to one of the hundreds of sponsoring companies for a summer internship. Once accepted, they officially become an Inroads participant and agree to work at the sponsoring company until graduation. Sponsoring companies include Shell Oil, Federal Express, Johnson & Johnson, AT&T, and Enterprise Rent-a-Car.

Inroads participants attend full-day workshops every Saturday during the summer. Workshop topics include time management, negotiation, presentation techniques, and other business skills. It is a challenging program that is well known and respected in corporate America. Sponsoring companies often pair senior management with an Inroads participant to create a mentor relationship and work hard to create a positive internship experience. Inroads is an excellent program that can open doors for people willing to put out the effort.

Connections: Inroads participants are a select group of people who are willing to work harder than their peers to attain the success they desire. The group workshops and training seminars give interns opportunities to network and create both professional contacts and lifelong friendships. Also, alumni include hundreds of middle managers in Fortune 500 companies, several chief financial officers and corporate vice presidents, and over twenty company presidents or owners.

How to Apply: Inroads seeks African American, Native American, and Hispanic American students who meet one of the following criteria: minimum 3.0 GPA, minimum ACT composite score 20, minimum combined SAT score of 800, or in the top 10 percent of high school class. The deadline is December 31. Approximately one-half of applicants are invited to attend the Talent Pool training. Performance in the Talent Pool determines if a candidate continues on to an interview with a sponsoring company.

Call or write to:

INROADS, INC.
10 South Broadway
Suite 700
St. Louis, MO 63102
(314) 241-7330

Microsoft

For people considering a career in the computer world, Microsoft represents an incredible internship opportunity. Opportunities are available at branches in Charlotte, North Carolina; Las Colinas, Texas; and Redmond, Washington. Unlike many computer internships, Microsoft both pays well and gives participants significant responsibility. Stories abound of nineteen-year-olds who write code for major MS products or work bugs out of systems just before delivery to stores. The selectivity of the program speaks volumes about its challenging nature; over 40,000 applicants apply for just over 600 positions. Those who make it are treated to the perks that go along with working for one of the most profitable businesses in history. Interns are provided round-trip airfare to Microsoft, a $250 allowance to ship personal necessities, subsidized housing with a private bedroom and a free biweekly cleaning service, and a choice between free use of a mountain bike or paying one-third of the cost of a rental car for the summer. Also, interns are paid between $3,050 and $3,800 a month.

Along with all the perks comes an intensive "trial by fire" in the fast-paced world of big-time computer programming. While interns are encouraged to follow regular work-week hours, many end up putting in significant time on weekends and late into the night. Interns report that the stress levels can run incredibly high at times and that the environment is fiercely competitive. The internship program is designed to develop future Microsoft managers so the expectations are high, but for people interested in a career in this field, few programs yield such a realistic view of the industry.

Connections: A mentor program ensures contact with higher-level management. Also, interns are expected to make significant contributions to the project teams to which they are assigned, which makes it certain that interns have constant contact with "real" Microsoft employees. Interns at the Redmond, Washington, branch have an end-of-the-program opportunity to meet Bill Gates at the huge outdoor mixer at his estate. All in all, the program introduces interns to some of the brightest talent in the programming industry and can open some significant career opportunities.

How to Apply: Microsoft recruits directly through 140 campuses across the nation. Students who do not attend one of these schools are invited to apply to the program by mail. Applicants who apply by mail and clear the first screening are given phone interviews to further determine their qualifications. Finalists are flown by Microsoft to Redmond, Washington, for a panel interview and a tour of the Microsoft campus.

Call or write to:

ATTN: RECRUITING
MICROSOFT CORPORATION
One Microsoft Way, Suite 303
Redmond, WA 98052-3303
(425) 882-8080
Web:www.microsoft.com/college

Other Internet Internships

While the ultra-competitive Microsoft internship is
the holy grail of computer internships, there is also an insa-
tiable demand for people who know anything about programming, computers, or web design. If your passion draws
you toward this field, incredible opportunities await. Small
start-ups looking to break into the market have been known
to compensate lowly interns with stock options and to give
even the most junior programmers major responsibilities.

To find Internet companies with internship opportunities, use the methods in Chapter 7 and find out who is in your
industry. Once you identify target companies, go after them.
Use the skills from this book to get past the gatekeeper and
talk to someone who can make the decision to hire you.
Remember, workers in this industry are in short supply, so be
aggressive and be prepared to jump into significant responsibilities.

Public Defender Service for D.C.

Rated by the *Princeton Review* as one of America's top-ten
internships, the internship program for the PDS for D.C. is
a great way to get a firsthand look at the criminal justice system in action. While most law internships are filled with
secretarial duties, participants in the PDS program get real-
world experience as "intern-investigators." The PDS represents indigent people who cannot afford a private lawyer

when they are charged with criminal offenses, incarcerated individuals, or respondents in civil proceedings. The one hundred interns selected for the program support the PDS staff of fifty trial attorneys, ten to twelve full-time staff investigators, and twelve appellate attorneys.

Interns are provided a one-week training that covers the basics of the criminal justice system and teaches the investigative techniques that interns will use at their jobs. Each intern-investigator is paired with an attorney who specializes in a particular area of law. Interns work mostly in the field, where they photograph crime scenes, interview witnesses, locate police reports, serve subpoenas, and conduct other support work. Visits to the Police Mobile Crime Unit, the autopsy room at the Medical Examiner's Office, St. Elizabeth's facility for the criminally insane, and the lock-down ward at Lorton Penitentiary ensure that participants see the reality of criminal law from the inside out.

Connections: The internship is not for the faint of heart. It attracts young men and women who are serious about a career in law or public service. Interns with the PDS for D.C. are a motivated and ambitious group, and the friendships made during the program often carry over into professional careers.

How to Apply: The deadline for applications for the summer session is April 1, while other semesters should be applied for at least three weeks prior to the semester beginning. The position is unpaid, so participants need to make arrangements for their own living expenses. Some past interns have been able to secure funding through fellowship grants and other public interest grants.

Call or write to:

PUBLIC DEFENDER SERVICE FOR D.C.
Criminal Law Internship Program
633 Indiana Avenue, NW
Washington, DC 20004
(202) 628-1200
(800) 341-2582

Alaska Fishing Boats

You have probably seen the ads in your school paper tempting you to Alaska with the promise of large amounts of money and adventure. "Make $24,000 for the summer and see the great outdoors." I love the Alaska fishing programs, but not because you can make some money or see some polar bears.

My reason for liking the Alaska fishing program is completely selfish and self-motivated. Every person I have hired who spent a summer in Alaska has the same great qualities: an incredible work ethic, adventurousness and willingness to take chances, the ability to take the initiative, persistence, and refusal to accept failure.

It could be some incredible coincidence, but the people I have hired also point to their Alaska experience as a formative time in their lives when they feel they truly acquired these character traits. The money can be great, but it usually is not. The experience is usually grueling and difficult, stretching you to your breaking point several times over the summer. It is not for the weak of heart and it can be extremely dangerous. Every year several ships are lost at sea with all hands.

It is for this reason that the experience can influence your life so profoundly. Adversity and challenge builds strengths and character traits that you might never experience unless you push yourself. The Alaska fishing trips are one way to do this—maybe not the most sane way to do it, but a way.

Connections: Like any intense experience, you will create strong bonds with people simply through survivor affinity. Be ready for some rough-and-tumble types. Alaskan fishing boats do not only advertise on college campuses, so you won't necessarily be able to critique Steinbeck with your boatmates.

How to Apply: Several companies will be willing to take your money to help you get information about this opportunity. Save some money and call the Alaska Department of Labor. It will be able to give you the same information for free.

ALASKA DEPARTMENT OF LABOR
Web:www.labor.state.ak.us/esd alaska jobs/ak jobs.htm
For a graphic video of what the experience looks like
($19.95 + $5.95 s/h) check out:
Web:www.ctvideo.com/order/form.htm

Procrastination is opportunity's assassin.
—VICTOR KIAM

Cop-outs: Why I Can't Do a Challenging Internship

■ **It's too late. I'm graduating soon and I need to find a job.** It is never too late to do an internship or take a new direction. Even a few years after graduation, internships are the best way to preview your career. I have recommended to several college graduates that they intern for the summer after their graduation rather than take a low-paying job outside their industry.

- **I have plenty of time before I graduate. I'm taking the summer off.** Everyone thinks he has a lot of time before he has to start planning for a career. Then you wake up one day with a robe on and someone puts a diploma in your hand. Congratulations, now go find an employer excited about someone with no tangible skills.

- **I need to take summer school to graduate on time.** This is my favorite one. On time for what? I can never find someone who can completely describe what "on time" means. Although impatience is a great attribute to have, the logic is a little off.

  If you graduate "on time" but have no significant work or internship experience, what are you prepared to do? You have a diploma but very few marketable skills. This might force you to accept a job instead of a career.

  The summer is your opportunity to do something that will make you stand out from your peers. It is the opportunity to create skills outside the classroom. When you take summer school, you add this line to your résumé:

  Not only did I go to school for four years, but during the summer I also . . . went to school.

  What does that add to your skills and qualifications?

  Companies do not hand out jobs for prompt graduation. They hire based on skills and qualifications.

  Also, don't forget that you can likely earn school credit with an internship. Contact your major department and find out what requirements it has. Requirements can include attending classes, developing a thesis, and making a oral presentation, or it can be as simple as writing a short paper. Interns can often receive anywhere from eight to twelve units, nearly an entire quarter of upper-division credit!

■ **I work hard at school and the summer is my time off.** It's difficult to grow up and finally lose the cherished summer vacation. However, you have to decide how serious you are about your goals and what trade-off you are willing to accept in your life. If you take the summer off, you have lost an opportunity to explore a career choice and create skills for yourself. Sacrificing a summer now can lead to a far greater enjoyment after college.

■ **I can't afford to stay another quarter/semester.** Whatever it costs for you to stay the extra quarter or semester will be more than repaid when you get a better and more appropriate career after you graduate.

Don't bother just to be better than your contemporaries or predecessors. Try to be better than yourself.
—WILLIAM FAULKNER

Top Reasons Why Good People Do Bad Internships

■ **Family Friend/Parents.** Your parents are so eager to see their son/daughter get a great job that they are more than happy to take care of your career choice for you. One day you are informed that you have an internship "blind date" with a family friend. While this could potentially be a great opportunity, it often backfires. Why?

a. It is usually in a field where your parents picture you, not where you picture yourself.

b. The family friend feels obligated to offer you the internship as a favor, but is unsure what to do with you. The person creates make-work projects just to get you out of her hair.

c. If the internship does not work out, you are certain to offend someone, usually your parents.

■ **Family Business.** While a job with the family business actually may give you more responsibilities than many positions, recruiters sometimes discount résumés with too much family business experience. It is assumed that allowances are made for family members that a regular employee would not receive.

Also, the experiences tend to be exaggerated and difficult to check. (It's hard to find out about someone's past job experience when his old boss is his mom.) While some family businesses are harder on relatives than regular employees, recruiters can't know for sure. Make certain that you have experience outside the family business.

■ **Designer Internships.** Do not be lured in by prestigious or popular brand-name internships. Evaluate the internship based on its merit, not just the company name. An internship at some posh corporate headquarters where you make copies all day still teaches you only how to run a copier. Entering the job market without strong work experience is a scary proposition. It often lowers the confidence level of first-time career hunters and causes them to lower their sights and accept dead-end positions.

- **Lack of Research.** You know that you should get an internship. Everyone else has one, so you jump on the wagon. After you look through the campus newspaper and circle every ad that has the word "intern" in it, you send out a few résumés, get a few offers, and choose the company that will be the easiest commute. Suddenly you are an unpaid receptionist in the middle of an office full of people playing a great game called "give it to the intern."

It isn't life that matters, but it's the courage you bring to it.
—HUGH WALPOLE

Grad School, Anyone?

Now that we have spent all this time on how to acquire practical, real-world skills, let's talk briefly about how to evade the real world for a few more years. I am, of course, talking about graduate school.

The thought of grad school usually makes people react in one of two ways, either relief or massive depression. Relief because it signals a respite from the reality of a nine-to-five job, mean bosses, idiot coworkers, commuting, and all of those other grown-up accessories. Massive depression at the thought of putting your life back on hold so that you can listen to overpaid professors wax philosophically about how they would change the world while you add another pile of money to your already monstrous student loans.

Before you discount grad school, listen to this statistic. For the first time in U.S. history, race and gender are no longer the greatest indicators of economic prosperity. The new leading indicator is *education*. There is a proven correlation between the level of education people accumulate and their economic well-being. Money certainly isn't the key to fulfillment, but advanced education can create greater opportunities for advancement and control of your environment, and can open doors that you didn't know existed.

So when is it a good time, if ever, to go back to grad school?

The answer really depends on your particular field and what you are trying to accomplish in it. For example, if your passion is child psychology and you want to open your own practice, it's not too difficult to figure out that you need additional education. On the other hand, if you are starting a business career, it may be less clear whether you should shell out the money for an MBA or not. It is a tricky decision, but here are five thoughts that may make it a bit easier.

1. **Make an educated decision.** Be as thorough about deciding to go to grad school as you are about choosing a career. Consult everyone that could have an opinion and weigh all of your options.

2. **Understand the return on your investment.** Find out from people in the field what benefits an advanced degree would give you. Interview people who have been successful with and without the extra credentials.

3. **Think long term.** Two years of graduate school may seem like an eternity right now, but it's a blink of the eye in the grand scheme of things. If the long-term

impact of an advanced degree would be two or three decades of more interesting and rewarding career opportunities, wouldn't it be worth it?

4. **Go for the right reasons.** Missing the college social scene and being tired of working (after your first six months of your first job) do not qualify. Graduate school can be an excellent avenue if your field requires it for advancement, if you feel the investment will equip you with the skills you need to achieve your goals, or because you are passionate about acquiring more knowledge about your field.

5. **Be careful not to become a professional student.** I had a friend in college who was on her fourth master's degree, all in very different areas. While she was well versed in subjects ranging from the mating habits of the North America bison to the impact of depreciating capital goods on an income statement, she had no intention of really *doing* anything. She loved hanging out on campus and living the student lifestyle, and taking classes just gave her a good reason to stay around. Watch out for the professional student trap. If you go back to school, do so with a mission in mind.

6. **Consider night classes.** Many good graduate programs cater to professionals by offering night or weekend courses. This would enable you to acquire your additional credentials while you continue to get an inside look at the career field you have chosen.

Ultimately, there is no such thing as too much education. You will never catch yourself later in your life thinking *Boy, I really wish I didn't have this master's degree hanging over my head.* However, there are other ways to be a lifelong learner and advance your knowledge of your field. Seminars, speaker programs, community classes, and professional organizations can provide you with educational opportunities specific to your field. The decision to enter a graduate program can be a pivotal point in your career progress, but it depends entirely on your field and your objectives. Seek out advice from those around you and do some serious soul-searching before you jump to a conclusion.

And just to make the decision even harder, don't forget that Bill Gates was a college dropout.

Good luck.

The Last Word

- It is never too early or too late to do an internship.

- Internships are a great way to create skills, make connections, build a résumé, and prove character traits.

- Set tangible goals for the results you want from an internship and take responsibility to fulfill those goals.

- Don't allow fear of failure or fear of hard work to deter you from the course that will give you the skills you need for your future.

- There is no such thing as too much education, but whether graduate school makes sense depends on your field and your objectives in that field.

- You are at the controls, so steer yourself in the right direction.

Five:
Strut Your Stuff

Destiny is not a matter of chance, it is a matter of choice; it is not a thing to be waited for, it is a thing to be achieved.
—WILLIAM JENNINGS BRYAN

Now that you have done your soul-searching to find your destination job, researched the opportunities you want to pursue, and prepared yourself with skill-enhancing internships and experiences, you are ready to jump into battle. Like most battles, the outcome will be determined by not only your skill but also by the weapons you utilize. Your weapons are the marketing tools that let employers know who you are and what you can do.

There is a saying that if you build a better mousetrap, the world will beat a path to your door. In today's economy, the most successful mousetrap company is the one with the best advertising campaign.

Marketing sells. Unless you can get yourself into the interview and ultimately into the job you want, you will never have the opportunity to prove yourself. We need to work together to create tools and strategies to give you the best opportunity possible to get that job and have that chance.

However, remember that marketing can do only so much. I might buy a mousetrap because of a great advertising campaign, but if it doesn't work, I'll never buy the same brand again. We are going to get you in the door, but you have to perform well enough to stay in the room!

Every production of genius must be the production of enthusiasm.

—BENJAMIN DISRAELI

How to Write the Best Résumé in the World

OK, so maybe that's false advertising. There is really only one way to write a truly great résumé: Be a truly great person.

However, this section will help you to write the most powerful résumé your experience will allow. It will cover the basics and some important tricks of the trade that can mean the difference between an effective résumé and trashcan fodder.

Recruiters want to see a standard résumé format. They have to look at thousands of résumés and they have a very low tolerance for anything out of the ordinary, especially if it makes the résumé difficult to read. (For you diehard rule breakers, check out the "Creative Options" section later in this chapter.) I understand that you want to show how individualistic your are, but I recommend that you pick a different time to do it. Your effort to stand out might get you thrown out.

> **If you want a place in the sun you've got to put up with a few blisters.**
> —ABIGAIL VAN BUREN

The Basics

- **Type and font.** Resumes need to be 12 point and a neutral font. Stay with Times New Roman or Courier.

- **Paper.** Use a high-quality, white or light cream paper. A 40- to 70-pound paper is perfect. Do not get fancy with marbled or shaded paper.

- **Style.** Never use italics, as they are hard to read. Use capitalization and bold to highlight items.

- **Length.** One page and one page only. There is nothing so important in your career that would require two pages.

- **No personal pronouns or abbreviations.** For you math majors, pronouns are words like "I," "he," "she," "you."

- **Never fold a résumé.** If you mail a résumé, use an 8½ by 11-inch envelope.

> **The secret of success is constancy of purpose.**
> —MARGARET THATCHER

1. ***Perfection.*** Nothing less than perfection is acceptable on a résumé. This document is your absolutely best foot forward. Your big chance to prove you can be a professional. Any error in the document is a massive strike against you. Check for spelling errors at least a thousand times and have it proofread by half the English department. Be consistent with your verb tenses and avoid grammatical errors.

2. **Visually appealing.** Your document needs to reflect the effort you put into it. It should be easy to read and well designed. A simple test: Turn your résumé upside-down and see what you think. It's surprising how much easier it is to see the balance on the page when you are not focusing on the words.

3. **Concise and easy to understand.** Your reader needs to easily pick out the information wanted and never have to read it twice. If your proofreader asks for a clarification, take that as a sign that you need to change something on your résumé.

4. **Don't overstate your skills.** Put your best foot forward when describing your past jobs, but if you exaggerate, you will ruin your credibility.

5. **Never lie.** People get caught in the most ridiculous lies all the time. Employers *will* check your past employment, your academic records, and your references. If there is something about you that you think will be a deal breaker with the recruiter, take the bull by the horns and explain it directly in the interview. If your GPA is in the basement, don't include it. If your

overall GPA is bad, calculate your major GPA and use that if the number looks good. If you have a poor GPA and it comes up in the interview, offer an explanation and follow up with why you think you would still be a good risk despite your academic shortcomings.

6. **Tailored.** Your résumé needs to be tailored to each interview you attend. The recruiter will appreciate the effort, and it will get the interview off to a strong start. If you do not have access to a computer, make sure you have some different versions on hand that you can use for different interviews.

7. **Current contact information.** If you are about to move, list a permanent address and phone number. Do not overload the recruiter with too many numbers, and make certain the phone numbers you give will be properly answered. There is nothing better than the recruiter from Goldman Sachs calling from New York and your fraternity brother answering the phone with a belch.

Do it big or stay in bed.

—LARRY KELLY

The Format

If you looked through a pile of 100 résumés you would see 100 different styles. However, some résumés would automatically stand out because they are well formatted and seem easy to read. There is no 100 percent correct way to write a résumé, but conventions serve as a good guide.

First, your name and current contact information are at the top of the page. Include an e-mail address if you have one. You can center this information or block it into a corner. Look at some sample résumés to see what style you prefer.

Your basic subject headings:

- **Objective**
- **Summary**
- **Education**
- **Work Experience**
- **Activities/Interests**
- **Skills**

Always bear in mind that your own resolution to succeed is more important than any one thing.

—ABRAHAM LINCOLN

Write an Incredible Objective Statement

You have a very short time to grab your reader's attention. The near perfection of your typesetting is a start. But the objective is your first line of defense. The objective is a concise statement of your immediate career goal. It allows you to directly communicate your purpose for pursuing the position in a well-thought-out and clear manner. Just make certain that it is well thought out and clear. I have read some long, confusing objective statements that served only to distract me from the interview. Keep it short and sweet.

A good trick is to read it out loud. If you could use your objective as an answer to an interview question, then you are in good shape. If you sound like you are reading

Chapters 1 and 2 of a Charles Dickens novel, you might need a little more work.

Try this formula for your objective.

1. List the job in which you are interested (Accountant, Architect, Programmer).

2. List the industry (Computer, Entertainment, Construction).

3. Indicate the geographical areas that interest you.

Examples: Staff accountant in the entertainment industry in the Los Angeles area.

Graphic Design Artist for a major daily newspaper—open to relocation.

Marketing position with major sports team—open to relocation and travel.

Not failure, but low aim, is the crime.
—JAMES LOWELL

Beware of the Thesaurus

These objectives just listed are concise and tell the reader exactly what you want. Most objectives that I read are long-winded, paragraph-long sentences with gigantic words. These two sentences say basically the same thing. Which one makes more sense?

Objective: Management position in a dynamic, growth-oriented company with strong opportunities for advancement.

Objective: To pursue a career path utilizing abstract thought process in the development of lasting team dynamics and interdepartmental synergies.

I don't even know what the second one *means*.

Leave the thesaurus in your desk. An objective statement is not the one-sentence proof that you passed English 101. It needs to be clear, concise, and simple. You are best served by always writing as you would speak to someone. If you regularly talk about "interdepartmental synergies," then feel free to let loose. Otherwise, use clear language to communicate your career intentions to the reader.

> *Sometimes success is due less to ability than to zeal.*
> —CHARLES BUXTON

Do I Really Need an Objective?

The objective is not optional. Do not let someone tell you that it is because you will hurt yourself by not including one on your résumé. Some say that an objective limits your opportunities because you are narrowing your job search. Yes, that is the point. You are communicating to the résumé reader that your are a viable candidate for their position because your goals match with the opportunity that is open. If you are worried about having too narrow a focus, then you can have different objectives for different résumés if you are unsure of what you truly want. In any case, make certain that you have an objective on every résumé you send out.

The difference between extraordinary and ordinary . . . is that little extra.

—ANONYMOUS

Summary—the Most Important Part of the Résumé You'll Forget to Do

The summary is my favorite part of the résumé. It is a quick snapshot of the candidate written in easy-to-understand language and designed to give me a lot of information in a short amount of time. A well-written summary will point out the candidate's important attributes or accomplishments, explain how these relate to the position in question, and encourage me to read through the rest of the résumé.

However, most résumés do not have a summary. Without a summary, the candidate is relying on my patience to read the entire résumé and pick out the most important points for myself. Because of my incredible lack of patience, I seldom read an entire résumé, but rather quickly scan it to pick out relevant points. Therefore, a résumé without a summary is relying on the most important points being seen during a fifteen- to twenty-second scan of the page.

I don't know about you, but I don't like those odds.

Every man is the architect of his own fortune.

—SALLUST

What to Include

The summary is a bullet-pointed highlight film of the résumé about to follow. It allows that recruiter to quickly identify the relevant experiences you have accumulated and enables you to draw attention to your greatest accomplishments. Use this format:

■ **Include three or four bullet points.**

■ **Emphasize past accomplishments relevant to the position.**

■ **Use concrete facts, nothing glossy or abstract.**

■ **Be concise. The résumé contains the details.**

The summary is your fifteen-second commercial about yourself. It has to convince the reader that it is worth her time to read the rest of the résumé. Imagine that the recruiter is only going to read the summary. (It often happens that way.) Is your summary enticing enough to make the recruiter want to talk to you? If not, try again.

> *Be bold and mighty forces will come to your aid.*
> —BASIL KING

Education

List the school you attended and the degrees you have earned or currently have in progress. List the most advanced degree first. Include your graduation date or your projected date. Include a GPA only if it is something to brag about. Otherwise keep that little bit of information to yourself until you can win the employer over in the interview. Also, do not assume that the recruiter will understand abbreviations. USD can be the University of San Diego or the University of South Dakota.

In an absorbing vocation, working hours are never long enough. Each day is a holiday, and ordinary holidays are grudged as enforced interruptions.

—WINSTON CHURCHILL

Work Experience

List all of your relevant work experience in reverse chronological order, with your most recent job first. Include your employer's name, the dates you worked, and your responsibilities. Make sure that you explain any gaps in your work history. This is your opportunity to showcase all of those long hours of training that prepared you to be a high achiever in your field.

When I conduct interviews, work experience is the first area I study and where I form my first impression of the candidate. I give a quick glance to the company name and go right for the job responsibilities. I do not care who you worked for; just tell me what you did and how that made you a good candidate for my position.

Resist the temptation to write a descriptive paragraph of everything you did in your past job. Use bullet points so it will be read. Include only the items that say the most about you and your abilities.

If you were promoted in your position, place that fact prominently in your job description. Include how long it took you to be promoted and why you were given more responsibility. If you paid for part of your education, prominently display that fact as well. It shows maturity and responsibility.

You are not limited to paid work experience in this

section. Any internships, programs, or volunteer work that you think is pertinent to the job you are applying for is fair game. Let employers know as much about you as possible, but try to make it only information they can use. Mind-numbing details will overwhelm the reader and cause him or her to miss the good stuff.

Students at my seminars often assure me that they have done so incredibly much that there was no way that they can fit everything on one page. Senior executives at major corporations can fit their careers on a one-page résumé, so you can. Keep in mind the picture you are trying to paint for the reader. If you are trying to say "leader," include clubs and activities where you have had a leadership role and give less space to academic accomplishments. If you are trying to say "analytic," include the academic accomplishments and exclude the summer job working at the country club as a golf cart attendant.

> ***Résumés should include what you did, not what you organized, experienced, or reviewed.***
>
> **—GLORIA FROST**

Activities and Interests

Generate the laundry list of interests that you pursue in your free time. Choose the top four to five most interesting things to include. An excessive activities can be distracting and usually boring if you only have the usual "Reading, Sports, Travel," so try to find something interesting about yourself. If you can't, maybe you should try to get out more. Also, avoid anything too strange if you are applying to a mainstream company. I interviewed a candidate who included role-playing games and body piercing as his activities. Hmmm.

I spend some time looking through this section when I conduct interviews. I want to see that the person is active and if we have something in common. A short conversation about a hobby or a sport allows me to see how the candidate reacts to a more social conversation. Also, I look for interests that show the character traits that the candidate has used to describe herself. If she describes herself as outgoing and adventurous, I want to see that she pursues activities that reflect that. If not, I will probe more to make certain she is representing herself correctly.

Several times a year, candidates fall apart under a simple question about their hobby. I love the outdoors, hiking, mountain stream fishing, and the like, so whenever someone has something similar on his résumé I like to ask him about his favorite spots to visit. I'm not trying to be tricky, I just like to find new places to go. There are always a few candidates who get flustered and admit that they don't really do much outdoors, but they thought it would sound good on their résumé. Not a great first impression. Moral of the story: Don't make stuff up. Being boring because you don't do many activities is not an interview crime, but frivolous lying will destroy your chances.

Skills

This section is pretty straightforward. Include specific computer skills, leadership qualities, and languages that you possess.

The world belongs to the energetic.
—RALPH WALDO EMERSON

References are an incredibly important part of the job search. The following section talks about how to use your references, but the first question is how to treat references on your résumé. A classic mistake made on résumés is that they don't end but rather just fade away. It's like a movie where all of the action happens in the first ten minutes with the next hour and a half spent winding down. This is what most résumés look like. Here's my objective, summary, and great work experience, then some skills, some activities, some of this, some of that. Where is the finale?

Whatever you do, don't use the line "References available on request." This phrase is used so often that it is essentially invisible to résumé readers. Use this opportunity to stand out and to create a finale for your resume. Try one of these:

- **Strong references available to prove outstanding work ethic and initiative.**

- **Strong references available to demonstrate exceptional work ethic and ambition.**

- **Strong references available to demonstrate exceptional creativity and work ethic.**

These lines will catch readers' eyes because they are not used to finding something original at the end of the page. I recommend that you put this one sentence in bold letters to draw even more attention to it.

Fortune favors the brave.
—TERENCE

Where to Find Incredible References

Your references can be an incredibly valuable tool if you use them properly. The number of times I have called a reference only to have the person not recommend the candidate for the position is amazing. A reference is supposed to be your best advocate. Take the time to choose and prepare your references to make sure that they will represent you well.

The quality of your references relies on the quality of the relationships you have built with people and the quality of work you have done in your past. The best candidates are:

- **Past employers—especially from the same field**
- **Extracurricular advisors—student government, club advisors, etc.**
- **Professors**
- **Personal professional acquaintances—friends of the family**

Do not include strictly personal references. (I don't want to talk to your mom.)

You can see why it is important to cultivate relationships with your professors and employers. You want your references to attest to a pattern of behavior over a period of time. A professor who barely knows your name and can only provide your class grade and attendance record does not do you any good.

An interesting reference source is the employer for whom you are still working. A couple of factors go into using this resource. If you are not in a career-type position and you have recently completed college, your employer likely expects that you'll be moving on soon. If you have a good relationship with him or her, there is no better reference. "I would love to keep Jane working for me, but she's overqualified for what I can offer her. I would definitely recommend her for your position." This is music to a hiring manager's ears.

What if you are job searching but you don't really want your boss to know about it? That makes the situation a little more challenging. Luckily, most hiring managers are very sensitive to this issue and will work with you to ensure the confidentiality of your job search. Be clear in your interactions with the company that you are pursuing that you are searching for a position confidentially. Strangely, this often makes you more appealing to the firm doing the hiring, especially if you work for a prime competitor.

Here's another twist. If you become frustrated at your current job because it seems like you're stuck on the advancement ladder, sometimes you can speed up a promotion by asking your boss for permission to us him as a reference. It is a simple and professional conversation. "I'm very happy working here, but I'm eager to tackle more responsibility. I've made some inquiries about positions in other companies and they have expressed a strong interest. I intend to pursue them so I wanted to be up-front with you and also ask permission to use you as a reference."

A few things to keep in mind. First, this is not a bluff. You need to have other things lined up and be willing to possibly lose your position in this process if your boss takes your shopping around as a personal affront. Use it only when you're sure you want to leave. Second, have a clear understanding about why you haven't been promoted. If it's because your boss thinks you're an idiot, I wouldn't recommend using him for a reference. Third, often the boss legitimately does not have any room for you to grow in the company and she can become a great advocate for you. And last, your boss might panic at the thought of losing you and offer you the long-overdue promotion. Overall, it's a risky move, but one that can produce results.

> **Nothing will come of nothing. Dare mighty things.**
> —WILLIAM SHAKESPEARE

Do a Reference Quality Control Check

If it bothers you that your fate might lie in the hands of your references, conduct a quality control check. Ask each of your references to write a letter of recommendation for you. This will:

- **Let you know what they will say about you.**
- **Make certain that they are willing to spend the time to be a good reference.**
- **Give you a valuable tool to use in the interview process.**

If they need a place to start, give them a few simple questions to serve as an outline.

- **How long have you known the candidate?**
- **What do you think of the person professionally/personally?**
- **Do you feel he/she would be good in the_____field?**
- **Why?**
- **Is there anything else you would like us to know about this candidate?**

Ask your references to type the letter on letterhead. Give them plenty of notice, but do ask for the letter by a particular date. It is easy to do this in an unobtrusive manner. "I have an interview in two weeks. Do you think I could come by and pick up the letter ten days from now? Will that give you enough time?" If you do not ask for the letter by a particular date, chances are you will have to call for it a few times, making you the annoying reference-letter seeker. Not the title you want to give yourself.

Once you have the letters of recommendation, make sure that you put them to good use. Always bring copies to any interview that you attend. At the end of the interview, offer the letters to the recruiter. Seldom will anyone decline the invitation.

Most often, the recruiter will take the shortcut and use the reference letters instead of making phone calls. This is great because you have effectively controlled the content of your references. You know what was said. You know that it was good.

> ### Knowledge is power, but enthusiasm pulls the switch.
> **—IVERN BALL**

Involve your References in the Process

You want your references to feel that they have a stake in your success. I love giving references for my past interns, especially the ones who did exceptionally well. I make it my mission that they get a job offer from every recruiter who calls me. I spend a great deal of time on the phone with recruiters giving concrete examples that support my recommendation and make the recruiter understand the challenging nature of the position the person held with my company.

Here are some ways to keep your references involved:

- Call your references whenever you give out their information to a company. Let them know that someone *may* call. If the interview did not go as well as you thought and no one calls, you don't look bad to your references.

- Tell them about the opportunities you interview for and ask for their input. This will prepare your references for the phone call from the recruiter and give you a chance to make your case as to why you would make a good candidate for the position.

- Ask your references for advice on what companies you should contact. Also, ask if they have a particular contact name they would recommend. "Pulling strings" is a time-honored tradition, and if your references have friends in the industry, you have a great way to get in the door.

- Send thank-you letters to all of your references once you are hired. You can expect several job changes in your life, so you will need references again in the future. It's always nice to keep in touch.

If you are applying for a competitive position, your references could be the deciding factor. Work hard to make certain that they make the decision go in your favor.

Final Résumé Tips

1. **Hire a professional to format your résumé.** Your résumé is so important, why not take it to a professional? There are many résumé services and they are not very expensive. Many of the large copy chains, like Kinko's, offer a great service. It is worth the investment.

2. **Get advice on content.** Show your résumé to anyone who will take the time to read it. Try your profes-

sors, your parents, your friends, your career counselors, even recruiters who are on campus to interview for a different position.

3. **Update your résumé constantly.** You never know when an opportunity will jump up and demand your résumé. Whenever something changes in your life, reflect it in your résumé. It is always a work-in-progress.

Scott Miller

123 Mill Street, North Liberty, IL 52317   *Phone: 319-438-9292*
                                        E-mail: smiller@aol.com

Objective   To obtain a staff accountant position in the Chicago area.

Summary
- Three summers of internship experience with Arthur Andersen.
- Extensive computer knowledge, including spreadsheet applications.
- Significant hands on management experience.

Education   1994–1999 University of Iowa
Bachelor's degree in Business-Economics
- Honors awarded

Experience   1996–1998 (summers) Arthur Andersen, LLC

Accounting Intern
- Assisted senior accountant with audit functions.
- Responsible for database management using Exel and Lotus software.
- Organized and helped coordinate new interns.
- Assigned and reviewed work performed by other interns.
- Conducted a departmental review as a senior thesis.
- Recommendations made in the review were adopted by management.

1995–1998 (school year) University of Iowa Bookstore

Assistant Manager
- Promoted to Assistant Manager within six months.
- Responsible for scheduling, managing, and motivating six employees.
- Designed and conducted training for new employees.
- Worked 30 hours per week while taking a full class load.

Activities   Accounting Association, Economics Association, horseback riding, fly-fishing, athletics, computer programming, and creative writing.

Skills   Fluent in Spanish. Extensive computer knowledge (Microsoft Word, Exel, Powerpoint). Strong leadership and public speaking skills.

References   Strong references available to indicate exceptional work ethic, determination, and initiative.

Beth Newsome

123 Celia Way, Long Beach, CA 90803   bnewsome@earthlink.net
                                         562-626-9089

Objective: To obtain a marketing position with a sports franchise—open to relocation and extensive travel.

Summary:
- Strong marketing background with professional ice hockey team.
- Designed and implemented successful promotions to boost ticket sales.
- Extensive industry knowledge gained through highly relevant internships.

Education: 1995–1999   University of Southern California
Bachelor's Degree in Marketing—3.89 Major GPA

Experience: December 1997–October 1998 Long Beach Ice Dogs

Marketing Intern
- Directly assisted Marketing Director for professional ice hockey team.
- Designed and implemented special ticket promotions and events.
- Responsible for public relations and media contact for special events.
- Designed and supervised "Meet the Players" ticket promotion.
- Awarded first-ever "Most Valuable Intern" trophy by Ice Dogs management.

February 1996–October 1997 Student Works Painting

Branch Operator
- Responsible for running all aspects of a small house-painting business for one of the highest-rated internships in the United States.
- Designed and implemented a successful direct marketing program.
- Estimated projects, drafted proposals, and conducted sales.
- Hired, trained, and managed a 6-person workforce.
- Responsible for wage setting, cost control, quality control, and customer service.
- Nominated *Manager of the Year* with $75k in sales and $15k in profit.

Activities: Marketing Association (President), Young Entrepreneurs Club, Woman's Intercollegiate Track, running marathons, charitable work, writing.

Skills: Fluent in Spanish, exceptional speaking skills, proven leadership ability, strong computer knowledge (Microsoft Word, Powerpoint, Exel, Internet).

References: Strong references available to indicate exceptional work ethic, ambition, and initiative.

Jason W. Bright

1322 Gainer Lane, Lauren, NY 11717   *(516) 555-1212*
          jbright@msn.com

Objective: To obtain a computer programming position with a start-up venture.

Summary:
- Microsoft intern at Redmond campus.
- Proficient in UNIX, HTML, JAVA, and LINEX.
- Four years entrepreneurial experience in software development.
- On-line portfolio available at *www.jbright.com.*

Education: Massachusetts Institute of Technology
BA Computer Science GPA: 3.87

Experience: **Microsoft Corporation**
June 1999–September 1999

Paid Intern
- Part of intern class of 600 selected from over 40,000 applicants.
- Developed software modifications as a MS Exel team member.
- Worked over 50-hour weeks and attended an additional 10 hours of optional classes each week.
- Responsible for solving code errors and eliminating system flaws.

BrightStar.com
August 1995–Present

Owner/President
- Designed and built *www.brightstar.com,* a portal for college students.
- Developed and implemented a marketing plan to drive site usage.
- Created site content and programmed extensive user database.
- Awarded Cool Site recognition by Yahoo!

Activities: Young Entrepreneurs Organization, volunteer with Big Brothers program, horseback riding, athletics, and music.

Skills: UNIX, HTML, JAVA, LINEX, proficient at identifying and remedying system errors, team leader, creative problem solving.

References: Strong references available on request to attest to exceptional work ethic.

Marty May

2305 E. Watrous Street
Hartford, CN 43232

Phone (415) 555-3333
E-mail mmay@home.com

Objective
A position with a leading talent agency on the West Coast.

Summary of qualifications
- Interned with Fine Line Films.
- Strong interpersonal skills demonstrated in past positions.
- Extensive knowledge and experience in the entertainment industry.

Education
Syracuse University
Business Economics and English Literature

Experience
Fine Line Films
Beverly Hills, California
June 1999–October 1999

- Production assistant on several Fine Line projects.
- Directly assisted Vice President of Acquisitions.
- Reviewed and critiqued project proposals.
- Participated with high-level executive meetings.
- Made significant industry contacts.

New York Film Institute
New York, New York
June 1997–March 1999

- Assisted coordination of annual film festival for two years.
- Liaison between NYFI and major film production houses.
- Helped design marketing campaign used in industry trade publications.
- Arranged schedule and welcome for visiting guests of NYFI.

Interests and activities
Film, music literature, outdoor activities, politically active for environmental causes.

Skills
Excellent interpersonal skills, able to delegate efficiently and coordinate multiple activities, proficient in computer applications, fluent in French.

References
Strong references available to attest to intense work ethic and ambition.

Riches are chiefly good because they give us time.

—CHARLES LAMB

How to Write the Best Cover Letter in the World

The purpose of the cover letter is to explain how you (the candidate) will benefit me (the company.) Unfortunately, 90 percent of cover letters are simply a paragraph form of the résumé I just read. I say "just read" because the cover letter is usually the last thing most recruiters read. That may be surprising to you, especially because you probably have received advice in the past that the cover letter is the introduction to your résumé. This is not true. Cover letters are seldom read, unless you clear the first two parts of the screening process first.

Here is the three-step process that takes place when a recruiter reads your résumé:

1. **Scan the résumé.** Look for keywords and experience. If still interested . . .

2. **Read the résumé.** Get details about past experiences. If still interested . . .

3. **Read the cover letter.** This means that I am interested in the candidate and I am willing to take the time to read what I hope is a well-written explanation of why I should pursue the candidate for an interview.

As I read through your résumé and cover letter, I am deciding where to allocate my interview time. Your job is to make your marketing tools so effective that I choose you from the stack of résumés that pile up on my desk every day. Some basic marketing concepts are important for you to understand for you to be successful.

> *Always aim for achievement and forget about success.*
> —HELEN HAYES

Argue Benefits, Not Features

People buy benefits. How a product or service will help them or improve their lives is what makes customers decide to buy. Features are the descriptive characteristics of the product or service. A health club has features, such as new exercise equipment, a pool, a spa, and tennis courts. It also creates benefits for new members, such as improved health, more energy, and a good-looking body. People purchase a health club membership because they picture themselves with a model's body, not because the equipment is in good shape.

Companies follow the same logic. They select candidates based on benefits, not features. Your résumé is all features: This is who I am and what I have done. Feature, feature, feature. The cover letter is where you sell the benefits that you represent. The features are your supporting evidence, but benefits will get you the interview.

Through your cover letter, you must convince the reader that you have skills and attributes that differentiate you from the other people applying for the same position. What makes you a good use of the recruiter's time is how these skills and attributes create benefits for the recruiter.

> *The most valuable of all talents is that of never using two words when one will do.*
> —THOMAS JEFFERSON

Writing the Letter

The cover letter should be written in the same font as your résumé and be on the same paper. Address it to the specific person who will be reading the letter. This may take a little research, but it is worth it to avoid the dreaded "To Whom It May Concern."

The letter should be three paragraphs long.

1. The first paragraph is a specific reference to the job for which you are applying and how you can satisfy the *need* the company has expressed. Also include how you heard of the opening. If you were referred personally by someone in the company, this is the perfect opportunity for you to shamelessly drop names. It is expected and, in fact, helpful to the person reading the letter.

2. The second paragraph is a summary of the benefits you can give the company. Use the bullet points from your summary to describe the most important features that you want the recruiter to remember about you. Follow up each feature with its consequences. That is, explain how these features translate into a benefit for the company. Limit yourself to four or five sentences, but make them good ones.

3. The third paragraph is a close. In sales, a close is a demand for action. You wrote the letter for a purpose: to interview for the position. Give the recruiter a specific way to contact you. Say that you will contact the recruiter on a specific day to discuss employment opportunities if you do not hear from him or her by a particular date.

We're all in this together . . . alone.
—LILY TOMLIN

■ **P.S.** If you want to grab a reader's attention, add a P.S. at the bottom of the page. It is somewhat gimmicky, but it can be effective. Make sure that you have something significant to say. If you really want to draw attention to it, hand-write the note. This will immediately draw the reader's eye and will be the first thing read on the page. Some options are to reiterate your most important accomplishment or your most relevant work experience. Always include how this feature will provide a benefit for the company.

Sometimes the idea of entering the real world is equated with blending into a depressing gray-flannel-suit, 9–5-workday, morning-coffee, rush-hour-commute, world of conformity. Thank God this description is only accurate for those poor slobs who didn't buy this book! You control your creativity and how you express it, and there is definitely room for creativity in the job search. Here are some ideas for creativity in cover letters.

■ **References.** If you have exceptional references, the cover letter might be another way for you to use them. You can include quotes from a reference in the body of the letter or include an entire paragraph in the middle of the letter. I have seen letters with quotes filling the margin surrounding the body of the letter. It looked too cluttered, but I still showed it around the office and still remember the candidate because of it. Use your creativity, but be careful not to lose your message in the fluff.

■ **Humor.** A friend of mine was turned down from every job possible in the entertainment industry. She couldn't even get an interview. As a last resort, she changed her serious reference letter to a script for a melodramatic radio drama of a poor farm girl (her) trying to make it big in the cruel world of Holly-wood. It caught somebody's attention and she landed a job reading scripts for a major production house. When she started, everyone in the office referred to her as the radio-drama girl because the recruiter had read the cover letter to everyone. Needless to say, the serious cover letters never received as much atten-tion.

■ **CAUTION.** Humor and creativity are very subjective. Funny to one person is insulting to the next. Using humor can be your ticket in the door, but it also holds the greatest possibility of total and dismal failure. It can work, but it can also backfire on you. Joke with care.

The road to excellence rarely has traffic.
—ANONYMOUS

Final Cover Letter Tips

■ **Treat your cover letter like your résumé.** Give it the same scrutiny that you gave your résumé. Let everyone read it and check it for errors at least a thou-sand times.

■ **Get the right name.** Work hard to find out who will read your letter. If it could be one of two people inter-viewing, bring two copies to the interview with you. Ask your interviewer if he received your cover letter, as sometimes an assistant will toss it aside when they screen the résumés (I know, how unfair!). If he does not have a copy, you will look like a superstar when you pull a copy out of your folder with the right name on it.

■ **Constantly work on it.** It can always get better. Ask more people for advice and update it with new information. It is the first thing the employer reads in depth if your résumé has enough on it to generate interest in the crucial first 15–20 seconds. It has to be perfect.

Mr. Michael Johnston
Los Angeles Lakers
123 Chapparel Road
Inglewood, CA 90802

October 17, 2002

Dear Mr. Johnson,

I am responding to your ad in the Sunday *Los Angeles Times* for "Marketing Executive—L.A. Lakers." My background has prepared me specifically for a career in sports marketing and I feel that I would be a valuable asset for your department.

I am a recent graduate from the University of Southern California, where I majored in Marketing. Many of my professors also consult with major corporations, so I was able to gain valuable insight into the latest trends in corporate marketing. Also, I interned for the marketing department of the Long Beach Ice Dogs. This experience trained me in promotions, special events, and media contacts, giving me a strong background that will enable me to quickly learn the position with your organization.

My previous experience, strong work ethic, and proven ambition make me a strong candidate for this position. I would like to discuss this opportunity with you more thoroughly at your convenience. I will call your office at 10 a.m. on July 12 to see if we can set an appointment. If you would like to contact me before then, I can be reached at 562-434-1818.

Thank you for your time and your consideration.

Sincerely,
Amy Ginsberg

Opportunity is missed by most people because it is dressed in overalls and looks like work.

—THOMAS EDISON

Prepare for the Response

Answering Machines, Roommates, and Parents.

Now that you have sent out your résumés, prepare yourself for the responses. Even if you did all of your research, chances are that your résumé-sending activity will be greeted initially with a deafening silence. Don't worry. It will take a little while for you to get your first interviews. Even though you will actively attract the recruiter's attention with follow-up calls, be prepared for a recruiter to take the first step as well.

- **Answering machines.** Change your answering machine to something you would want an employer to hear. The latest rap hit pounding in the background is probably not a first impression you want to make.

- **Pager.** If you anticipate a problem with receiving messages, get a voice-mail pager specifically for your job search. Record a professional message that you wouldn't mind a recruiter hearing and use this number on your interview materials. Let the recruiter know that you are giving him a pager number and explain why. Do not use a pager without a voice-mail. You end up calling back a number that you don't recognize without any idea whom you are calling or why. Voice-mail will give you the opportunity to collect your thoughts before you call back and make you much more accessible to the recruiter.

- **Roommates.** Tell your roommates that you expect an important phone call. I called a candidate once and was told by her giggling roommate that she was in the bathroom and would probably be there for a while. I didn't care, but when the candidate called back, she was obviously very embarrassed. Also, make a special message board where they write down only messages from employers so you don't miss an opportunity.

- **Parents.** If you live with your parents, let them know what is going on. I once called a candidate at 10:30 on a Monday morning. His mother answered the phone and complained to me for five minutes about how lazy her son was to still be in bed. She never asked who I was.

- **Yourself.** Be prepared for a phone call from a potential employer. Think about what you want to say and how you want to come across on the phone. Have your schedule ready so that you can come across as organized when the employer sets a time with you to interview.

What happens to us is less significant than what happens within us.
—LOUIS MANN

The Last Word

- Résumés and cover letters are representative of your best abilities. Anything less than perfection is an unforgivable shortcoming.

- Get help. Have your résumé and cover letter reviewed by someone with expertise in the field. Spend the money on a résumé service that will format your document professionally.

■ References can be an incredible asset if they are used correctly. Conduct a quality control check to make certain that your references are working hard for you.

■ Argue benefits, not features, in your cover letter. Features say what you've done while benefits describe how what you've done will help the employers to whom you are applying.

■ Prepare to handle the response from the companies you have contacted in a professional manner.

Section Three:
How to Find the Best Opportunities

Six: Evaluate Your Job Opportunities

What Is the Purpose of Your First Job? ■ Evaluate Your Opportunities ■ Networking ■ Opportunities for Advancement ■ Paying Your Dues, or Shouldn't I Like Going to Work? ■ Evaluate Your Opportunities ■ Job Evaluation Worksheet ■ The Perfectionist and the Unemployment Line ■ The Last Word

Seven: Find the Right Companies and the Right Job Openings

Cast a Wide Net ■ Keep a Journal ■ Network of Friends and Contacts ■ Campus Career Center ■ Job Fair Success ■ Pre-Job Fair Preparation ■ Classified Ads—Worthwhile or Worthless? ■ Research Guides—Books and CD-ROMs ■ Professional Journals ■ Narrowing the Search ■ The Last Word

Eight: The Electronic Job Search

Résumés in Cyberspace ■ How to Make Sure Your Résumé Gets Into the Database ■ Important Things to Remember ■ Best Job-Related Internet Sites ■ How to Maximize Your Time On-Line ■ The Last Word

Six

Evaluate Your Job Opportunities

Success isn't measured by the position you
reach in life; it's measured by the obstacles
you overcome.
—BOOKER T. WASHINGTON

What Is the Purpose of Your First Job?

Your first job right out of school may not be the job of your
dreams. Unless you have taken the time to get some serious
work experience while you were in school, your first
employer is going to put you wherever you can do the least
amount of harm.

This can be disheartening. You have done your
research into the industry, focused your job search, thought
of a thousand ways to change the world, landed your ideal
job, and now you find yourself stuck into a dark corner and

asked not to speak until spoken to. What happened? You're a college graduate! You deserve some respect!

Well, not really. In the real world, people respect achievement and a track record. While you have an academic background that says you are smart and capable of passing an essay test, you still have to prove that you can perform when it's for real. People are risk averse by nature, and when you first come out of school you are a high-risk proposition. Employers may not be eager to pay you very much or give you too much responsibility until you start to prove yourself. You should be ready for this and expect it.

Evaluate your first job on these criteria: (1) learning opportunity, (2) networking opportunity, and (3) opportunity for advancement.

> *It is not enough to have a good mind. The main thing is to use it well.*
> —RENÉ DESCARTES

Evaluate Your Opportunities

Since your first job is not going to make you a fortune, what is it going to do for you? What will you learn from this position? Although the job might not be exactly what you are looking for, does it give you exposure to the industry where you want to work?

Many people go back to graduate school if they can't find an ideal job. Imagine that there is a graduate school specifically tailored to your industry. It focuses on practical skills and exposure to the day-to-day activities of a person in the industry. At this graduate school, the top students are guaranteed to get a great job. Sounds pretty good!

Your first job is a graduate school program. You received the academic background from your classes, and now you are ready to acquire practical skills for your career. You would expect to pay big money to attend a graduate program that taught you career-oriented skills, but this program pays you! (This rationalization makes it easier to swallow the small paychecks!)

Basically any job can give you skills that you will need to progress in your career. It is up to you to take responsibility to learn from these positions. If you are stuck as an assistant to someone higher in the food chain, use that opportunity to understand that person's job as well as he or she does. Don't just do enough to get by. Your second responsibility is to find a better job or ask for a promotion as soon as you stop learning. The key is to perform well enough in your position to create these options for yourself.

Whatever you are, be a good one.

—ABRAHAM LINCOLN

Networking

Someone said, "It's not what you know, it's who you know."

I prefer, "Who you know will get you in the room, but what you know will keep you there."

In either case, connections don't hurt. Your first job is harvest time for networking and your crop is every person you meet. Other people new to their careers are incredibly eager to network, mostly because it's a great buzzword and they know they are supposed to be doing it. People up the food chain will respond well to your networking attempts because they are always on the lookout for new talent and enjoy being around youthful enthusiasm.

It is truly amazing how networking can work in your career. The person you meet at company training probably will give you the lead to your next job. Your boss might start her own company some day and need some young executives to help her. A receptionist might drop your name to her next boss when he is looking for a key employee.

The secret to networking is to get your name out and get everybody else's name in. This includes your old professors, teachers, bosses, associates, and friends.

> **One doesn't discover new lands without consenting to lose sight of the shore.**
> **—ANDRÉ GIDE**

Networking Tips

1. Make a database and send out cards on every major holiday.

2. Hand-write cards to important contacts.

3. Send or fax newspaper articles or cartoons that are pertinent to your contact's industry.

4. Call people to check in with them.

5. Let people know when you are considering a job change.

6. Send thank-you cards for absolutely everything. Good service at a restaurant, a good public speaker, a well-organized event. *Everything.*

7. Do favors often. Never remind people that you did them, they already remember.

8. Join professional organizations in your industry.

9. Collect business cards.

10. Give unique gifts that people will talk about.

> *I was seldom able to see an opportunity until it had ceased to be one.*
>
> —MARK TWAIN

Opportunities for Advancement

Your first job is always your stepping-stone to your next job. It's like playing chess. When you move a pawn forward one square to start the game, you don't expect to win from that move. The pawn is part of a larger strategy to win the game. Your first job is your opening move in your career, but you have to think five or six moves ahead. You can advance either within the company or by transferring to a higher position in another company after you have created a track record for yourself.

Does this position have strong possibilities for advancement? Will I be rewarded for being outstanding, or are promotions seniority based?

> *The difficulties and struggles of today are but the price we must pay for the accomplishments and victories of tomorrow.*
>
> —WILLIAM BOETCKER

Paying Your Dues, or Shouldn't I Like Going to Work?

I absolutely hated the phrase "paying your dues" when I was in college. "What do you mean, 'pay my dues'? Wasn't I paying my dues by going through college?" I was ready to get out in the world and start running things. When I realized that wasn't going to happen, I decided to become an entrepreneur, but I had to pay my dues for that as well. I'm afraid the concept of paying your dues is alive and well, but there have been some changes to the old rules.

At my seminars, students have asked whether I see a contradiction in encouraging people to follow their passion but also to accept less-than-ideal jobs where they have to pay their dues in a role where they are not passionate. (It's hard to make photocopies with very much passion.)

Pursuit of your passion takes hard work and dedication and requires all the same sacrifices that the pursuit of any career would require, and often much more. Whatever your goal, the commitment and drive required for your success will be amazing. The difference is that the result you are working toward is something that drives you and excites you.

Does this mean that you are going to love your job every day? Of course not. Part of paying your dues and working toward a goal entails some challenge and work that may or may not excite you. The beginning of a career is like working out at the gym. Sometimes you enjoy it because it feels good to exercise and get the blood pumping. Other times it's the last place on Earth you want to be. You're tired, bored, whatever, but you know that you don't want to work out that day. But if you stick to your guns and still work out, you will stay on course to achieve your goal of good health.

Later, long after you have forgotten how much you didn't want to work out, you feel great because you're in shape.

People always want to feel healthy and energetic, but not everyone is willing to put in the hard work at the gym to make that happen. The same is true in the workforce. If you want the enjoyment of pursuing your passion, you have to put the time and effort into it.

The work required of you to achieve your career goals is like the training regime for a professional athlete. The passion comes from competition, the desire for excellence, and winning on the field. Yet the *ability to win* does not come from the action on the field but from the conditioning, practice, and preparation that happens off the field. Hours of drills, lifting weights, and running are hard, unrewarding activities. The reward is to win the game if you train hard enough.

Long hours at your first job, when you are engaged in repetitious, sometimes unchallenging work, can be difficult to stomach. The reward is to win the game if you work hard enough. Remember, the goal is for you to achieve your passion. As long as you keep your focus on that objective, your career will evolve and you will have the opportunity to showcase the skills you developed from your long hours of preparation.

A common question I get at seminars is "When I'm frustrated with my job, how do I know it's because I'm paying my dues and it's not that I made the wrong career choice?" It's a great question, because either way you would experience the same sense of dissatisfaction with the day-to-day activities that your work gives you. The difference between the two is the light at the end of the tunnel.

It is your responsibility to use your position at the bottom of the food chain to find out as much as you can about your destination job, the position that makes paying your dues worthwhile. If you do your research and still like what you see, then keep your nose to the proverbial grindstone and get there. If, on the other hand, the more you learn about your destination job the more you doubt your decision, then it's time to reevaluate. Use the exercises in this book again and find out if you are on the right path. If not, then make a change.

> **The test of vocation is the love of the drudgery it involves.**
> **—LOGAN PEARSALL SMITH**

Evaluate Your Opportunities

It is difficult to search for something if you are unclear what exactly you are trying to find. The next chapter shows you how to find hiring companies and how to do the research that will give you the edge in the interview process. However, just finding a job is not enough. The goal is to find the *right* job.

I talk to so many students who get caught in the "I-just-need-a-job" trap. They want me to tell them what companies will be most likely to hire them. They don't care too much about details, as long as they have a job. A popular rationale for applying to a company is "My friend works there and says it is easy." Not quite the path to high achievement!

All job opportunities are not created equal. Sometimes you get lucky and the perfect job comes to you (job fair, on-campus interview), but most likely you will need to work hard to find the right fit. Your first career job is important because it will set the tone for your professional career. Obviously it's important enough to merit a little effort.

Do your research in the context of the attributes that

you find important. Go back to the worksheet in Chapter 3. If you skipped it the first time, take the time to do it right now. This is an essential tool as you research your opportunities, so make the investment to fill it out thoughtfully.

The following Job Opportunity Worksheet is similar to the worksheet in Chapter 3. However, the questions are in the present tense instead of in the abstract. The question is no longer what you want but what the position at hand offers.

Make photocopies of this sheet and fill it out completely for every position you seriously consider. Doing so will help you to think through each opportunity clearly and in the context of your overall goals. Keep a file as you consider more opportunities. This reference will help you to compare the pros and cons of different positions.

Job Opportunity Evaluation Worksheet

Company name:

Position offered:

Job description:

What will I learn in the first two years?

What type of responsibilities will I have?

What kind of people will I meet?

What advancement opportunities exist from this position? What kind of mentoring will I receive?

What attracts me to this field? To this particular company?

How does this position fit into my overall goals for my career?

Is there something else I would rather do? If yes, why am I not doing it?

We create our Fate every day.

—HENRY MILLER

The Perfectionist and the Unemployment Line

Even with all of this soul-searching and exhaustive research, you probably will not find a position that meets all of your criteria. (Unless, of course, you have very low expectations.) The point of all this effort is to find the best possible fit, to find the opportunity that will set a positive tone for your professional career and place you on the path toward achieving your passion.

Don't get weighed down trying to look for perfection.

Get as close as possible and then make the best of the opportunity by being determined and exhibiting a strong work ethic. Don't settle for something because it is the easy thing to do; nevertheless, don't discard a good opportunity because it is slightly imperfect.

For example, imagine that you find an opportunity that meets all of your requirements, but requires you to relocate. If you have never considered relocation as a possibility, you might discount the position automatically. Yet, *this* could be the great start that you are looking for and might really open some doors for you.

Stay open to new ideas and opportunities that present themselves during your job search. The adventure that you end up on might be very different from the one you thought you were going to take. It would be a shame to miss out on a journey because you closed your mind to unexpected opportunities.

The great and glorious masterpiece of man is to learn how to live with a purpose.
—MICHEL DE MONTAIGNE

The Last Word

■ It's important to get your career off to the right start, so carefully evaluate your first job before you accept it.

■ Your first job after college will likely not be the most exciting position in the world. The most important criterion for a first job is that it is the proper stepping-stone to the position you want.

■ Use your first job to go through the learning curve as quickly as possible in your new field, network with people in your industry, and position yourself for quick advancement.

Seven:
Find the Right Companies and the Right Job Openings

The nice thing about meditation is that it makes doing nothing quite respectable.
—PAUL DEAN

The key to any good decision is to have as much information as possible. Collecting that information is not that difficult. You just have to take the time to tap into the resources that are available to you.

First, you should decide exactly what you want to find out. Whether you are interested in a general field, a particular company, or a specific position, creating some goals for your research will be helpful. At the very least, you should find out the basics. It always amazes me when I interview candidates who swear that they want to do so-and-so or work for such-and-such a company but have absolutely no idea why.

This chapter discusses research at two levels: First, general research that will help you to decide on a handful of prospective employers; second, specific company research that will tell you whether the company will be a good match for you.

> *Don't spend too much time collecting information.*
>
> *Unless you get out there and start interviewing, you will be the most well-informed unemployed person in America.*

Cast a Wide Net

An incredible amount of opportunity is out there just waiting for you to discover it. Thousands of companies and organizations that you have never heard of would be a great match for your aspirations. But if you have never heard of them, how can you be expected to find these opportunities?

You may not realize it, but you have excellent resources at your disposal to make this discovery easier. They include:

- Your network of friends and contacts
- The Internet
- The career center at your school
- Job fairs
- Classified ads
- Research guides—books and CD-ROMs
- Professional journals

All these sources represent an invaluable tool for you to use in your general job search. They will guide you toward the handful of companies that may hold opportunities of interest to you. After you identify these companies, you can utilize the techniques discussed later in this chapter to get the sordid details.

> **To move the world, we must first move ourselves.**
> —SOCRATES

Keep a Journal

As you start your initial research, it is important that you keep a journal of the companies that you are considering. It does not have to be anything fancy, just a simple book where you can jot down suggestions you get from your different sources. Your future employer might come from a suggestion someone gives you while you are waiting for a bus. Unless you religiously write down the companies you are considering, you may pass up the best opportunities simply because you forgot about them. Write everything down. Doing so will simplify your life.

> **The purpose of life is a life of purpose.**
> —ROBERT BYRNE

Network of Friends and Contacts

Your network of contacts is often the best place to start to generate a list of potential companies. Let everyone know that you are looking for a job. I mean everyone. The best suggestions tend to come from the most surprising places. Your barber might have a brother in the financial field, or your uncle Bob might have a contact in the entertainment industry. These people might have an insight into a particular company that you might not have considered in your job search.

Professors

Your professors are an excellent source of information. Although some academics become detached from the "real world," some do have extensive contacts and a great amount of industry knowledge. They will be able to suggest companies that match up with your criteria. Great questions to ask are "If you wanted to get started in this industry, what five companies would you contact?" "Do you have a specific name that you would recommend I get in touch with?"

Recruiters often pay a visit to professors to ask for recommendations. Let your professors know that you are interested in learning about any opportunity that they might hear about. Give them a few copies of your résumé and ask for any job search suggestions. The more time they spend helping you, the more invested they feel in helping you succeed.

Alumni

This is an avenue that I completely discounted when I was in college. I couldn't imagine why someone would take the time to help me simply because I went to the same school that they had years before. Now that I am on the other side of the equation, I understand that it is a great tool to use for your job search.

It still doesn't make any sense to me, but I love to talk to people who go to school at UC Santa Barbara. It's fun to talk about the school and about the professors who are still there. I am more than willing to spend some extra time with UCSB graduates, simply because they are UCSB graduates. Is it an unfair advantage for me to give these people? Sure, but I want to find out what's going on in my old stomping grounds.

Your school most likely has an alumni association in one form or another. Contact this group and find out if there is a registry, phone book, or mailing list that you can use. Find alumni in your field of interest and contact them. Whether by phone, or by letter, the contact is very simple: "Hi, my name is_____. I am graduating from UCSB and I want to go into finance. I am contacting alumni for advice on how to conduct my job search. Do you have a few minutes?"

You will be surprised at how much assistance you receive. The secret is to choose the oldest alumni on the list. This gives you the best chance of finding someone who has worked to get to a position of authority and who has strong industry knowledge. You never know: The graduate you call for information might be the person who gives you your first job.

Friends, Friends of Friends, Friends of Friends of . . .

Your friends are probably (I hope) doing job research of their own. Take the time to share notes on your research so far. I have hired friends who did not realize they were in the same internship program until they saw each other at a training seminar. Older friends are an even better source of information. They have been in the job market for a few years and will be able to give you some insight into the company they work for as well as the reputation of different companies in their field. If you do not have many older friends, try to network through the friends of an older sibling or an older relative.

Parents

Although your parents probably already give you more than enough advice, you might be surprised how valuable their input might be. Discuss your plans with them at length and ask for advice on companies you might contact. Put your parents to work for you. If they work on their network of friends, they probably will turn up some good information for you to use. They may have some off-the-wall suggestions, but it is hard to find people more eager for your success than your parents. Don't overlook them as a resource.

> **No act of kindness, however small, is ever wasted.**
> **—AESOP**

Campus Career Center

The career center on your campus is an incredible resource. Unfortunately, it is also one of the most underutilized resources. The career center exists for two purposes: career planning and career placement. The first will assist you in choosing a career, researching possible fields of interest, testing for aptitude, and so on. The second is to help you move from student to the world of the gainfully employed. It's nice to have people whose job is to help you find a job. And it's free!

The problem is that most people look for help from the career center either late in the process or not at all. Not using the service at all is inexcusable. Going to the career center can make an incredible difference in the effectiveness of your job search, and all it costs is a few hours of your time. Not a bad trade-off.

This is essential. Visit the career center as soon as possible in your college career. Get acquainted with the staff and how to use the available resources. The career counseling, aptitude tests, and personality tests are best done early. However, even if you are about to graduate, do not skip this step. Make an appointment even if you think you have decided on a direction. The career center staff are full-time employees who make it their business to know the state of the job market and what opportunities exist in different fields. It makes sense to get their opinion about your plans.

> *I prefer the errors of enthusiasm to the indifference of wisdom.*
>
> —ANATOLE FRANCE

Career Center Staff

Career center staff are usually very talented individuals who are truly interested in your success. However, there are always exceptions. Do not accept career center advice (or any advice, for that matter) as fact. View the staff's input as just one more resource to help you reach your own conclusions. Students have told me some absolutely horrible advice they have received from career counselors. Statements like "Don't worry about getting a challenging job this summer. The only thing companies really look at is GPA." If you think the advice sounds a bit off, don't hesitate to ask to speak to someone else. You can be polite and explain, "You have been very helpful, but I would like to get as many different views as possible. Can I make an appointment with another counselor?"

A general theme in all of my advice so far has been to get other people to feel an investment in your success. The more time people spend with you and the more advice they give you, the more obligated they feel to make sure you succeed. If you are following their advice, your success or failure is a reflection on them and the advice they gave you.

Career center staff are great because they already have a direct interest in your success. It's their job. However, there's doing your job and then there's going way beyond the call of duty to help someone. If you befriend the people who can help you the most, you will find that doors might open unexpectedly for you. Get to know the staff in the career center. Take the career center director out to lunch to pick her brain about your career path. You know, kiss some butt. Remember, these people have a direct line to on campus recruiters and you might need favors from them in the future. Invest some time in building relationships, because these relationships can make a huge difference in your future.

Career Center Resources

The career center staff will not find a job for you. They will show you the tools you need, but the hard work is still up to you. The career center can provide several different resources and services. Here is a brief list.

■ **Career Counseling Tests**

a. Personality tests: Myers-Briggs Type Indicator (MBTI), the Kiersey Temperament Sorter, and others will show your personality type and evaluate career options based on the results.

b. Interest: The Strong Interest Inventory is the best-known interest text. It quantifies your interests in a variety of areas, then matches your interests with the interests of people who have been successful in different fields.

c. Values: The System for Interactive Guidance and Information (SIGI) analyzes your value system in the context of particular careers.

d. Aptitude: The Structure of Intellect (SOI) will test for your aptitude in different areas in the context of specific career choices.

- **Books and Directories.** Most career centers have an extensive library of books ranging from specific industries to general career advice. Save some money and camp out in the career office to read through this material. Most career centers are very liberal in allowing you to photocopy specific pages that interest you.

- **Employer Listings.** You should be able to find some very good information about employers, especially those who do on-campus interviews. Often there is a file on each employer who actively recruits on your campus. Books and directories covering similar ground for employers who do not come to your campus should be available as well. It is important to remember that more companies exist than the ones who come to your campus. Don't make the mistake of confining your search to the employers listed in the career center. It is a good place to start, not a good place to end.

- **Job Listings.** Find out what the format is at your school. Some have old-fashioned job boards, while others are computerized with sophisticated search engines. Whatever the case, you may be able to find some good opportunities from this listing. It is also a good way to identify hiring companies and to get some company names to research. (See Chapter 8 for job listings on the Internet.)

■ **Computer Databases.** Career centers often have CD-ROMs with incredible amounts of information: databases on labor statistics, occupational trends, employer information, and so on.

■ **Seminars.** Career centers often sponsor seminars and workshops to assist you in both career planing and career placement. I went to a two-day seminar on the medical field when I was a freshman. It was great. It made me realize I definitely did not want to go into medicine, a path that I was seriously considering at the time. What a relief to find out then and not three years into a science curriculum that I did not want to become a doctor. Your career center may have workshops on particular careers or have how-to seminars on résumés and interviews. Keep your eyes open and invest the time to attend these events.

■ **Practice Interviews.** If your school offers practice interviews, I can't stress enough how important it is for you to take advantage of this service. Some schools have great practice interview programs. At one school, students attend a class on interviews and then go through a formal panel interview where they are videotaped. The interviewers are professors and professional recruiters. After the interview they watch the tape with the student and give suggestions. However, most practice programs are not so elaborate. Usually your career counselor will interview you and give you suggestions.

I understand that interviews can be a nerve-wracking experience, so why should you subject yourself to the pain of practice interviews? Trust me, you will be less nervous about your actual interviews if you have gone through interview training and practice. It's better to make the mistakes when there is nothing on the line. Practice interviews will give you the best possibility of success when you have to do it for real.

- **Counseling.** One-on-one attention of a job-search strategist is a luxury that is easy to take for granted. You pay the salaries of the people who work in the career center (through your student fees) so make certain that you get your money's worth. Spend time working with your counselor and take advantage of his or her knowledge about the job market and job hunting. This counseling can be an incredible asset if you choose to use it properly.

- **Relocation Assistance.** If you intend to relocate to a different part of the country after graduating, your career center can provide an invaluable service to you. Most career centers are very strict on allowing only their own students access to the resources they provide, which makes sense because students are the people paying for the service through their fees. However, your career center director can open some doors for you. Most colleges belong to the National Association of Colleges and Employers and will extend other NACE members the professional courtesy of providing services to relocating students. This includes résumé help, interviews with local companies, and all the other regular services. The key to this red-carpet treatment is to ask your career director to make the contact for you.

Life has a value only when it has something valuable as its object.

—GEORG HEGEL

HOW TO STAND OUT AT THE CAREER CENTER

Remember that everyone who uses the career center is getting essentially the same information and the same advice. If you limit yourself to the advice from the career center, you will blend in with the other students who follow the same advice. You can do a few things to stand out.

1. **Use the résumé format from this book.** Everyone else will use the format that the career center recommends, and their résumées will look identical. Using a different format is especially important if you are doing on-campus interviews where you are competing only with other students from your school.

2. **Be original with your cover letter.** Use the advice from this book and from other sources, but create an original letter. I have done several back-to-back interviews on a campus where the letters are literally identical except for a few words (such as the candidate's name!). It didn't crush their chances, but it did make me wonder why they wouldn't spend the time to write their own letter. Do you want to inject this kind of doubt at the beginning of the interview?

3. **Create a relationship with the career center staff.** I talked about this earlier, but it is important enough to mention again. If you can create relationships with the staff, then you become more than a

number, you become a person. Staff members are more likely to do favors for people than for numbers. You can stand out from the masses because a staff member wants you to stand out.

4.   **Actually use the resources.** Most people will use only 10 percent of the services that the career center can provide. Take the time to get as much of the benefits as possible.

5.   **Go beyond the career center.** Do not allow anyone to place limits on your career search. If a career center staffer tells you that IBM is not hiring, call IBM. The career center is only *part* of your search strategy, not the limit of your options.

Adversity causes some men to break and others to break records.
—WILLIAM WARD

Job Fair Success

Job fairs have become progressively more popular with companies trying to fill a large number of entry-level positions quickly. They are the meat market of the recruiting world. Companies set up booths covered with company propaganda and masses of students filter past to size up the opportunities available to them, possibly stopping long enough to pick up some company literature and to talk with a recruiter staffing the booth. One thing is true for both the students and the recruiters. A job fair can be a very productive outing, or a complete waste of time. It depends on what you do while you are there.

It is essential that you prepare yourself before career fairs. They usually last only a few hours, and you want to be able to maximize your effectiveness during that time. The best way to understand how to prepare for a job fair is to view it as a series of five-minute interviews. All the recruiters you speak to at the fair are thinking one thing: "Is this person a viable candidate?" If not, they don't want to waste their time talking to you. Prepare yourself so that you don't miss out on an opportunity because you do not make a good first impression.

■ **What you need to bring.** This is basically the same checklist for interviews: several copies of your résumé, letters of recommendation, briefcase or attaché case, pen, and something to write on.

■ **What to wear.** Dress the part of the eager overachiever. Even if you don't think that any companies that you are interested in are going to be there, come prepared. Assume that you are going to stumble across your dream job. Assume that the recruiter at the booth is going to say "The president of the company stopped by to see how the fair was going and wants to talk to a student to see what type of recruits we can look forward to this year. Would you mind talking to him?" Your jeans and polo shirt ensemble wouldn't feel so comfortable all of a sudden! Dress to impress. Anything less will be noticed.

■ **Find out who will be there.** The list of participants usually is printed well in advance of the job fair. Get this list and circle the companies that you find most interesting. If you have not heard of a company, do a little research to see what it is all about. The first question most students ask recruiters is "What does your company do?" That question becomes very annoying after a while. Recruiters will remember people who ask intelligent questions because they have done their research.

- **Set your objective.** What do you want to accomplish at this career fair? What companies do you want to learn more about? What companies do you want to find a contact name to call after the fair? What companies do you already know you want to interview with? Make a list of your goals in order of priority. Cross off your goals as you accomplish them and maintain your focus until the list is complete.

- **Prepare your commercial.** Job fairs are all about sound bites. Can you make a quick first impression that will leave a concrete image with the person who spoke to you? You have to be ready to answer questions about yourself and your goals in a concise and clear manner.

- **Wish your friends luck.** Wish them luck before the fair, because you don't want to see them until afterward. Don't travel around the fair with your buddy and especially don't travel in a group of people. You have specific companies you want to talk to and you have a limited to time to do it. Also, you want to make an individual impression with recruiters. It is hard to do that if the recruiter has to share attention between two people. Your friends might also get bored and encourage you to skip companies: "That company is horrible, let's get out of here." Go solo and work your plan. Compare notes with your friends afterward and try to learn from each other's experiences.

If you aren't fired with enthusiasm, you'll be fired with enthusiasm.

—VINCE LOMBARDI

Tips for a Successful Job Fair

Armed with your prioritized list of objectives, your first task is to figure out the layout of the fair. Arrive early to avoid the midday crush and walk through the entire area. Plan your attack now that you know the lay of the land and then get to work. If you are nervous, talk to a few companies that hold no interest for you. This will give you a feel for the types of questions normally asked, and you are not risking anything. After you have talked to a few people, start on your list.

■ **Exude confidence.** Walk up boldly to the person at the booth. Extend your hand and initiate the handshake with solid eye contact. The person you are talking to is a trained professional, who makes her living analyzing body language, so this is no time to be a wimp.

■ **Eavesdrop.** It's much easier to answer a question after you have had some time to think of the answer. Pick up some of the company literature while the recruiter is talking to another candidate. Listen to the conversation (I know, bad manners) and be prepared to answer the same questions when it's your turn to introduce yourself.

■ **Sell yourself.** Put yourself in the recruiter's role. What is going to get you excited enough to remember someone? A viable candidate who might get hired. That equation has two parts. First, you have to be good enough for the position, and second, you have to have an interest in the position. Recruiters at a job fair spend 95 percent of their time selling the position they have available. Reverse the tables and spend some time explaining how you can benefit the company. Do it succinctly, but make the point that you are interested enough in the position to sell yourself.

- **Close the deal.** Students who go to career fairs and come back with a bag of company literature and nothing else are professional visitors. A job fair is not social hour. You are not there to meet new friends. You are there to produce a result—your list of objectives. If you find a company that interests you, you have to close the deal:

"I am very interested in pursuing this position. My past internship in finance with Goldman Sachs and my strong work ethic have prepared me to be a strong asset for your company. What step do I need to take to get an interview?"

"Leave your résumé and we'll call you."

"Here's my résumé. I am extremely interested. Could I please have your business card and call you to ask a few more questions and coordinate an interview?"

There is no such thing as being pushy. The scenario just presented shows an enthusiastic display of initiative. You have to get the point across that you are extremely interested and that you are a viable candidate for the position. Get some kind of commitment from the recruiter, either an actual interview date or a date and time when you will call to schedule an interview. *Close the deal.*

The human spirit is stronger than anything that can happen to it.
—GEORGE C. SCOTT

After the Job Fair

Sit down for an hour after the job fair and write down the important notes from your meetings in your notebook that you used during your company research. Once again, create a business card file, filling out the back of the card with as much information about the person as you can remember. Organize the company literature that you want to keep and toss the rest. Make a list of the companies that impressed you and create an action list. Send thank-you cards to all of the recruiters you met from companies that you might pursue. The sooner you send these cards, the better. It is easy to procrastinate and lose the window of opportunity. A thank-you card is an incredibly effective way to separate yourself from the huge stack of résumés the recruiter probably acquired during the fair.

> *Of all the advantages which come to any young man, poverty is the greatest.*
>
> —JOSIAH HOLLAND

Classified Ads—Worthwhile or Worthless?

The classified ads are the stereotypical source for job seekers. In every movie where a character is looking for a job, there is a scene where she circles ads in the newspaper and crosses them off one by one in frustration until she finally settles on a job as a waitress. If you rely only on classified ads to find a job, your life may imitate art.

I don't recommend that you put too much faith in the classified ads as being your savior from table-waiting hell. These ads are the least favorite way for recruiters to fill a position, one they turn to often as a last resort. Why? Because hiring through the classified ads requires a lot of work by the recruiter. A one-day ad will produce hundreds of responses, a small percentage of whom are qualified for the position. The recruiter has to screen through these hundreds of applicants in order to find the few who meet the criteria.

The response from newspaper ads really gets ridiculous. I have put ads in the paper for office personnel and received résumés and cover letters from people seeking everything from sales positions to engineering positions. I couldn't figure out why these people were responding to my ad until I learned more about résumé services. These services automatically send your résumé to hundreds of companies for a small fee. While it might sound like a neat idea to send your résumé out to a thousand companies in one mass mailing, it is a waste of your time and your money. It only ends up annoying the recruiters who receive them because they are not tailored to the position that was advertised.

However, classified ads remain a staple in most recruiters' marketing mix simply because it is the traditional way to recruit and old habits die hard. The following four ways to approach classified ads may yield some good results.

1. **Start by writing your own ad.** Imagine that you were going to write an ad for the position you want. What would the ad say? Take the time to create your ad, and use it as your guide when you scan through the ads. By doing so, you will find you are much more directed and more realistic about the amount of information you can get from an ad.

2. **Use the ads as a starting place.** The classified ads are most useful as a source of new companies for you to research and explore. You will see companies that you may never have heard of if you hadn't checked out the ads. Compile a list of potential target

companies and include them in your research strategy.

3. **Tailor your résumé and cover letter to the position.** Do not send out generic résumés. With a little more effort, you can impress the recruiter by addressing the cover letter to the proper person. If there is no name in the ad, use directory information to get the company phone number and find the name with a little detective work. Avoid "To Whom It May Concern" at all costs.

4. **Write a cover letter itemizing the needs listed in the ad.** When you respond to a classified ad, you are saying that you meet the requirements listed in the ad. Why not directly approach this issue? List the requirements in the ad, point by point, and provide a short paragraph answer describing how you meet or exceed those criteria. If you can show that you possess everything that the employer wants, why wouldn't you get an interview?

Standing Out

Although classified ads are mostly helpful only from a research stand point for entry-level positions, sometimes you can find some good opportunities there. The problem is that if you found the opportunity simply by opening the newspaper, so did about a thousand other people. Once you send off your résumé, your chances of a phone call back are exceptionally low. Your résumé has to end up in the right part of the pile, catch the recruiter in the right mood, and have the right buzzwords. That's a lot that has to go right in order for you to be successful. If it doesn't all come together, you've just become a number. The trick is to stand out. How?

■ **Apply in person.** Hand-deliver your résumé to the recruiter. Even if you only get a thirty-second meeting, that's thirty seconds more than anyone else. Have your personal commercial ready and be prepared for an impromptu interview—in other words, dress appropriately.

- **Send your résumé Priority Mail.** Big packages usually get opened first. A Priority Mail package is bright red, white, and blue, and it just begs for attention. It costs three bucks, so make sure that you are serious about the opportunity. If you are, it's a great investment.

- **Always follow up.** The longer you wait to call the company, the deeper your résumé will sink to the bottom of the pile. Do not be a pest but be professionally insistent. You are a viable candidate, and you want a chance to present your case.

A gem cannot be polished without friction nor man perfected without trials.
—CONFUCIUS

Research Guides—Books and CD-ROMs

You can use several publications in your hunt for companies that are hiring. Many of these books are also available on CD-ROM, which makes searches easier. Your career center will have many of these on file. Otherwise, your school bookstore will carry them or will be able to order them for you. My preferred source for books is Amazon.com—online shopping at its easiest and best.

The National Job Bank
Adams Media Corporation, 260 Center Street, Holbrook, MA 02343
1-800-872-5627

This publication includes information on over 20,000 major employers throughout the United States. Adams also publishes city-specific books: *Job Bank Los Angeles, Job Bank New York*, and so on. It does a good job of describing the company and the opportunities available, and it will provide you with contact information.

Job Opportunities in Business, Job Opportunities in Engineering and Technology, and Job Opportunities in Healthcare.
Petersen's Guides, P.O. Box 2123, Princeton, NJ 08543
1-800-338-3282

Petersen publishes three different guides, each of which target a particular field: *business, engineering and technology*, and *healthcare*. These books are effective at describing the industry leaders in these fields. All of the usual information is provided: company function, size, opportunities, contact information, and so on. The guides are not comprehensive, but they are good places to start your search.

The Career Guide: Dun's Employment Opportunities Directory
Dun & Bradstreet, 99 Church Street, New York, NY 10014

This guide will give you an excellent index of major employers listed by industry, geography, and job types hired. It will also let you know what educational and professional backgrounds are required. This is a good source for information about the players in the industry, but it is not geared to the entry-level market.

Directory of American Firms Operating in Foreign Countries
Uniworld Business Publications, 50 East 42nd Street, New York, NY 10017

Many students express an interest in working overseas. However, opportunities to work in another country are often difficult to find. Your best bet is to work for an American company that has international operations. This directory will make it easier to find those companies. If your goal is to work overseas, make that clear in the interview process. Just because the company you work for has overseas branches, it does not necessarily mean that your job type will have the opportunity to transfer internationally. Find out before you accept a job for the wrong reasons.

Encyclopedia of Associations
Gale Research, Inc., Book Tower, Detroit, MI 48266
1-313-961-2242

This is a great resource. It includes over 14,000 national and international organizations and will help you both in collecting company information and networking in your industry. Find out what associations exist in your area of interest and get involved.

> *If you see a bandwagon, it's too late.*
> —JAMES GOLDSMITH

The Best CD-ROMs

CD-ROM technology enables you to have easy access to a huge amount of information. Most of these CD-ROMs are very expensive, so your best bet is to use a copy from your school library or career center. If your school does not have a copy, call schools in the area to see if you can get access that way. I include the company addresses and phone numbers, so if you have difficulty finding access, contact the company and they may be able to point you in the right direction.

Dun & Bradstreet Million Dollar Disc Plus
3 Sylvan Way, Parsippany, NJ 07054
800-526-0651

This database is a library favorite. It has information on over 400,000 companies, all of which have a least $3 million in sales or at least fifty employees. Listings include the number of employees, sales volume, name of the parent company, and corporate headquarters. It also includes the names of the top executives in the company and has some biographical sketches. This immense amount of information is easily handled through a user-friendly search engine. You can search based on several criteria, including size, geography, and the type of business. Search results give you only the basic facts, but they are good starting points.

Business U.S.A.
5711 South 86th Circle, P.O. Box 27347, Omaha, NE 68127
800-555-5211

This is similar to the Dun & Bradstreet CD-ROM. It is a fairly comprehensive listing of companies in the United States, both public and private. It is searchable using a variety of criteria such as industry, geography, products, and size. It also contains contact information, usually in the Human Resources Department.

Hoover's Company and Industry Database on CD-ROM
1033 La Posada Drive, Suite 250, Austin, TX 78752
512-454-7778

This CD-ROM contains three different databases: *Hoover's Handbook of American Businesses, Hoover's Handbook of World Business, and Hoover's Handbook of Emerging Businesses*. It has a very broad scope but is very helpful to conduct your initial research. You can search by industry codes and find contact names for companies all over the world.

Discovering Careers and Jobs Plus
835 Penobscot Building, 645 Griswald Street, Detroit,
MI 48226
800-877-GALE

This resource give you contact information for more than 45,000 companies, 15,000 in-depth profiles, and 1,000 company histories. It also includes self-assessment tests, college profiles, and financial aid information for graduate school.

Encyclopedia of Asociations: National Organizations of the U.S.
835 Penobscot Building, 645 Griswald Street, Detroit,
MI 48226
800-877-GALE

From the same publisher of *Discovering Careers and Jobs Plus,* this is the CD-ROM version of the book I recommended earlier. It contains descriptions and contact information of over 23,000 national organizations. You can search by name, geographic location, and keywords.

> **The harder you work, the harder it is to surrender.**
> **—VINCE LOMBARDI**

Professional Journals

Another excellent resource to find hiring companies is professional journals and trade magazines. Almost every industry has its own trade publication that discusses trends and current issues. Also, many of the contributing authors are industry leaders. Reading these publications will give you some great contact names and some insight into the industry. Also, the ads in the magazine will give you some good leads on companies in the industry. Many libraries and career centers subscribe to a variety of trade journals, or you may want to subscribe to one yourself in order to become well read in your industry.

> *Human happiness and moral duty are inseparably connected.*
> —GEORGE WASHINGTON

Narrowing the Search

Once you have found the handful of companies you want to target, you need to get more specific information. There are some great resources available that will help you.

- **Annual reports.** Public companies are required to issue an annual report that outlines their status. It includes a financial statement, an overview of the business, and a list of key executives. The best (easiest to read) part of the annual report is the "Letter from the President." This provides a descriptive report of the state of the company and its future growth plans. You can get a feel for how business is going and what vision key executives have. To get an annual report, call the company directly and ask for investor relations, or check the library for annual reports of larger companies.

- **Internet sites.** Most companies have their own Websites that contain extensive company information. (See Chapter 8.) Also, many on-line stockbrokers offer free access to company research.

- **Current employees.** Call the company and start asking questions. Your best source of talkative people is the marketing department. Their job is to sell the merits of the company to potential customers, so they are well suited to give you the quick rundown on the company.

- **Competitors.** While current employees will give you a good view of the organization, some of the company's competitors may be able to give you a different perspective. Once again, call the marketing department. Staff members have to explain their competitive advantage to customers every day, so they will have answers to questions about most companies in your industry.

- **Newspapers and journals.** Search for any recent newspaper articles written about the company. Use the search engine at your library or conduct a search via the Internet. Doing so will allow you to find out what issues are currently facing the company and give you some good talking points when you go into your interview.

These resources will give you a good start in your search. Remember that the first interview serves two purposes: (1) You provide information to the recruiter, and (2) you receive more information about the company. While you need a lot of information to shine in the interview, be careful that you don't spend too much time collecting information. Unless you get out there and start interviewing, you will be the most well-informed unemployed person in America. While you have to prepare for action, you have to act to get results.

> *Waste no time debating what a good person should be. Be one.*
> —MARCUS AURELIUS

■ Information is the most crucial component of any decision, and collecting information is an essential part of the job search process.

■ Your best source of information might be right in front of you. Use your network of friends and family to research potential career paths and opportunities.

■ The campus career center can be an extremely useful resource as long as you know how to use it. You might be amazed by the help you receive if you simply ask for it.

■ Job fairs are great opportunities to window-shop for careers and make initial contact with companies that interest you. Success is when preparation meets opportunity. You can never tell what kind of opportunities will present themselves. Prepare for a job fair seriously, and you will be able to create some serious contacts.

■ The Internet and other electronic media have made information more accessible than ever. Do your research and give yourself an advantage over your competition. If you don't, I guarantee that someone you're competing against will. The research you do could be the difference between getting the job and getting the rejection notice.

Eight

The Electronic Job Search

**There is no force as powerful as an idea
whose time has come.**
—EVERETT DIRKSEN

More and more jobs are being advertised for and found on the Internet. Human Resource managers are starting to realize the potential of the Net as a tool to broaden their reach to job candidates and make their jobs more efficient. Every Human Resources conference is sure to include a seminar or a featured speaker on the subject, and private companies are working hard to keep up with the demand for service.

The electronic job search follows most of the same job search rules as a traditional search, but the Internet provides you with greater and more immediate access to some incredibly helpful resources. This technology brings you closer to decision makers and enables you to do deeper research about potential employers. As technology and services improve, more and more hiring will be done through the Internet.

Three benefits of electronic job placement are:

1. **Broader reach.** Both employers and individuals are able to reach a broader pool. Employers can reach out beyond their geographic boundaries and offer positions to a larger applicant pool. Whereas a company in the past would have to invest thousands of dollars to place a national ad, a simple job posting on a large job search engine will draw not only national but global responses. Individuals also are no longer restricted geographically but can easily search for positions in any area.

2. **More information.** Job hunters can easily access a company's Website to understand the company's products, growth, and culture. Most companies will post a page of job openings with detailed descriptions of job duties and a contact e-mail address. You can access company research that once required weeks of phone calls and letter-writing in one evening from your home.

3. **Companies come to you.** Many job-related Websites enable you to do research about companies and post your résumé to their database. Client companies search the database for the qualifications and background they require and initiate contact. Companies from industries that you might not have considered in your primary search may have incredible opportuni-

ties. You can never have too many options available to you.

Résumés in Cyberspace

The centerpiece of the electronic job search is the electronic résumé. Most major companies have long since given up on the piles of paper résumés they receive every year. This is good news as most of those unsolicited résumés used to end up in the circular file—the trash can. Now you at least stand a fighting chance with your résumé being scanned into an electronic database.

Optical Character Recognition

OCR (optical character recognition) is the software owned by the company you are applying to that translates your masterpiece résumé into a computerized format and stores it for later use. The scanner compares the patterns on the page with known images; therefore it is important to use common styles and fonts. Anything too stylistic will not be read properly by the scanner and will decrease your chances of being contacted.

Most large companies (1000+ employees) use OCR software. Some of the big names include American Express,

Coca-Cola, General Electric, and Microsoft. If you send an unsolicited résumé to a particular department at one of these companies, it will go through the following four-step path.

1.   **Résumé review.** The recruiter in charge of the position for which you are applying receives your résumé. It may end up in the hands of an anonymous HR staffer if you send it unsolicited (which you will never do after you read Chapter 7).

2.   **Résumé scan.** After being reviewed quickly, your résumé is scanned into the database. Some companies will scan in your cover letter, but many will simply toss these to the side. The computer creates two files of your résumé: a snapshot photo of it and one that qualifies your skills. It does this by registering keywords it finds in your résumé.

3.   **In with the masses.** Your résumé is now in a gigantic database with thousands and thousands of other résumés. People from every department can search the database to find your qualifications. Searches are conducted by defining search criteria based on keywords.

4.   **Purge.** Most résumé databases will automatically toss you out if your résumé is not brought up on a search over a certain period of time, ranging from a month to a year. You might be surprised to receive a phone call from a division of a large company to which you submitted a résumé months before . . . but don't count on it. Once you are in with the masses, your chances of getting out are pretty low. You can resubmit your résumé periodically to increase your chances of escaping database hell. If you insist on banging your head

against this wall, here's a hint. Each time you resubmit you résumé, change the wording as much as possible and use different buzzwords. You'll understand why after you read the next section on keywords.

Keywords Are the Key

Keywords are the driving force behind electronic résumés. A computer will sort and categorize you based on keywords, and recruiters will search the database the same way. For example, a recruiter might use the keywords "finance" and "business" to find a candidate for a position. The first search might return 1,000 matches, so the criteria will be further defined by additional keywords.

The tricky part is trying to guess what keywords recruiters will use to identify candidates they want to pursue. Suppose that Microsoft wants to hire a financial analyst. The recruiter plugs in some criteria into the résumé database and receives hundreds of matches. She further defines her field using the keyword "Excel," referring to the spreadsheet program. You might be the world's most proficient user of Excel, but if you described your skill as "Extremely proficient with computer spreadsheets," your name will not come up. On the flip side, if you know nothing about Excel but described yourself as "Proven to excel in leadership positions," the keyword will still activate your résumé.

How to Choose the Right Keywords

It is hard to accept that after all your hard years of work and preparation, a job offer hinges on whether you choose the right three words to include somewhere on your résumé so that your name comes up on a computer. Well, the point behind this book is that you should never allow yourself to be in this position. But if you insist on not following my advice and want to send out a bunch of unsolicited résumés, I'll help you get a better-than-average response. It starts with keywords.

Keywords and scanning are nothing new. When the first recruiter faced the first pile of a hundred résumés to fill one position, he created the ten-second review of a résumé. This is a quick visual scan of the résumé for industry buzzwords and any experience that would be applicable to the position at hand. If nothing jumps out at the recruiter, the résumé falls into the trash. Obviously, that is not where you want to be. The following exercise pertains to your paper résumé as much as to your electronic one because human eyes also actively use keywords.

Imagine that you are a recruiter for the position that you want. You have a deadline to hire five people for the position and you have two weeks to get it done. The only source of people you have is a résumé database with thousands of people in it. You don't have time to do a hundred interviews to find the five people you want to hire, so you need to narrowly define your search.

Choose the first five keywords that you would use to start this search.

If you need some help, think of these headings.

■ **General words associated with the industry—business, finance, medicine.**

- **Skills associated with the industry**—laboratory experience, financial analysis, recruiting skills.
- **Specific computer programs or languages**—Excel, Microsoft Word, Java, HTML.
- **Licenses or group affiliations associated with your industry**—CPA, Series 7, American Management Association member.
- **General attributes**—leader, organized, energetic.

Remember, these five keywords are to represent the essential elements you need a candidate to have for this position. Write a keyword in each space provided below.

1. _____

2. _____

3. _____

4. _____

5. _____

Suppose that you, the recruiter, use the first five keywords for your search and you get back a list of three hundred names! There is no way that you will be able to sort through all of those people, so you have to come up with five more keywords to further narrow your search.

1. _____

2. _____

3. _____

4. _____

5. _____

Use What You Have

Now that you have identified the keywords, make sure that they appear in your résumé. Some search programs also rank résumés by the frequency of keywords. That does not mean that you should write the word "valedictorian" ten times across the top of your résumé. However, you should make sure that the best keywords appear at least two, sometimes three times. You can do this in a very natural way in your description of past work, your skills, and your objective.

For example, suppose that I have decided to apply to a large investment banking firm. I decide that the basic keywords are going to include *finance, investment banking*, and *leader*.

1. Right in my objective statement I would hit all three: "To obtain a position in the corporate finance department with the leader in the investment banking industry."

2. If I majored in business and my school did not offer a specialization in finance, but I took a lot of finance classes, I would include "Major: Business—course work emphasized finance."

3. Each of my work experience areas would describe "Demonstrated leadership skills by . . ."

4. I would sign up for the investment banking club, attend one meeting, and include "Member of Investment Banking Club."

I think you get the idea. Obviously, I wouldn't dare be so redundant on a regular résumé. Then again, I also wouldn't dare count on an unsolicited résumé to get my dream career. Ultimately, if you choose the right keywords, you get lucky. "Luck" is not my favorite word when it comes to a job search, so I recommend revisiting the earlier chapters to give yourself the tools to make your own luck and take control of your job search. Your job search is too important to rely completely on some recruiter thinking the same way that you do and choosing the right keywords. Use résumé databases, but use them in conjunction with the other, more proactive, methods available to you.

> *Follow your bliss. Find where it is and don't be afraid to follow it.*
>
> —JOSEPH CAMPBELL

How to Make Sure Your Résumé Gets Into the Database

If your résumé does not scan correctly into the database, your chances of getting a phone call disappear. You could be a valedictorian with ten years of relevant industry experience, but if you don't get into the database, you don't exist. Here are some guidelines to follow to make sure you get your information into the system.

■   **Avoid paper.** When you print your résumé and then scan or fax it, the quality tends to be very poor. Whenever you can, send your résumé electronically by e-mail or fax directly from your computer without printing it first. Many ads request that you fax a résumé to the company. Ninety-five percent of the time this is a clear indication that your résumé will go directly into a résumé database. When you fax a résumé, it is received by a computer. This helps because there is less chance that the scanning will break down at the company.

However, you do have to worry about the quality of the fax machine that you are using. If it is an older machine and has a low resolution, then the clarity at the receiving end will be low. To avoid problems, remember to fax directly from your computer.

■ **Format in ASCII (text only).** If you have no idea what ASCII format is, tap one of your computer science friends on the shoulder to help you out. Here are the basics. When you save a document on a computer, the program you are using saves it in a particular format. Every program has its own method of saving fonts, borders, margins, and the like. For a different user to see exactly what you saved, he or she has to open the file with the same program that you originally used. Otherwise, the file will open and look like gibberish.

ASCII is the most basic format to save a text file. It is plain as plain can be. No crazy fonts, no tabs, or margins, no italics. In most word processing programs, you save a document this way by selecting "Save As" and choosing to save in ASCII or "Text Only" format. After you save your résumé, make sure you look it over and make certain that it translated properly.

You résumé will not look pretty, but it will be functional. Remember that OCR programs do not grade for creativity and style, but do care whether they can read data. However, be aware that human eyes may also look over your ASCII résumé, so do take some time to make it look good.

■ **Don't rely on computers.** I recommend that you send a backup paper résumé to any job position that you care about. If you are responding to an ad that asks for faxed résumés, do some research and mail a paper résumé as well. State in your cover letter that you did fax a résumé, but you sent the paper to ensure that it was received.

Some career books do not agree with this advice because employers asked for "faxed résumés only" for a reason and a paper résumé will only anger them. This advice usually comes from someone who studies recruiting and hiring but has never done it himself. I have placed ads that request faxed résumés only and received a great response from them. A few days later, I received five résumés by mail with cover letters to inform me that these were hard-copy backups for electronic résumés. I read each of those five résumés completely, was impressed with the senders' initiative, and hired two of them.

No one can produce great things who is not thoroughly sincere in dealing with himself.
—JAMES RUSSELL LOWELL

Important Things to Remember

- **Keep it simple.** OCR has difficulty with italics, underlining, small print, graphics, and unusual fonts. Stay with 12 point Times New Roman or Courier, and no shadow boxes or graphics.

- **Use keywords.** Employers will search for you based on keywords, so use a lot of them. Every industry uses these buzzwords. They include computer programs commonly used in your industry, accreditations or licenses, languages, and geographical references. If you find it hard to choose keywords for your industry, pretend that you are the recruiter and you have to come up with ten keywords to use in a database search. Make sure that all of these are on your résumé.

■ **Send it electronically.** If a large company requires you to fax your résumé, send it through a fax modem or a high-quality fax machine. Old machines may send blurred images. This will increase the risk that your résumé will not be processed correctly, and you will be lost in the system. If you e-mail a résumé, send it in ASCII format. This is the standard format used by OCR programs and is usually requested by employers.

■ **Be virus free.** Nothing makes a poorer impression at a company than crashing their computer system with a virus attached to your résumé.

■ **Do not send large graphics files.** They will tie up the time and computer space of the person you are trying to contact. If you have an electronic portfolio, architectural designs, art samples, ask permission to send them via e-mail. You can offer to send this information in your cover letter, so the person knows the option is available. More and more candidates are creating personal Websites to showcase their talents. Doing so makes it simple for contacts to look up your information. If you create your own site, include the URL prominently in your cover letter and résumé. In only a few years, tech firms will likely require all candidates to have a Website portfolio as part of the hiring process.

Each of us makes a difference. It is from numberless acts of courage and belief that human history is shaped.
—ROBERT F. KENNEDY

Now that you are ready with your electronic résumé, I suppose you want to know the best places on the Web to spend your time. Like most things on the Internet, there are literally thousands of possibilities for you to pursue to help you with your job search. Also like most things on the Internet, there is a lot of "noise" among job-related sites. Noise refers to incomplete, abandoned, and otherwise useless sites that threaten to waste your time.

Next I provide the largest and more worthwhile sites to visit. Do not limit yourself to these sites because great new companies spring up all the time to offer new services. The best thing about being a job seeker is that the services provided by these recruiting sites are free. You are the product that they sell to their clients, either through your résumé or through your viewership (Website advertising). Take advantage of all this attention and let these sites serve your interests.

CareerCity
Web: www.careercity.com

The Adams Media Corporation operates this site. It draws extensively from the Adams career books and has a lot of very good information. The site is laid out in an easy-to-use style. You can do research on companies, read articles about job-hunting, and add your résumé to a résumé database. The résumé service is free to students and may generate some interest from CareerCity client companies. It is a worthwhile site to visit.

CareerMart
Web: www.careermart.com

This site has some good features geared specifically to recent college grads. It allows you to research companies, read job-hunting advice, and obtain job listings. The "NewsStand" gives you access to electronic versions of publications such as *USA Today, Fortune,* and *The Economist.* The "Advice Tent" provides career outlooks, employment prospects for college grads, career fair information, and access to college home pages.

CareerMosaic
Web: www.careermosaic.com

An all-purpose career site, CareerMosaic has several helpful resources for new college grads. The site has an on-line job fair, 250 links to career-oriented sites, résumé posting, and a forum for job seekers. You can post your résumé, conduct company research, and look through the articles listed by subject.

CareerPath
Web: www.careerpath.com

This site allows you to search the classified ads in more than thirty newspapers based on keywords, job category, or by newspaper. Some of the papers included are the *Atlanta Journal-Constitution, Baltimore Sun, Boston Globe, Chicago Tribune, Cincinnati Enquirer/Post, Columbus Dispatch, Rocky Mountain News, Los Angeles Times, Miami Herald, New York Times,* and *Washington Post.* Over 200,000 job openings are listed on this site. It is exceptionally useful if you are trying to conduct a job search in a distant city.

JOBTRAK
Web: www.jobtrak.com

This site is one of the few specifically geared to college students. JOBTRAK is an excellent source for job listings because it has strong relationships with campus career centers. In fact, many career centers use JOBTRAK instead of conventional job posting boards. This little monopoly means that many employers are forced to use JOBTRAK to get exposure on campus. The drawback is that ads are campus-specific, so you can view ads only if employers have paid to target your school. You also have to get an access code from your career center to use the service. If your school does not use JOBTRAK or if you attend a small university, the site will not be very helpful. JOBTRAK has also started a résumé database where you can post your electronic résumé.

JobWeb
Web: www.jobweb.org

JobWeb is sponsored by the National Association of Colleges and Employers (NACE). It has great resources for college grads, including job and employer listings for entry-level positions. You can search the extensive database with a simple keyword search or read through articles regularly posted by career search professionals.

Online Career Center
Web: www.occ.com

One of the pioneers, Online Career Center remains one of the premier career sites. It contains an extensive job list that is easily accessed through a keyword search. You can post your résumé to the site and read up on major employers. OCC.com also has international listings.

Monster Board
Web: www.monster.com

Another general career site, the Monster Board is popular for its trendy graphics and edgy features. Chat rooms, hiring events, career links, and access to career search professionals to answer your questions are some of the features available. The site can be a little confusing and crowded on your first visit, but it is one of the most entertaining and helpful once you get used to the interface. The "Career Center" will help you to develop an electronic résumé that will be automatically posted to the site.

Yahoo!
Web: www.yahoo.com
Yahoo! is the most visited site on the Internet. It has evolved from a search engine to a search engine with a lot of good stuff of its own. Check out the headings under "jobs" and "employment." You will find links to the sites I have already listed and many, many more.

> *Even if you're on the right track, you'll get run over if you sit there long enough.*
> **—WILL ROGERS**

How to Maximize Your Time On-Line

The most important thing to remember is that the Internet is just part of your overall job search strategy. It is very easy to lose yourself in cyberspace as you bounce back and forth between sites, looking at all the bells, whistles, and flashy graphics. Minutes suddenly become hours, and you can blow a whole day on the Net. You may confuse this activity with progress and feel like you are doing a lot for your job search. Eight straight hours on the Internet can feel as if you are searching for a job full time, but it is very easy to accomplish absolutely nothing in those eight hours. Here are five tips to help you work smarter, not longer, when you use these Internet resources.

1. **Get professional help.** Career center staff should be able to guide you through the maze of job-related sites. Rather than spend hours learning through trial and error on your own, have someone walk you through the best sites. Don't let anyone give you a list of sites and send you on your way. Make an appointment with a counselor to actually sit down in front of a computer with you. It's not that you wouldn't be able to figure it out for yourself, but you have better things to do with your time.

2. **Create an electronic résumé.** Most major sites will invite you to post an electronic résumé in a résumé database. This database is a major source of funding for the site (sites sell access to the database to major corporations) and also a harmless form of passive marketing. Don't expect miracles from the database, but you may get some interest and it's free. If you create an electronic résumé, you can quickly post it to a database when the option is given to you.

3. **Don't click on the banner ads.** For non-Internet users, banner ads are the small boxes on a web page that link to other sites. They are Internet commercials. They pop up everywhere and can be for anything, from ads for credit cards and new cars to ads for phone service. These are a major source of revenue for the site so they are placed prominently and they look very appealing. Once you start clicking banner ads, it's all over. You wake up eight hours later from an Internet-

induced stupor and realize that you haven't done a single thing to help yourself find a job.

4.   **Have a plan.** Before you jump on-line, sketch out an outline of what you want to find out or accomplish. It is fun just to bounce around different sites to see what is available, but doing so can use up too much valuable time. Try to accomplish your tasks first, then allow yourself some time to surf. Remember, these sites charge advertising fees to companies based on site traffic. They want you to linger as much as possible and jump from page to page. While a site's ability to lure you into a time suck is great for the owner of the Website, it also means that you have figure out how to get the information you want from a site without having to spend three days reading every page.

5.   **Don't chat.** Internet chat rooms are popping up everywhere. These are dialog screens where you can exchange messages with other people on-line. Some career sites have them "as a way to share experiences with other job seekers." However, the chat is limited in content and intelligence, best used if you are looking for some truly safe sex. They are great for Website owners because they keep you on the site, where you can be barraged with banner ads. Don't waste your time.

If your daily life seems poor, do not blame it; blame yourself, tell yourself that you are not poet enough to call forth its riches.

—RAINER MARIA RILKE

■ The Internet has grown more quickly than any technology the world has seen. As it continues to evolve, the Internet will play an even more important role in the job market. The resources available right now are very good and can help you tremendously. The technology changes so quickly that you need to keep your eyes open for new opportunities. Use the Internet to broaden your reach. It can make a huge difference.

■ Electronic résumé databases rely on keywords to pick out candidates from the masses. If you mass-mail a résumé, include repetitive buzzwords to give yourself a fighting chance.

■ Career-related sites on the Internet can be a good resource for information, but this book teaches you better, more proactive methods. Definitely check career-related sites out, but don't rely on them to find your dream job.

Section Four:
How to Interview and
Get the Job

Nine:
The Interview

Act the part and you will become the part.
—WILLIAM JAMES

You have done a lot of work to get to this point. You did some serious soul-searching and bared your soul to pick a career to pursue. You researched the industry to determine the companies to contact. You created the perfect résumé and cover letter and dutifully sent it off in an 8½-by-11 envelope to your potential employer. Now there is only one thing between you and your objective: the interview.

Depending on your personality, this word either excites you because you finally have the opportunity to get in front of a living, breathing decision maker, or it has you gasping for air as you hyperventilate through an anxiety attack. Whether you have a cool demeanor or sweaty palms, this chapter will prepare you to give the best interview you can give.

Years wrinkle the face, but to give up enthusiasm wrinkles the soul.
—WATTERSON LOWE

The Purpose of the Interview

The Interviewer's Perspective

1. **Screen the applicant.** Make a quick judgment whether the applicant is even a serious candidate for the position.

2. **Evaluate the candidate.** Use the candidate's performance during the interview as a measure of competence and ability to perform in the offered position.

3. **Convey information.** Make the candidate aware of the details of the position that is being applied for. This lays the groundwork in case the applicant is accepted for the position.

4. **Minimize risk.** Employers, especially professional recruiters, have a lot at stake when hiring someone. They bear the responsibility if they make a poor hiring decision. For that reason, they want to protect their reputation and hire the "sure thing." They want to see concrete skills and credentials, so that if you turn out to be a bad apple they can provide evidence of why they hired you. When an employee steals the company car or sells the company secrets to a competitor, it is easier for the recruiter who hired her to say "How

could I have known? She was a Harvard MBA" than it is to mumble weakly "Well, she seemed nice in the interview."

5. **Rank you.** Employers have X number of positions open and $X + Y$ number of applicants. They need to determine where you fit into the overall applicant pool.

6. **Reach a conclusion.** Employers say that they wait to make their decision after they conclude all of their interviews and review their notes. Sometimes this is true, but often the decision is made directly after an interview. I walk away from many interviews knowing that I want to hire a candidate. Unfortunately, I walk away from more interviews knowing that I definitely do *not* want to hire a candidate. There is a mid-level of candidates who I withhold judgment on until I see what the candidate pool looks like. However, your goal should be to make the interviewer's decision easy.

The Interviewee's Perspective

1. **Impress the interviewer.** The person who conducts your interview holds the key to your future. If you make a bad impression, an interviewer has the power to close and lock the door. You want to impress the interviewer with everything you do and say from the first handshake to the closing of the door behind you on the way out.

2. **Present your case.** You need the interviewer to be aware of your strengths and how they make you a viable candidate. When you leave the room, the interviewer needs to have tangible evidence that you are the right person for the position.

3. **Learn about the position and company.** Your research should give you a very clear idea what the position entails before you reach the interview, but this is your opportunity to get some in-depth answers.

4. **See if the people at the company mesh with your personality type.** Interviews are an opportunity for both you and the company to learn about each other and avoid surprises in the future. At some point in the process you should try to interview with the person you will work under. Sometimes personality types can make or break an employment opportunity.

5. **Ask for the job.** If you do not ask, you will not get. Offers of employment are like offers of marriage. They are rarely given unless the answer is already known. If the idea of saying "I want the job, so give it to me" makes you break out in hives, there's an easier approach. If you know that you want the position, just let the interviewer know it. It's as simple as saying "I find this position very appealing and, if offered, I would definitely take the opportunity." If you are still a bit unsure but you want to make sure the interviewer knows you are interested, say "I find this position very appealing and I am interested in moving the process forward. Where do we go from here?"

I've been absolutely terrified every moment of my life—and I've never let it keep me from doing a single thing I wanted to do.
—GEORGIA O'KEEFE

The only way to be great in an interview is to do great preparation. This is true even if you have strong social skills and feel that you can just "wing it" through an interview. I have sat across from many competent and confident people who suddenly freeze in an interview setting. A simple *"tell me about yourself"* can create a nervous shudder through applicants and suddenly the only thing they can remember is their name and where they were born. It is amazing what can happen to you in an interview. I have seen everything you can imagine. I have had an applicant:

- Have such sweaty palms that our handshake made a loud sucking sound. I had to wipe my hand on my suit to get it dry.

- Freeze when I asked him to tell me what accomplishment gave him the greatest amount of personal pride. His eventual answer: "I can't think of anything I'm proud of."

- Start to cry because she became tongue-tied on an answer.

- Sneeze all over me by accident.

- Use a two-minute memorized objective statement twice in the same interview. She realized what she had done at the end and recovered well with "I just wanted to reiterate that point as exactly as possible."

- Bleed through an entire interview because of a shaving accident in the rest room right before the interview.

- Spill a glass of water over my notes.

- Excuse himself to go to the bathroom in the middle of the interview because "I just can't hold it."

- Have a piece of salad in her front teeth for the entire interview.

- Completely lose his train of thought midsentence. He was so boring and long-winded that I couldn't help him when he asked me what he had been talking about.

- Have such a dry mouth that every word created a sticky *click* sound. There was water on the table, but he was too nervous to take a drink.

- Give me a résumé with his name spelled incorrectly.

- Give me a résumé with the wrong company name on it.

- Stare to the side or at the wall behind me for the entire interview.

Keep in mind that I am a benevolent interviewer. I do whatever I can to make candidates feel comfortable and help to get rid of the jitters as fast as possible. These types of interview missteps happen even more frequently in trial-by-fire interviews when the interviewer actually tries to shake you up.

You have only one chance to make a good first impression. Take your preparation seriously, regardless of how confident you are in your abilities. Trust me, you do not want to become a recruiter's funny story at the office the next day. If you are not prepared, you will be noticed, but for all the wrong reasons.

Life shrinks or expands according to one's courage.
—ANAÏS NIN

Before you step foot into the interview, you need to know everything possible about the company. The interviewer wants to know that you have made the effort to do some research and will consider you more seriously if this is evident. Also, you need to know if the company meets your requirements. You should know the company's products, competitors, corporate structure, principal locations, industry rank, strategic plans, recent and projected growth, industry trends, and any recent events that could impact it.

There are several possible sources for this information. Try to go on-line to the company Website or use a search engine like Yahoo! or Excite to find any recent press coverage the company has received. Other sources include trade publications, the company's literature, family members who have heard of the company, and, if it is a public company, the most recent annual reports. For smaller companies, call and speak with someone at the company who is willing to answer some of your questions.

Make a minireport of your findings using the following worksheet so that you can review them when your interview date approaches. This is a great tool to have when you create a list of questions to ask the interviewer.

Preinterview Company Information Sheet

Company name:

Contact name:

Position offered:

Industry:

Years in business: *Public or Private:*

General description of products/services:

Has this company been in the news recently? Why?

Describe the company culture:

Why is this opening available?

Where is this company ranked in the industry? (leader/midlevel/new-comer)

> **How many cares one loses when one decides not to be something, but to be something.**
> **—COCO CHANEL**

Candidate, Know Thyself!

You are going into the interview to sell yourself, so be clear about what you have to offer. It is very easy to get tongue-tied when you are trying to make a pivotal point about yourself. Suddenly you become the town idiot and your answers sound like the same ones you gave in a third-grade essay contest. As soon as you leave the room, you become the most eloquent orator the world has ever heard as you think of all the great things you *could* have said. The following exercise can save you some of this second-guessing.

You should have already done the soul-searching for this exercise when you decided what career to pursue. The purpose here is for you to clarify your answers and put them into a usable form for your interview. Take out paper and pen and answer these questions. Write for at least five minutes on each subject. If you finish early, work hard to keep writing. This is usually when the good stuff comes out.

The Essential You Worksheet

1. *My five greatest strengths/character traits are:*

_____   _____

_____   _____

_____

2. *Actions and past behavior that tangibly demonstrate these strengths are: (Give one or more detailed descriptions for each strength.)*

_____

_____

_____

3. *My five greatest weaknesses are:*

_____   _____

_____   _____

_____

4. *Actions that demonstrate how I overcome each of these weaknesses are:*

_____

_____

_____

_____

_____

5. *My three greatest accomplishments are:*

_____   _____

_____

6. *I am proud of these accomplishments because:*

_____

_____

_____

7. *I respect myself because I:*

8. *I am motivated by_____because I:*

Now take each of the answers and rewrite them as concise answers to an interview question. Read them out loud to make sure they do not sound forced or obnoxiously formal. Keep each answer under two minutes so that you do not make a series of speeches but engage in a conversation. When you have it nailed, memorize the answers word for word. This will give you a solid framework to work from when you answer any question that an interviewer can throw at you. No matter what the question is, it always comes back to the core issue: Who are you? What have you done that is impressive? What is it about you that will make you excel? You have the answers in your head, but you need them at your fingertips when you are in a pressure situation.

> **Progress always involves risks. You can't steal second and keep your foot on first.**
> **—FREDERICK WILCOX**

What to Bring

Be prepared for every possibility.

- A good-looking briefcase or attaché. If you do not have one, go pick up a synthetic leather case from Target for twenty bucks.
- Copies of your résumé and cover letter in a professional-looking binder.
- Typewritten questions.
- Notepad.
- Pens.

- Your Daytimer or organizer (if you set up another interview on the spot).

- The Essential You answers. Review them right before the interview.

- Extra everything. Be paranoid and assume you will spill coffee on yourself ten minutes before your interview or that you will forget to brush your teeth after your pastrami sandwich at lunch. Fight back against Murphy's Law.

> *There are no secrets to success. It is the result of preparation, hard work, learning from failure.*
> —COLIN POWELL

What to Wear

Amazingly, there are entire books written about this one subject. It really does not need to be that complicated. However, what you wear *does* matter, so it is important to understand the rules of the game. You may not like the rules and some of them may really offend you, but fight them after you get the job. Here they are:

1. **No statements, please.** I know that you are dying to wear that cartoon tie to your first interview. Don't. You will have many opportunities in your life to demonstrate your free-spirited ways, so resist the temptation to do so in an interview. Regardless of the statement you mean to make, unconventional dress signals to a recruiter that you do not take the interview seriously. It is an insult to the recruiter who has made a time investment to interview you. This goes for all shock-value clothing and accessories.

2. **Conservative is the word.** Dark suit, white shirt, and conservative tie for men. Suit with a skirt for women. (Some recruiters consider pants too informal.) Both sexes should pull long hair back neatly and remove any unconventional piercings. Wear minimal jewelry and makeup.

3. **Dress for your destination job.** Look better than you will ever need to for your job. Your goals are set high and you are going places. Dress like it.

Again, you might not like the rules, but there they are. While these rules apply to most interviews, be ready to adapt your dress to the industry you want to pursue. If you interview on a construction job site, a suit may be out of place. If you apply to a record label to manage a punk-rock group, you might want to go *get* some body piercings. A good rule is, when in doubt, ask. If you are still in doubt, assume the most conservative.

> *A turtle travels only when it sticks it neck out.*
> —KOREAN PROVERB

Top Ten Rules for Interview Brilliance

1. **Confirm and be on time.** Being habitually late and being unemployed are closely linked. Always arrive fifteen minutes early for your appointment. If you have a long drive, assume you will have a flat tire, run out of gas, and get lost. Plan accordingly. Call the day before the interview to confirm.

2. **Prepare and have an agenda.** You can never be too prepared. Use your parents or roommates to con-

duct mock interviews so you can practice the questions. Define your personal objectives before you walk into the interview. Is it to decide if you want to enter the industry? Is it to get the job? Is it to find out information specific to that particular company?

3. **First impressions are everything.** Dress as if you own the place. Stand up as soon as you see the interviewer, walk toward him/her, and offer your hand. Recruiters love it when candidates initiate a handshake. Make immediate eye contact and introduce yourself with confidence, using your first and last name.

4. **Watch the eyes and display the teeth.** Strong eye contact is absolutely essential. If you know or have been told that this is a weakness for you, then you need to work on it. Smile pleasantly through the interview. You don't need to grin like a fool, but be pleasant and warm. This is also the best ammunition if you get stuck on a tough question. Just smile broadly and start over.

5. **Be concise.** Completely answer the questions put to you, but be concise. Try to limit your answers to a maximum of three minutes. If you are not sure if you have answered a question completely, ask, "Does that answer your question, or would you like me to elaborate?"

6. **Showcase the Essential You.** The biggest complaint that recruiters have is that applicants are too general. Use concrete examples to back up any claim that you make about yourself. If you say you have strong leadership skills, back it up with a brief description of your leadership experience. Use the Essential You exercise to help you.

7. **Be genuine.** Don't tell your interviewer what you think he or she wants to hear. Say what you believe. Remember that recruiters earn their living by reading people in interviews, and they will see right through you if you try to be someone you are not. Be yourself.

8. **Ask intelligent questions that show your research.** Have your list ready and make every one count. Keep them concise and easy to answer. Do not ask questions that you could have easily answered yourself with a little research.

9. **Ask for the job.** Even if you don't know if you want it. Get the job first and then make your decision. Remember the closing question: "I want to move forward. Where do we go from here?"

10. **Thank you, thank you, thank you.** Always send a personal thank you to your interviewer the same day you interviewed. Its arrival will be noted and its absence will be noticed.

Energy will do anything that can be done in this world.

—JOHANN VON GOETHE

A Quick Little Interview Story

The hardest interview I have had in my experience was when I was going through the nomination process for Boy's State when I was seventeen years old. Boy's State is a week-long program where high school boys learn about politics by actually running a political system with elections, campaigns, a visit to the state capital, and so on. It is run by the

American Legion, an organization comprised of veterans of foreign wars. There were seven candidates and two spots.

I knew about the interview weeks ahead of time, and I knew the format. It was going to be a panel interview with ten American Legion members, and the questions were designed to see how fast you could think on your feet. Word was that these guys liked to see the candidates squirm so they always had tough questions and liked to grill people with follow-up. I really wanted to go to Boy's State, but I was scared to death.

The big day came and I showed up a half hour early wearing one of my dad's ties and a suit that didn't fit quite right. The interviews were done individually in a private room off to the side from the main hall. While one of the candidates was in there getting grilled, the rest of us just milled around, joking about the questions we were going to get. The door opened and out walked one of the candidates, a kid I knew from the high school across town. One of the Legionnaires filled the doorway behind him and called out, "Gunhus, Jeffrey." The Legionnaires always talked like that, very military, very intimidating.

As I walked to the door, I noticed that the kid from across town didn't look so good. He looked pretty shaken up and kind of pasty. And his hands were shaking. Just the confidence boost I needed before I faced the firing squad.

I walked into the room, where a single chair in the middle faced a long table of the prosecutors/interviewers. Each of the Legionnaires wore his Legion hat, which showed the outfit he fought with during his war, dating back to World War II. It was an impressive show of force, clearly not designed to put a candidate at ease. The interview began.

The questions were pretty simple at first. What were

my interests after school? Why did I want to go to Boy's State? Who were the public figures I admired? Piece of cake. Not only was I acing the thing, but I was actually enjoying it. Then one of them pulled out the heavy artillery.

"Mr. Gunhus. Do you feel that an American citizen ought to have the right to burn the American flag?"

Remember the audience. I was just asked by a room full of American Legion members, men who fought under the flag they were talking about, whether I support a person's right to burn and desecrate our national symbol. Kind of a touchy question. I happen to believe that burning the American flag is protected under the First Amendment and so should be allowed. For some reason, I figured that the men in the room with me didn't want to hear that answer.

"Mr. Gunhus, do you have an answer to the question?"

Let me tell you, I *really* wanted to go to Boy's State. My friends and family knew I was nominated and were pulling for me, but it just seemed unlikely that my stance on flag-burning was going to help my cause. The silence stretched out a little longer, so I figured I had to say something.

"I believe that the burning of the American flag is a treacherous and shameful act." The smiles started to appear around the table.

"An act that I could never condone nor take part in." More smiles.

"And an act that I feel is completely protected by the First Amendment." No more smiles.

"I feel that the flag is a symbol of the ideals of freedom and liberty, ideals that founded our country and for which we fought wars. Freedom and liberty require us to protect even those things that we disagree with, because unless we do, we are not truly free." Goodbye, Boy's State.

There was a good full minute of silence in the room (give or take fifty seconds). Then I was excused without any further questions. Two weeks later I was notified that I was chosen to go to Boy's State. The notification letter had a handwritten message on the bottom from one of the Legionnaires: "Leadership is doing what you believe is right even when you believe it will be unpopular. Good luck in your future. Stay the course."

The moral of the story: Being genuine is the most important thing to remember while you interview. Say what you believe and refuse to compromise yourself for any opportunity. Integrity cannot be recovered after you violate it, and no job is worth that price.

> *The proper function of man is to live—not to exist.*
>
> **—JACK LONDON**

How to Have Uncommonly Good Answers to Common Questions

If you want to blow away an employer, practice for an interview the same way you would prepare for an important college final. If you were given the test questions ahead of time, you probably would research the answers and make sure that you studied the right information. You might even write out practice answers to get ready. Well, this is a pretty important exam, so it makes sense to follow the same strategy. Work with the most common questions asked by employers and spend some serious time deciding how you want to answer them.

Do not, I repeat, do not use this exercise to guess what the recruiter wants to hear. That is not the purpose. Your goal should be to accurately represent yourself, but to do so in a well thought out and intelligent way. As the saying goes, you have only one chance to make a good first impression. Why risk a tongue-tied disaster that doesn't reflect your skills? With a little effort, you can prepare yourself to be polished and articulate, a masterpiece of interview charm and finesse.

Common Interview Questions

Personal Questions

- Tell me about yourself.

- Why are you interested in this field?

- Why did you choose your major?

- Why did you choose to attend your university?

- Do you feel you received a good education? Why, why not?

- What activities meant the most to you during college?

- What was your favorite class in your major? Why?

- What was your least favorite? Why?

- What was your favorite elective class? Why?

- What was your least favorite? Why?

- What do you do to relax?

- Describe a stressful situation that you have excelled in.

- What are you most proud of in your life? Why?

- What skills would you bring to this position?

- Why do you think you would be an asset to our company?

- What do you know about our industry?

- If you couldn't be in this industry, what career would you choose?

- What would you personally or professionally do differently?

Questions You Need to Be Ready to Nail

- What are your strengths and weaknesses?

- Why are you the best person for this position?

- Why will you be successful?

- What motivates you?

- Where do you want to be in five years? Ten years?

- What is the single most important thing I should know about you?

The self-explorer, whether he wants to or not, becomes an explorer of everything else.
—ELIAS CANETTI

When It's Your Turn to Ask the Questions

The interviewer will give you the opportunity to ask your own questions at some point in the interview. *I don't have any questions* is the wrong answer. This is a very important part of the interview because you will be evaluated by the questions you ask. A good interviewer will analyze the content of your questions, your choice of words, your delivery, and your body language. Prepare questions in advance and memorize them.

Guidelines

1. **Use your questions to show that you have researched the company.** A question like "What other products do you manufacture?" shows ignorance, not interest. Instead ask: "I understand that the company recently expanded to Japan. Will there be opportunities for advancement to this division?"

2. **Make your questions reflect your ambition.** Ask about the career path for someone in your position. Make it clear that your intention is to grow quickly. Ask about what opportunities exist for professional growth, such as company-sponsored classes or mentor programs.

3. **Ask about your interviewer's personal experience.** You are in front of a living, breathing member of the company you are trying to join. Find out why that person applied to this company and if his or her expectations were met. Don't suck up. Just ask the questions that are interesting to you.

4. **Do not ask about money or benefits.** Doing so is inappropriate in a first interview. Get the job offer first and then worry about that. If they are not what you expect, then do not accept the job. If the employer inquires why you have not asked about it, reply that you are more interested in the opportunity than the money at this point.

5. **Ask easy questions.** Do not put the interviewer on the spot with a tough question that you doubt he or she can answer. Archaic, little-known bits of trivia dredged up by your research are not great opportunities to make you look smarter than your interviewer. No one likes to look foolish, and it will create a negative impression in the interviewer's mind.

6. **Bring written questions with you.** Type them and write them out in complete sentences. Place them in front of you at the beginning of the interview. Some recruiters ask to keep them. Do not read directly off your list. Use it as a point of reference and then ask the question with good eye contact.

7. **Take notes.** Write down keywords from the answer. Don't write down every word, because you lose eye contact by doing so. Also, don't try to write without looking down at all. I once had an applicant who wrote entire paragraphs when I spoke without ever looking down. All the lines ran together and it was a complete mess. It was funny but distracting.

8. **Never interrupt.** Let the interviewer go on as long as he or she wants. Do not interrupt and never finish a sentence for him or her. While it's only bad manners in a regular conversation, it can be disastrous in an interview.

9. **Keep your questions short.** Restrain yourself. Remember it is a question, not an essay.

10. **Ask the closing question.** "I would like to pursue this position. Where do we go from here?"

> *Every page of your life is a passage of your history.*
>
> **—ARABIC PROVERB**

The Secret to Exceptional Answers

Keep in mind that an interview is not a conversation. A conversation is simply conveying information, while an interview is an exercise in persuasion. If you answer questions in a conversational style, all you are doing is giving an oral version of your résumé.

Answers in an interview have to go beyond providing information. They have to make an argument for your aptitude and convince the interviewer that you are the right person for the position. Every part of the interview creates the overall impression (your confidence, the way you dress, your handshake), but the content of your answers is most important. The formula for answering questions was actually taught to me by a candidate I interviewed.

I asked, "Suppose you find yourself overwhelmed by the stress in your job, what would you do?"

She replied, "Let me give you two examples of when that happened to me in past positions and how I resolved the problem. . . . Finally, I feel this has prepared me for this position because . . ."

I asked, "Suppose you had a problem with a co-worker, how would you resolve it?"

She replied, "That happened when I was with so-and-so company and here is what I did. . . . However, looking at it now, I think I would have resolved it in this fashion. . . ."

She was a great interview . . . and she still works for my company! Most candidates will answer these questions fairly well, but they make me work to form a conclusion. I have to decide what character traits the experience shows and how it relates to the position I want to fill. I have to do this mental exercise on the fly, as the question is being answered, because I have to ask another question once the answer is done. The need to make a snap analysis can cause an interviewer to miss a key point and make a poor decision about a candidate.

Answer questions in a way that takes the burden off the recruiter's shoulders. Help the interviewer to reach conclusions by showing him or her the link between your past experience and how it relates to your future position.

A simple pattern to follow is:

- **Give examples of past experience relevant to the question.**
- **Discuss character traits proven by experience.**
- **Summarize the relevance to the position.**

The questions I asked in the preceding conversation followed the traditional interview format. They revolved around what she could offer the company in the future and how she intended to add value through her efforts. The candidate's answers were a persuasive argument about the character traits she developed from her past experience and why these proved that she was a good candidate for the position: *"Here are the character traits that make me a great candidate. I understand everyone says they have the same traits, but here is my proof."*

Recruiters have found that the past is the best indicator of the future. That is why relevant work experience is so welcome. If you have performed well in the past, there is no reason to think you will not continue to do so. On the same logic, if you were a real slacker the last time you had significant responsibilities, there is not much reason to doubt that you will be a slacker again.

This may seem like a very narrow way of thinking, but it makes good business sense. Hiring people is like approving a credit card. The first thing a bank does when it receives your credit application is review your past credit and payment history. The person reviewing your credit does not want to read an essay on all the reasons why you are a trustworthy investment for the bank. All the bank wants to know is "Have you paid your obligations in the past?" If you have not, the bank will not be willing to take a risk on you.

I do believe people can change. The past is not a prison that traps you to a predetermined fate. Every individual has the power of personal change. Just like the person who goes bankrupt and then rebuilds credit over a period of time, a person who makes bad choices early in life can rebuild credibility over time.

However, when I hire someone, I want to know the person can do the job right now. Traditional interviews test how well you can think and imagine solutions to future problems. Behavioral interviews try to determine behavior patterns as demonstrated by the problems or situations you have dealt with in the past.

To be successful in a behavioral interview, you need to demonstrate a link between your past actions and actions you will need to take in your new job. The following worksheet will help you to identify the behaviors you will want to highlight in the interview and prepare you to have specific examples at your fingertips.

Behavior Worksheet

Directions: List two specific stories that demonstrate positive behavior in each of these areas. Use the most recent examples first.

1. *You have demonstrated leadership in past roles.*

   a. _____

   b. _____

2. *You have demonstrated work ethic by doing whatever it takes to complete a job.*

   a. _____

   b. _____

3. *You have demonstrated perseverance by overcoming repeated failure to finally succeed at your goals.*

   a. _____

   b. _____

4. *You resolved a conflict with a supervisor or a coworker in a professional manner.*

   a. _____

   b. _____

5. **You have demonstrated initiative by creating a new project or solving a problem that was not your responsibility.**

a. _____

b. _____

6. **You had to handle stress to achieve your goals.**

a. _____

b. _____

7. **You have demonstrated creativity in your problem-solving.**

a. _____

b. _____

8. **You have demonstrated your ambition by the determination required to achieve specific goals.**

a. _____

b. _____

It is important for you to take the time to fill out this exercise. Draw from as many different experiences as possible. Behavior that you demonstrate in a nonwork setting is just as valid as what you do on the job. The interviewer wants to know what kind of person you are, not necessarily what kind of worker you have been in the past.

I spend a lot of time in my interviews talking about leadership. I can't tell you the number of times candidates have told me that they really don't have any leadership experience. I always probe to see if they have done any sports or clubs. Suddenly the floodgates are open. "I was the varsity football captain." "I was the founder of the Business Club on campus."

Everything you do has a bearing on the kind of person you are and the behavior traits that you will demonstrate in your career. Go back in time and show a pattern of behavior that demonstrates positive character traits. It can be something that happened in your family, while you were playing sports, or in a past job.

A Quick Story

I once interviewed a candidate with extremely limited work experience and marginal interpersonal skills. Ten minutes into the interview I made a decision not to hire him. My last question was whether he could describe to me a circumstance where he had to show incredible determination and perseverance in order to reach a goal.

Honestly, I didn't expect a great answer, but I received one that I will never forget.

This young man had been nearly beaten to death by his father when he was three years old and raised in poverty by his single mother. He was surrounded by gangs, drugs, and crime throughout his adolescence and became involved in all three. After barely passing high school, a strong male role model convinced him to attend junior college to further his education. He did so and married his pregnant high school sweetheart that same year.

Determined to set a good example for his newborn, he maintained a 4.0 average throughout his first year in college and transferred to a four-year university. After he transferred, his daughter was diagnosed with a rare brain disorder that required several surgeries. The prognosis gave his daughter a 10 percent chance to live past her third birthday. To help pay the medical bills not covered by his insurance, this man worked nights at UPS, attended school during the day, and still wanted to do my program so he could show his daughter that hard work creates success.

This was the person I was about to turn away because I didn't think he possessed the determination and the willpower to be in my program. He went on to be a valuable employee, and the interview taught me a lesson about judging too quickly.

If you can give a recruiter a concrete image of positive character traits, you have won half the battle. Skills can be taught, but character traits are incredibly hard to instill in someone. Demonstrate through exact, detailed examples that you have the skills and behavior patterns that you claim to possess. Do not leave recruiters guessing whether they can believe you can handle the job, make your case through the evidence of your past actions.

> *A man can succeed at almost anything for which he has unlimited enthusiasm.*
>
> **—CHARLES SCHWAB**

Interview Secrets That Professional Recruiters Don't Want You to Know

Secret #1

Some recruiters do not interview well. Everyone you interview with will have an individual style. Some recruiters will provide you with great opportunities to showcase your talents and past experiences. Some recruiters will give you a half-hour lecture on the importance of your work ethic and a not-so-brief history of their own lives.

Bad interviewers can be dangerous to you. They still represent your link to the company or the position that you want, and their lack of ability could seriously impact your ability to showcase your attributes. Do not allow poor interview skills to sabotage your chances.

Take responsibility in the interview to get your most important points across. If the interviewer does not ask very good questions, use your questions as a stepping-stone to the answers you want to give.

Ask the interviewer, "How important do you feel leadership skills are to this position?"

After they give their answer, respond with, "Great, because I have consistently shown leadership ability throughout my college career. For example . . ."

Do not let an interviewer take away from your ability to get your main points across. If you are frustrated during the interview, give a strong closing argument at the end.

"In closing, I would like to reiterate why I would be a good investment for you and for the company. Every hiring decision you make is an investment decision. And like any investment decision, I'm sure you base your decision on risk. Although I am confident that I would be a good choice for you to make, I understand it is my responsibility to convince you why I am a good risk.

"First, the best indicator of future action is past results. I have been a consistent high performer in any activity where I have applied myself. For example. . . .

"Second, the most important precursor to achievement is commitment. I am committed to my career goals and I believe that ABC Corporation is the best vehicle for me to realize my ambitions. I would be an asset if hired for this position.

"I am very interested in this position. How can I move forward from this point?"

Secret #2
Mirror the person who interviews you.

This is an old sales technique. The theory is that people respond to people who are like them. A hard-hitting, down-to-business type will not like to work with someone who is easygoing and soft-spoken. Likewise, a quiet, diminutive personality will go into shock when confronted with someone who is brash and overbearing.

When you enter an interview, determine the personality traits of the interviewer and mirror what you see. If you get a rapid-talking showman, you had better step up the energy level. If you get a mouse, don't feel like you have to stoop all the way to his level, but you might want to tone down your delivery a little. People like to hire people who are like them. The more similarity you can make the interviewer see in you the better. The old joke about interviewer egos: *How was the interview?* That guy was perfect. He was just like me! You may laugh, but this is the way it works. Mirror your interviewer as much as possible and let him hire a young version of himself. Your interview success rate will increase dramatically.

Secret #3
Recruiters are bored to death. Try having the same conversation twenty times in a row and you will have a flavor of what it means to be a full-time recruiter. If you can break the monotony, you will stand out. Do whatever it

takes to be interesting. Dare to be bold and outgoing, but don't overdo it. Find one thing you have in common with the interviewer and use that to have a brief non–work-oriented conversation. Show how friendly and easy to get along with you will be once you're hired.

Secret #4

Recruiters have egos. Yes, it's true. Recruiters, like most people, like to talk about how great they are. Don't shamelessly pander to their egos, but show an interest in their careers and background. Be careful, because some people need very little prompting to open the floodgates, and you are not there to find out interviewers' life stories. Ask enough to make them feel good and to get some insight into what their experience with the company has been.

Secret #5

Recruiters will forget everything you say. The exact words that you use in the interview are going to be forgotten. The only thing a recruiter will remember is an overall impression. The words you use are important, because they create the impression, but your mannerisms are just as important.

When I review my notes the day after a full interview schedule, I remember the candidates based on their aptitude and their overall presentation. Were they confident? Quiet? Were they forceful with their answers? Was it an enjoyable conversation, or were they difficult to talk to?

Mannerisms count, so be aware of how you carry yourself. Your words and answers will prove your aptitude, but employers look at attitude just as strongly. Say the right things, and remember to say them well.

Success is going from failure to failure without loss of enthusiasm.

—WINSTON CHURCHILL

The Last Word

■ Don't confuse an interview with a snapshot of the true you. An interview is you on your best professional behavior with the advantage of intense preparation and extensive research.

■ Preparation for an interview includes knowing specific background about the company with which you are interviewing and being able to clearly articulate your skills, interests, and goals.

■ You are judged by the quality of your questions as much as the quality of your answers.

■ The key to excellent interview answers is to use specific examples from your past that demonstrate the claims you make about the character traits you possess.

Ten

Top-Down Job Hunting: The Secret Method to Get Any Job You Want

An ounce of action is worth a ton of theory.

—FRIEDRICH ENGLES

Everything we have talked about so far is fairly conventional. We have identified the primary methods to land good interviews and how to shine once you get there. This is great to find average job opportunities and to have an average chance of getting hired. There is nothing wrong with being average. By the strict definition of the word, most people are.

However, if you have your sights a little higher, we need to approach job hunting from a different angle. The traditional methods discussed so far have all pointed you toward human resource departments and professional recruiters. While you will receive job offers using these entry points, approximately 70 percent of jobs are filled outside of this avenue. A majority of positions are filled through referrals, networking, and personal relationships. Therefore, if you confine yourself to traditional job-search techniques, you are severely limiting your options.

So, if this hidden job market is filled through connections, how do you magically get the connections to help your career?

Instead of starting at the bottom of the interview food chain with the assistant recruiter-in-training, I am going to show you how to start at the top and work your way down. You may not have the connections right now to enter the hidden job market, but if you work hard using the methods in this chapter, you will have connections that will help you throughout your career.

> **The tragedy in life is not that a man loses, but that he almost wins.**
>
> **—HEYWOOD BROUN**

The Premise

- The only time you want to visit Human Resources or the Personnel Department is after you have been hired or after you have a ringing endorsement from a senior executive.

- The more people you meet in your industry, the more opportunity you have of job offers.

- The most powerful people in your industry will be able to open the most doors for you.

- People love to help college students and will give you incredible access to try to help you.

- Access is only the beginning. You still have to shine once you get there.

Little strokes fell big oaks.

—BEJAMIN FRANKLIN

Define Your Targets

- **Identify the industry you want to target.** This is the easy part. We have already worked on this together, and you should have a pretty good idea of what you are interested in by now.

- **Research the industry and find out the names of principals.** Create a target list of the heavy hitters in your industry. Start off with the easy ones: the big names. If you want to go into the film/entertainment field, start your list with Michael Eisner, Steven Spielburg, and Robert Zemekis. If you want to go into investment banking, find out who are the current heads of the top investment banking firms in the industry. Make the list as extensive and as extravagant as you want.

- **Identify some of the midlevel players in the industry.** Doing this can be a little more difficult because the celebrity factor is gone. A good source of information is the annual reports for public companies. Another good source is a publication called the *Who's Who in American Business.* This book is categorized by industry, which makes it a very useful tool for your purpose.

    The people to locate are the midlevel movers

and shakers. These are the ones who are playing the game and playing it well. They have rocketed through the ranks, experienced early success, and are eager to tell someone about it. If you are interested in advertising, find a young ad executive who recently received a big promotion. If you are interested in sales, find someone who has recently won an award or set a company record. You can find this information in your local newspaper's business section. Most papers usually have a column with a title like "Executives on the Move," "Movers and Shakers," or something similar.

Never stop. One always stops as something is about to happen.

—PETER BROOK

Send a Great Letter

Now that you have identified your targets, it's time to write a great letter. The letter serves only one purpose; to open the person up to the possibility of some type of interaction with you. Whether it is a phone call, a personal meeting, or a message left with a secretary, all you want is contact. Here is a sample of what this letter might look like.

Sample Top-Down Letter

Spencer Pepe
1234 Prelife Crisis Street
Needajob, CA 90001

October 5, 2000

Dear Mr. Spielberg,

My name is Spencer Pepe and I am writing to ask for a ten-minute meeting with you to discuss the film industry.

I will graduate from the University of California at Santa Barbara later this year and am considering a career in film production. However, I have several concerns about what that career would be like. I write to you because the impact of your work is one of the reasons I feel compelled toward a film career.

I understand that your time is incredibly valuable. However, I was hoping that you could find ten minutes to meet with me to answer a few questions. I will call your office at 9 a.m. on Monday, September 13, to ask your assistant if there would be a convenient time for us to meet.

Sincerely,
Spencer Pepe

P.S. If your schedule does not permit a meeting, can you suggest someone I could contact to answer my questions?

The key is to make it clear that you are not looking for a job but simply want to discuss the concerns you have about a career in the field. That is the key phrase. Remember that you are writing to an industry leader, someone who loves what he or she does. Such people are eager to make others understand why they love their field. The thought of someone with concerns about such a great career is almost too much to bear.

Be completely honest in your letters, and be respectful. Do not tell some midlevel ad executive that she is the reason you want to go into advertising. But you can say, "I saw the announcement of your promotion in the *Wall Street Journal.* Congratulations! I recently graduated from the University of Florida and am considering a career in advertising, and I found it encouraging to read about your success. . . ."

The P.S. at the bottom is essential. The top-down method assumes that the big-time players will shoot you down. Sometimes you get some amazing luck, and you will actually get the ten minutes you request. Usually the best you can hope for is an answer to your last question: Whom can I contact? If you get an answer to this question, you are doing great.

If Steven Spielburg refers you to someone, you need to understand a few things. First, accept the fact that Steven Spielberg probably did *not* see your letter but that it was answered by an assistant. Second, realize that you shouldn't care because all that matters now is that you can write a letter to your new contact that says "Dear Mr. Smith, Steven Spielberg suggested that I contact you." How powerful is that?

Make sure that you immediately send Steven Spielberg and his staff thank-you cards and some flowers for their help. Include a note with the flowers that explains what they are for and that you intend to contact Mr. So-and-so. Again, Steven Spielburg never sees the flowers, but you have reminded the staff in his office who you are. If Mr. Smith calls to ask who you are, you now have a chance that someone in the office will say something good about you.

I know it sounds like a lot of work, but the contacts you can make with this method can be incredible.

Success, in general, means the opportunity to experience and to realize the maximum forces that are within us.
—DAVID SARNOFF

Be Sharp on the Phone

In your letter, you need to give a definite date and time that you will call your contact. This makes it harder to chicken out and decide not to call. Make sure that you call on time and are prepared to be sharp.

If you are calling a midlevel player, there is a fifty-fifty chance you will speak with someone who expects your call, whether it is your target person or a personal assistant. Ten to 15 percent of the time, you will make the phone call and be put directly through to the person you want to reach. When you call a big shot, there is a 1 percent chance you will talk to the person, but there is always the possibility, so be ready.

You have to make this a *great* phone call.

Write an outline for the phone call before you make it. Double-check your contact information and clearly define the purpose for your call. Have your schedule ready so that you can set an appointment. If you are calling a heavy hitter, cancel everything on your schedule if he or she agrees to a meeting. Be prepared to conduct your ten-minute interview over the phone if that is all the person can offer you. There is nothing more embarrassing than going through all this trouble and then not having a single question to ask.

Remember that your goal is to get a personal meeting, so make certain that you ask for one. Be considerate of the person's time. Try to set up an interview time early in the conversation and then let the person go back to work.

If you can reach only an assistant, explain your situation and ask whether your contact received your letter. Executive assistants govern the world, so take the time to gain their approval. They can be great allies. If you can win over personal assistants, your letter might reach the contact's desk instead of the trash can. It's amazing what a little kindness can accomplish!

I never learn anything talking. I only learn things when I ask questions.

—LOU HOLTZ

The Meeting:
Only the Brilliant Need Attend

Treat this meeting as you would any interview. The difference is that you are the one who gets to conduct the questioning. This may be uncommon ground for you, so you have a great reason to do a lot of preparation.

■ **Ask great questions:** You are not there to apply for a job, so don't feel as if you need to throw softballs. Ask about the drawbacks of the industry, find out what the trade-offs for success are, and learn what steps you need to take to achieve prominence in the industry. Write down twice as many questions as you think you will have time to ask. You will be surprised how fast you go through them.

Ten Great Questions

1. Why did you go into this field?

2. What has been the biggest challenge in your career?

3. How has the industry changed since you started?

4. How do you see the industry evolving in the next five years?

5. I want to be a leader in the industry. What kind of career path would you recommend?

6. What character traits does a leader in this industry need to possess?

7. What are the negatives to this industry?

8. What is your reading list like? What books would you recommend?

9. If you were me, an overeager, confident, impatient, recent college graduate, what would you do to make certain that you were successful?

10. What businesses and individuals do you respect the most in this industry? Why?

Eight Questions Not to Ask

1. How can I get your job? *Cliché*

2. How can you help me? *Clumsy*

3. How much money can I make? *Immature*

4. How much free time will I have? *Lazy*

5. Why would I want to be in this industry? *Arrogant*

6. What can you tell me about your job? *Nonspecific*

7. What mistakes have you made that held you back in your career? *Awkward*

8. Do you feel like you had to be unethical to be success-
    ful? *Judgmental*

- **State your purpose and do not bring a résumé.**
  Reinforce the point you made in your letter that you
  want to consider a future in the field and requested
  the meeting only to find out more about what such a
  career would entail. If the person asks for a résumé,
  say "I didn't bring a résumé with me because I am
  truly here only to find out more about this career. I
  would love to give you a copy to get your insight and
  suggestions."

- **Share information about yourself.** The person
  you are meeting with will inevitably ask you questions
  about yourself. Be open, but do not use your regular
  interview style. Be much more conversational so that
  the meeting does not turn into an interview.

- **Ask the best question.** "If you were me, and you
  decided that you wanted to be a player in this industry, what would you do?" There is wisdom to be
  learned in the answer to this question. Often, if you
  have made a good impression, the contact will offer
  assisstance to you at this point. As in: "If I were you, I
  would get into the trainee program at corporate headquarters. I can't get you the job, but I can make sure
  that the right people see your résumé." Bingo.

- **Be considerate of the person's time.** This is
  where I always mess up. I lined up a ten-minute meeting with the vice president of ICM, a Hollywood talent
  agency with a client list including Schwarzenegger and
  the Beach Boys. I asked that man questions for an hour
  and a half! Granted, he never asked me to leave, but the
  signs were there that the interview had dragged on too

long. Don't cut an interview short if you are rolling, but respect people's time. They will appreciate it and be happy to help you in the future.

■ **Ask for help.** Sometimes people are willing to help you, but they need a little encouragement. If you have established a good rapport with contacts, ask whom they could refer you to in the industry to get some more insight. If you do not feel comfortable doing this, simply ask if you can contact them in the future if you think of any more questions. Just make sure that the door is left open for you.

Nothing is particularly hard if you divide it into small jobs.

—HENRY FORD

Following Up/Sucking Up . . . Same Thing

You worked hard to make this contact, so don't ruin all of your effort because you forget to follow up. Send an immediate thank-you card. If you were able to keep the meeting focused on questions about industry and escaped without the meeting turning into a formal job interview, send a small gift as well. Some small bit of memorabilia from your school will do nicely. *Never* do this after a regular interview, as it can come across as extremely unprofessional. But it can work wonders after an informational interview. Is this sucking up? Of course it is! And it works great!

If the interview went well, you probably were offered

some kind of assistance: a contact name, an offer for a job interview, or some good advice. Follow up as soon as possible on whatever action your contact suggested. Keep your contact informed of your progress and always ask for more advice. To avoid being a nuisance, limit your calls to a maximum once every two weeks.

> *Somehow we learn who we really are and then live with that decision.*
> **—ELEANOR ROOSEVELT**

Why It Works So Well

- **People are basically good. They like to help students and people about to start their careers.** People who are very successful in their field often become teachers later on to fulfill the need to "give back." Often, when heavy hitters grant you an interview, you will find that they had a similar experience when they were your age. Bill Clinton was famous (and notorious) for spending time with the interns and students who visited the White House. His formative experience meeting John F. Kennedy when he was a student compelled him to provide others with the same experience.

- **People all have the same favorite subject of conversation: themselves.** You provide them with a forum to brag a little and to feel important. This is especially true for midlevel players who have recently received a promotion.

- **People look out for their investments.** After you have an informational interview with people, they tend to take an interest in your success. This is because they have invested their time and they want to see their investment pay off. Also, contacts are eager to see if you follow their advice. They are able to live vicariously through your experiences, and want their recommendations to be proven correct. "See, I told you that if you called So-and-so you would get a good job offer."

- **Informational interviews are easy work.** You are not explicitly asking for anything other than some advice. The person you are interviewing does not have to make any decisions or take any actions as a result of your meeting. It usually represents a nice break from a heavy schedule.

- **Interview rules are suspended.** While you need to be polite, well dressed, and the like, you can ask much tougher questions and be much more conversational than if you were in a formal interview. The people you interview recognize this and look forward to an interesting dialog instead of the usual rigid formality of an interview.

- **You cannot have a bad experience.** Any contact with someone in your industry is educational. Meeting a legend in your field can be a transforming experience. Go into every meeting with an open mind and be ready to learn. After the interview, immediately write down everything you can remember from the conversation.

Success usually comes to those who are too busy looking for it.
—HENRY DAVID THOREAU

- Top-down job hunting is a technique designed to put you in touch directly with the decision makers in your industry.

- Successful people enjoy talking about themselves and usually are very willing to grant you an informational interview. Such interviews often lead to job offers and can create an impressive networking list in your industry.

- Prepare for each meeting as if it is the interview that will change your life. It very well could be just that.

Section Five:
Job Offers, Negotiation,
And Other Fun

Eleven:
Get the Job Offer

If opportunity doesn't knock, build a door.
—MILTON BERLE

The moments right after a big interview are great, especially if you did well. Even if you blew it, you're just happy to get out of there. After the adrenaline rush wears off, the inevitable question will come to you: "Now what?" There are two parts to the answer. First, you have to ensure that you get a job offer. Second, you have to decide what to do with the offer.

The First Step is a Thank-You Letter and a Personal Phone Call

The fact that you had an extremely long or an extremely short interview really has no bearing on how well it went. Never assume you blew it and give up, and, more important, never assume you already have the job and forget the follow-up. The first steps in the follow-up are a thank-you note and a personal phone call. You already know that this is what you should do. It's not an original idea. However, you wouldn't believe how many people blow it on this simple gesture. They procrastinate and stall until they just give up on it. Huge mistake. *Huge.*

The recruiter who interviews you probably will meet dozens of people to try to fill one position. Your face and name will slowly slip away unless you do something to ensure that you get noticed. One of the finest resources regarding job offers and negotiation is Brian Krueger's *College Grad Job Hunter.* In it, he recommends that you get a thank-you letter in the recruiter's hands by the end of the day that you were interviewed or by the next morning at the latest. If you send it by regular mail, it will be days until the person receives it. By that time, the recruiter might have difficulty remembering any details from your interview.

The letter should be typed and directly related to the content of your interview. Some people recommend a hand-written note, as it is more personal. These are fine, but a few words of warning. First, make sure you have good handwriting. I have received thank-you cards that I could barely read. It detracted from the gesture the person was trying to make. Second, your hand doesn't have spell-check. Double-check your spelling. It sounds obvious, but I have received many thank-you cards filled with errors. Not the impression the candidate was trying to make. Also, I believe thank-you notes are expressing personal sentiment, so they should be kept private. Don't send postcards or faxes that anyone can read. I recommend against faxing a thank-you note, as fax machines are often shared among several people and your note could easily end up in a trash can before it has time to work its magic.

In the note, reiterate the key points from the interview and make your case as to why you are a good candidate. This is a good opportunity for you to include facts that you may have forgotten to include in the heat of interview battle. Now that you have more time to form your thoughts, you can present a more coherent argument. Often the recruiter will remember you more by this letter than by the content of the interview.

I have invited candidates in for a second interview solely because of a strong follow-up letter. Sometimes these were candidates who were unimpressive in the interview but made such a good argument for themselves on paper that I had to give them another chance. If you do not feel that you did well in an interview, spend some quality time on a great thank-you letter.

Make a quick thank-you phone call to the interviewer as well. This needs to happen in the same time frame as the letter, either the same day or early the next morning. Simply thank the person for his or her time and consideration and reiterate your desire to move to the next step of the process. Every interaction that you have with the recruiter will help to make certain that you are remembered.

Get a thank-you letter in the recruiter's hands on the day that you were interviewed or by the next morning.

There is a fine line between annoying and persistent, but there is also a line between polite and so passive that you find yourself unemployed. Don't be afraid to remain engaged with the recruiter or interviewer as the hiring decision is being made. Specifically ask about the time frame in which the decision will occur. If you cannot get a straight answer, call back once a week to get an update.

My favorite line that a candidate used on me was when he called me up a week after the interview and said, "I know that I would be a good person for this position. If you are still undecided, I would welcome the opportunity to sit down with you for another five minutes to sell myself to you." I laughed and said, "You *are* persistent." The candidate replied, "I'm persistent because I know that this position is a great opportunity for me and I am willing to work hard to get it. Let me sit down with you and answer any concerns you have. I believe that I will be able to show you that I am the best candidate for the position. Do you have time later today?"

This approach is not for the weak-hearted, but neither was the position that this candidate wanted. I was impressed by the confidence and the initiative displayed by the phone call. I looked at his behavior as an indication of what I could expect from him as an employee. I let him come to a second interview to sell himself, and I bought it. He was hired that day.

> *Do your duty and a little bit more, and the future will take care of itself.*
> —ANDREW CARNEGIE

Rejection is part of the job search. It can be a very humbling experience if you receive the thin letter in the mail from the company you are sure that you were born to work for. REJECTION. Oh, well, you tried. Your friends and family will give you their support and tell you to keep on trying. You might be depressed for a couple of days, but you'll get over it. You might even open the want ads and start circling those little boxes in between your bouts of self-pity.

Don't be such a wimp. A rejection letter is just the first no. Most people look at it as the last no, but it is still six or seven nos away. If salespeople accepted the first no they heard and just said "OK, have a nice day," there would be a lot of hungry salespeople in the world.

In sales parlance, a no is either an objection or a condition. Objections are concerns that buyers have that keep them from making a buying decision. Conditions are unsolvable issues that make it impossible for buyers to make a purchase. An objection would be that the interviewer is not sure that you have the skills necessary for the position. You can handle this objection by arguing your case more effectively. A condition would be that the position was given to the CEO's son or that there were other candidates that were simply more qualified for this *particular* position. However, conditions are often just objections in disguise, so don't be too quick to give up in the face of a perceived condition.

> **Everything comes to those who hustle while he waits.**
> **—THOMAS EDISON**

Your first objective after you have been rejected is to find out why. This can be accomplished with a simple phone call. "Hi, this is _____. I received your letter that I am no longer being considered for the accounting position. I was hoping that I could get some feedback from you to help me in my job search. What was it that I specifically lacked to meet your needs?"

You can start by talking to the initial recruiter who did your first interview. Sometimes you can glean some important information from this person. Think about it. He or she recommended you for an interview with the boss as a good candidate for the position, and the boss disagreed. First, the recruiter will be just as curious as you about why you didn't get the job and will likely have received feedback from the boss. Second, the recruiter also has a vested interest in you eventually working out: It makes the recruiter look as if he or she knew what was going on when recommending you for the interview in the first place.

Take notes and ask questions to get as specific as possible. You are trying to get all of the objections out in the open. Once you know what the objections are, you can handle them head-on. Sometimes you might find that the decision was based on inaccurate information. A recruiter tells you that she made her decision because she needed someone who was willing to relocate overseas and her notes indicated that you were unwilling to do that. In fact, you would love to move overseas and her notes were wrong. This gives you the opportunity to set the record straight and possibly put yourself back in the running.

If the objections are more subtle, then you have to be ready with some persuasive arguments. For example, if the recruiter says that your GPA was too low, then you have some work to do. First, you have to make sure that all of the objections are on the table. An easy question is "If my GPA were higher, would I still be considered for this position, or were there other areas where I did not meet your needs?" This might pull out some other objections or commit the recruiter to the GPA answer.

After you have the objections on the table, you have to handle them one by one. "I understand my GPA might be lower than other applicants'; however, I also worked a job throughout school to pay for my own tuition. I believe that this speaks well of my work ethic and proves that I could handle the long hours required of this position . . . etc."

Next, don't be afraid to call the higher-ranking decision maker who did your interview. However, it's important to realize the pros and cons to this course of action. The cons are that you might be seen as something of a pest and hurt your chances if you want to reapply at a later date. The pros are that you can receive some very good feedback that will help you in your future interviews and there is a slight chance that you will work your way back into the job. One thing is for sure: You probably will be remembered more than the other candidates the interviewer met with with. This can be either a good or a bad thing depending on the tone and style you use in your phone call.

Remember the outcome you want. Once the interviewer gets off the phone, you want her to think "That was a very professional call. The tone was sincere and the candidate clearly stated the purpose of the call (to get feedback to improve her future interviews). That candidate is obviously dedicated to succeeding in this industry. Maybe I should keep his résumé on file for the future." What you are trying to avoid is the person you call thinking "What a strange phone call. I wonder which part of 'no' he didn't understand? And that whining about how I didn't give him a chance . . . I'm glad I avoided the mistake of hiring him."

Make the same phone call to each person you interviewed with in the recruiting process. Say something along the lines of "I wasn't offered the position, but I wanted to sincerely thank you for the time you invested in our interview." Again, remember the end result you are trying to achieve: for the person to end up thinking "What a class act. I can't believe my boss didn't hire him." If you handle those phone calls correctly, your name might be brought up by more than one person the next time there is an opening at the company.

The feedback method can be very useful, but there is danger inherent in this approach. You are inviting criticism, so you have to be ready to take it and learn from it. People don't enjoy hearing negative things about themselves, but it can be very constructive. The reason you didn't get a job might be because the interviewer simply didn't like you. Not a nice thing to think about, but it happens all the time. Be ready for some negativity and be thankful for it; the feedback will help you in the long run. If you simply can't stand any negativity in your life, don't call. Just remember that you might be missing out on a great opportunity.

There is no failure except in no longer trying.
There is no defeat except from within.
—ELBERT HUBBARD

The Puppy-Dog Approach

This is one of the oldest closes in sales. Imagine a father and his kids standing in a pet store. The kids desperately want a dog, but the father is resisting. The kids promise that they will take care of it, feed it, give it baths, and so on. Enter the pet store salesman. He has a great idea. Why not take a puppy home for a week and see how it goes? The father does not even have to pay for the dog . . . yet. The salesman offers to come by in one week and either pick up the dog and take it back to the pet store, or the father can give him a check at that time to pay for the dog.

We all know how that story turns out. Once the dog gets into the house, it's not leaving. Even if it eats everything in the house, the family becomes attached and the dog has a home for life. When the salesman come by a week later, he knows he's there to pick up a check, not the dog.

Use this approach with a company that gives you a big no. Find out what the objections are first and then offer to handle them by proving them false. In response to "We are unsure that you have the skills for this position," say "I am confident that I do. I am willing to work for free for two weeks to prove that to you. At the end of the two weeks, you and I can sit down and evaluate my performance. If it is satisfactory, which I know it will be, I have the job. If not, it has not cost you a thing. This is a measure of my commitment to success in this position." Once you are there for two weeks (and you have to shine during this time), you will most likely have the job. This method is a little harder if the company has already hired someone for the position you want. The best scenario is to get in there before the company has a chance to hire someone else. (Often the powers that be will be impressed with your enthusiasm that you will get a shot at the position.) If you don't, go for the part-time puppy-dog approach: Intern ten to fifteen hours a week to get your foot in the door. At least you'll be there when the next opening develops.

*I'm a little wounded, but I am not slain; I will
lay me down to bleed a while. Then I'll rise
and fight again.*

—JOHN DRYDEN

The Work-Your-Way-Up Approach

The work-your-way-up approach involves offering to
accept a position below your target job. Doing so will show
the employer your high level of commitment to achieving
this position. Make sure that the job you take is one that
gives you exposure to the position you want in the future.
Establish some conditions with your employer if you are
going to take this approach.

1. Create a time line (either based on time or perform-
    ance) with your employer as to when you will be able
    to move into the target position or at least apply for it
    again.

2. Agree that you can attend the training program for the
    your target job, even if it is on your own time.

3. Get these agreements in writing and be ready to leave
    if these conditions are not honored. You are taking the
    position to get your target job, not to get stuck answer-
    ing phones for three years.

*Study as if you were to live forever. Live as if
you were to die tomorrow.*

—ISIDORE OF SEVILLE

The Whatever-It-Takes Approach

If you desperately want to work for a company but doors keep getting shut to you, try something drastic. Don't take hostages or anything crazy, but be a little adventurous. I met a student who applied for a position with a commodities trading company. He went through two interviews and felt like he did very well. Then came the letter saying that he was no longer being considered for the position. He called the interviewers and discovered that he was rejected due to his lack of industry experience. No amount of fast talking could get him back in for another interview. It seemed he had come to the end of his road.

With nothing to lose, the student wrote and called the owner of the company, who was a nationally syndicated financial writer, the author of several books on commodities, and a sought-after public speaker. This student called and asked for five minutes of his time. "I have been denied employment with your firm and I want five minutes to convince you to reverse that decision. I am a good investment for you to make, but I know it is up to me to convince you of that. I need five minutes." The owner loved the aggressive approach, invited the student in, and gave him the job.

People respond well to aggressive pursuit of a position. It makes them believe that you will be just as aggressive once you are in the job. If you try this approach, there are a couple of caveats. First, it may not work. Many senior people simply do not have the time to deal with staffing issues and will not want to go over the heads of the people they have hired to provide this function. Also, you might fail to be very convincing in that five minutes. This is not a high-percentage close. Krueger's *College Grad Job Hunter* calls a similar approach the "Kamikaze Technique." Be careful not to offend the people who interviewed you the first time. Speak highly of them if you get your meeting with the senior person. Why? If you get the job, you will have to work with them. Most people will not bear you a grudge. In fact, they probably will be impressed with your initiative. Just remember that you have nothing to lose. The company has already said no; the worst it can do is say no again.

> **Life is a mirror and will reflect back to the thinker what he thinks into it.**
> **—ERNEST HOLMES**

Prepare for Contact

When you sent our your first résumés, you prepared for the responses and the requests for interviews. It is doubly important that you take the same precautions now that you are expecting job offers. I recommend that you purchase a pager with voice-mail for the duration of your job search. Chances are that you already have one. Ask recruiters to use this number to contact you. Using voice-mail gives you a few advantages.

- **Time to think.** If you answer the phone in the middle of a *Monday Night Football* party at your house and it's IBM on the other end, it can be hard to focus. If IBM pages you, then you have time to collect your thoughts and go to a quiet room to make the phone call.

- **No lost messages.** If your roommates are anything like mine were in college, the chances are better that a message will be lost than that it will find its rightful owner. Don't rely on others to take messages for you. They are too important.

■ **Quick response.** You can call the company back right away, which continues to build your on-the-ball image.

When you call a recruiter back (as soon as possible), have your thoughts collected and have a purpose. If you get rejected, what is your response? If another interview is requested, do you have your schedule in front of you? If you are offered a position, what do you say? Mentally go through these questions before you pick up the phone. Play out each scenario in your mind and be ready for anything.

The quality of our expectations determines the quality of our action.

—ANDRE GODIN

What to Do Once You Have the Job Offer

What if everything goes the way it's supposed to and you get a job offer? What do you do? The biggest mistake most people make is that they accept the first offer they receive. It's as if they are so relieved they actually got a job that they feel the need to grab it as quickly as possible. Don't be in such a hurry.

Once you receive an offer, how you react depends on how you feel about the position being offered. If you get an offer of your dream job with your first-choice company, it's not time to play hard to get. Instead, move to the negotiation section of this chapter. However, if you are uncertain about how this offer compares to other opportunities that are still pending, then it's time to have some fun.

Big shots are only little shots who kept shooting.

—CHRISTOPHER MORLEY

Once you receive an offer, let the other companies you are interviewing with know right away. It is human nature to want what someone else wants. (Hence the term "love triangle.") If a recruiter knows that you have a job offer on the table, she will look at you in a different light. Instead of an unemployed, desperate college grad, you are now a sought-after commodity coveted by the competition. Feel free to tell the recruiter the name of the company that has offered you a position, but do not feel obligated to disclose the specifics of the offer. Simply say that you have been made an offer but that you are still very interested in weighing all options before making your decision.

Also, tell the company that made you the offer that you are interested in the position but still have other firms whose offers are pending. Although you believe the offering company offers the best opportunity, out of professional courtesy you feel it necessary to listen to all offers before making a decision. Ask for time to make your decision. One or two weeks is the norm.

Suddenly your position has improved dramatically. On one side, firms that are thinking about you now feel that they need to make a decision and somehow convince you to choose them over the competition. On the other side, the firm that has offered you a job feels that it needs to chase you. It may sweeten the offer in order to compete with the other offers you will receive. Your sudden popularity gives you greater negotiating leeway later in the process and also can hurry the process along with firms that have not yet made a decision.

If you think it's going to rain, it will.

—CLINT EASTWOOD

Negotiation for entry-level positions is always a difficult issue. New college grads seldom negotiate when entering their first jobs, mostly because they do not feel that they can. Some companies will be very specific in the interview process that the job offer, if made, is set in stone with no negotiation possible. This is not always true.

There is an old saying, "Everything is negotiable." Everything *is* negotiable, but you can also negotiate yourself out of a job if you are not careful. High-handed, know-it-all tactics by fresh out-of-college job candidates can make recruiters rethink their hiring decisions. Said another way, if you are a pain in the butt trying to negotiate your contract, you'll probably be a pain in the butt as an employee. I don't mean to imply that you cannot do some negotiation with your first job. You just have to do it carefully.

> *If you would hit the mark, you must aim a little above it; every arrow that flies feels the attraction of the earth.*
>
> **—HENRY WADSWORTH LONGFELLOW**

The Easy Lead-in Negotiation

Once you have a job offer from a company, you have a little more power. The people there want you and now you know it. However, your power may not be as much as you think because the company undoubtedly has candidates waiting in the wings ready to jump at the opportunity if you say no. But for right now, you are the first-choice candidate, which gives you a little breathing room.

The easiest negotiation is the I-have-a-few-questions technique. Tell the recruiter who offers you the job that you are honored and would like to sit down to discuss a few questions in finer detail. This is also a good time to let her know that you are entertaining offers from other companies, as discussed.

Sit down with the recruiter, or your future boss, and ask specific questions about the person's position and your career path. This is best done in person so that you can read the body language to make sure you don't go too far.

"What are my opportunities for advancement in this position?"

"How do you measure performance, and when can I expect to have my first review?"

"What kind of access will I be given to senior management for purposes of mentoring?"

"What kind of support can I expect for career growth? Does the company encourage seminars and conference attendance?"

What you are doing is getting your future employer to commit to a series of promises about your position. Take thorough notes and repeat the answers to make sure that you understand what is being offered. Notice that all of the questions are geared toward achievement, self-improvement, and ambition. You are not demanding vacation days or a salary increase, but you are concerned with excelling in the company if (when) your work is exemplary. Once you have the meeting, indicate what specifics you would like to see included in their offer. A casual "And compensation for professional growth seminars is included in the agreement, right?" gets the point across that you would like things in writing. If this gets an angry reaction from your potential employer, it might indicate you have a problem. Promises are written down in the real world. If someone reacts strangely when you ask for something in writing, it's a strong indication that the person was not too concerned about keeping that particular promise to you anyway.

Use common sense, though. If your boss says that the company is growing quickly and there could be chances for quick advancement, don't ask him to commit in writing to your forthcoming ascendancy into senior management. Remember, you are still the unknown factor. But if he says that you'll be eligible for stock options after your first year, get the details of what you need to do to earn them in writing.

Once you accept the offer, your boss probably will not be as forthcoming with the answers to these questions. A current employee who asks these questions can be a nuisance, but when you are the prized recruit who is considering other offers, the employer is eager to put the best face on the job opportunity. By asking direct questions, you force the employer to make a commitment to future action. For example, if you are an employee asking when you can have a review for promotion, the answer will probably be "Let's just see how it goes." When the boss is trying to sell you on the position, you are likely to be given a specific time frame. Write it down and hold her to it.

Victory belongs to the most persevering.

—NAPOLEON BONAPARTE

The value of the offer is the sum value of all its parts. A common error made by recent college grads is to fixate on the salary. Although it is nice to win the who-has-the-largest-salary-offer competition with your college friends, it doesn't make that much difference in the long run. Sometimes an offer with a high salary is actually less compensation than a competing offer that combines attractive benefits with a lower paycheck. Before jumping at the first sign of a lump of cash, make sure that you look at each part of the job offer.

A starting salary is usually the highest amount that a company is willing to risk on an unproven talent (you). Given this definition, it shouldn't surprise you that it will be extremely low. Here are some average starting salaries for recent college grads in different majors.

Humanities and Social Sciences		Business and Technology	
Education	$22,898	Chemical Engineering	$40,689
Human Resources	$22,760	Computer Science	$32,762
Social Science	$22,600	Accounting	$28,022
Liberal Arts	$21,124	Business Administration	$23,950

Source: College Placement Council of Bethlehem, PA, "Salary Survey for 1993-94"

An offer has three categories: salary, benefits package, and long-term opportunity.

1. **Salary.** You have to decide if the salary offered is acceptable. Not what you hoped for, or dreamed of,

but acceptable. It will increase dramatically in a short period of time if you prove your worth.

If you simply cannot survive on the amount offered, you have to ask for more. Before you do, make sure that you are willing to lose the offer, because often you will. Look for other avenues first. Can you borrow money from your parents until you get your career going? Can you make changes in your budget to fit the salary? Remember, your first job, if chosen properly, should be the equivalent of attending graduate school. It will teach you practical skills and provide a strong network of future contacts. If you were in school, you would be spending $30k a year, not making it!

If you try to negotiate salary, here are some tips:

- **Never base your need for more money on your budget or lifestyle.** Why should the recruiter care if you need to make payments on an expensive car? The only exception is if you have a family. This is a legitimate and often accepted reason to negotiate.

- **Be ready to walk away from the table.** This is the most essential tool in negotiation. If you need the position, do not play hardball.

- **Be ready to sell.** Don't expect an ask-and-ye-shall-receive reception at the negotiating table. You have to have a strong argument why you need and deserve more salary. Find out what the going rate is for your position and come armed with the numbers. Something like "The industry average is $5,000 higher for this type of position than what you've offered. I really like the opportunity here so

I'm willing to accept less than the average, but can we close the gap a bit?" Keep your tone courteous and respectful. Remember, confidence will get you the job, but arrogance during negotiations can lose it for you.

2. **Benefits package.** A benefits package can be as simple as general healthcare coverage or as complicated as healthcare plan, stock options, 401(k), tuition reimbursement, pension plan, and dependent care facilities. A common mistake is to dismiss the details of the package with a wave of the hand and assume that it has everything you need. Here are some guidelines to follow.

■ **Do your research.** Get a copy of the benefits package and work your way through it. Yes, it is incredibly boring, but the details can be important.

■ **Get advice.** Sit down with someone in the company and have everything explained to you. Ask a lot of questions and get specific. You probably will need to talk to someone in Human Resources because chances are that your new boss doesn't fully understand the details of the benefits package either.

■ **Don't think you're invincible.** You actually might get sick or injured one of these days. Make sure that you are properly covered. Also, if you intend on having a family soon, find out what your insurance provides. The most common complaint with insurance plans revolve around care during pregnancies, so check the details.

■ **Maximize your savings plans.** Whatever the form, whether it is stock options, 401(k), or other pension vehicles, choose the maximum contribution allowed by your plan. You can learn not to miss the money each month, but that money will grow quickly into the nest egg for your future.

■ **Pursue tuition reimbursement.** More companies are using tuition reimbursement to lure and retain top employees. Even if the company has not done it in the past, ask if it would be open to you attending night or weekend graduate courses on the company tab. You might be surprised to see how receptive it is.

■ **Understand sick days, vacation time, etc.** It is quite a shock when you enter the workforce and find out that you have one week of vacation for the entire year. (A big selling point for being an entrepreneur.) If you have planned events, put them on the table right away to make sure they work with your new schedule. (Hint: A trip to Iowa for your brother's wedding counts as an appropriate event to discuss with your employer; a trip to Mexico with your fraternity brothers does not.)

3. **Long-term opportunity.** If you feel that the position offered to you creates a strong long-term opportunity for your career, the rest of the offer doesn't mean much. A good example is the entertainment industry. There are so many talented individuals trying to get into the field that entry-level starting wages are in the basement and benefits are few and far between. However, for people who work their way up from the entry-level position, the rewards in the industry are incredibly huge salaries and amazing benefits. You have to take the short-term poverty to get to the long-term opportunity.

    If you receive an offer that is your dream job and

it is something that you can be passionate about, take it. Make certain that you have enough money to survive and coverage if you get sick, but beyond that, pursue excellence. If you take advantage of an opportunity because of the long-term potential to pursue your passion, you can't help but find yourself on the right track in life.

Sometimes you have to take short-term poverty to get to the long-term opportunity.

What to Do Once You Accept the Job

Congratulations! Once you have done the proper soul-searching, gone through the research process, created great marketing materials, sold yourself in the interview, and negotiated the best deal possible, you are ready to accept the job. It's hard to believe, but this is just the beginning. Here are six things to think about as you prepare to enter your new position.

1. **Contact all other firms to which you've applied.** Even if you never received a reply from a résumé that you sent, be sure to send a letter to every single company where you applied. In the letter, you want to politely thank the company for its consideration but inform it you have accepted a position with XYZ company in the _____ department. If you have to inform a company that you have chosen not to accept their job offer, you need to precede the letter with a phone call to your main contact with the company. Voice-mail will *not* do. You actually

have to speak with the person who interviewed you and then send the letter.

Contacting every firm who may be considering you for a position is a courtesy that is almost second nature among professionals, yet almost never seen from entry-level college grads. The recruiter will remember the way you handle yourself. When you say no, it hurts the recruiter for two reasons. First, you represent a time investment that did not pay off, especially if you have gone a significant distance in the interview process. Second, it is reflection of the recruiter's ability if you are a candidate that he or she wanted to bring on board. Recruiters need to select the best candidates, but they also need to attract the best candidates. If you were a top candidate (which I'm sure you were if you followed the tactics in this book), it is easy for recruiters to view your rejection as a measure of their recruiting ability.

Be extremely conscious of how you deal with these people when you accept a different offer. Use this opportunity to build some bridges and transform your interview contacts into professional contacts. After all, they are in the industry and represent the companies you admire, so they are a perfect fit into your network. Also, there is a good chance that you will be interviewing with them again some day. Professionals move between different companies on a regular basis, and every industry becomes a fairly inbred group. Don't burn any bridges. Start to build a reputation of professionalism and courtesy.

2. **Contact all of your references.** If you have used your references properly (Chapter 7), they will have been keys to acquiring your new position. Contact

them right away and give them the good news. Go into detail with them and explain how the position you accepted fits into your game plan. The message is "You haven't gotten rid of me yet." You are still trying to invest your references as much as possible in your career decisions. Contacting them continues to make them feel the need to assist you and give you advice on direction.

You want to be able to use these references for many years to come. A reference is more powerful if it comes from someone who has known you through the formative stages of your development, so you want to keep in touch with these people. You don't want to be a pest, so a drop-in call every one to two months should be enough. Also, ask if you can continue to use them as references in your new profession, for new clients, new suppliers, and so on. This lets them know that you are still networking with them. Your references can be a very important tool in your professional career. Cultivate these relationships and hold yourself to the level of professional conduct that will make your references proud and confident in their recommendation.

3. **Set goals for your new job.** Not only did you get your foot in the door, you are actually in the room. Now you have to decide what you are going to do with the opportunity. You accepted this position with some kind of purpose. (If you accepted the job just to have a job, quit and turn back to page 1.) Before you get caught up in the day-to-day activity of your new job, it is important to set some strong goals for yourself. Once you get into the grind, it becomes hard to solidify mid- and

long-term goals. You start to focus on more immediate concerns, such as making it to the weekend.

Write down the reasons you took the position. Why did the job appeal to you? What opportunities for personal growth did you see? What time line do you see for your advancement? What did you think you would learn from the position? What time line do you see for learning in these areas? What concrete performance criteria can you use to measure your success?

The answers to these questions will outline your goals for the position. The last question varies depending on your industry. If you go into sales, it can be volume, closing rate, commissions, or a thousand other measures. If you are writing the great American novel, it can be the number of chapters completed, short stories published, or acceptance by a publisher. Find a way to measure your progress toward your goal so that you can be honest if your actions start to fall behind your promises to yourself.

4. **Ask your new boss how you should prepare for your new job.** I love it when I am asked this question. It shows tremendous initiative, and it makes me think that I made the right hiring decision. More than that, you truly want to prepare as much as possible for your new position so that you can make an immediate positive impact. As the new kid on the block, you have a lot to prove, and everyone will be watching you closely in your first few weeks. If you can prepare by doing additional research, reading company material, or attending a seminar, make sure that you take advantage of the opportunity.

My own recommendations for how to prepare for your new job are:

- **Read as much company material as possible.** This includes annual reports, promotional materials, and newspaper articles. Do the same with your company's biggest competitors.

- **Read Stephen R. Covey's *The 7 Habits of Highly Effective People*.** This is a tremendously effective book that gives you a realistic approach to problem solving and personal development. It is one of the most widely read books among professionals and will give you a great philosophical framework to use as you tackle your new job and your new life.

- **Read Kenneth Blanchard's *The One Minute Manager*.** This skinny little book has an amazing amount of wisdom in its 121 easy-to-read pages. Regardless of what field you are entering, you need to interact with people to be successful. *The One Minute Manager* will give you a strong insight into what makes people tick. It is helpful if you are the one being managed and absolutely essential reading if you have management responsibility.

- **Read Cynthia Kersey's *Unstoppable*.** This is the book I wish I had written. It is a collection of forty-five stories of people overcoming incredible odds to accomplish incredible things. You will be amazed at the power of the human spirit as it is demonstrated time and time again that true human determination is indeed *unstoppable*. Put a copy next to your bed and read a story a night. You will find that you face your personal challenges with more courage once you have read this book and realize that much harder tasks have been attempted and accomplished. You will give yourself a gift if your take the time to read this book.

■ **Read George S. Clason's** *The Richest Man in Babylon.* This quirky little book (you can read it in one sitting) is a great lesson in personal finance. The tone of the book is like that of a biblical parable. It is a simple story of a son sent off to build his fortune, only to immediately lose all of his money in get-rich-quick schemes and other bad investments. He spends the next few years learning from his mistakes and building his true fortune. Along the way, he (and you) learn valuable truisms about investments, negotiations, and wealth. This is a book that you will recommend to other people after you read it.

■ **Read Anthony Robbins's** *Personal Power.* I believe few motivational speakers truly make a difference in people's lives. Most are powerful speakers who get their audience excited for a few days with some snappy one-liners and analogies, but they do little to make a lasting change. Anthony Robbins is different. He has taken the best aspects from hundreds of motivational and life-changing techniques and created an incredible system for personal change. His writings have had an impact on my life because they contain the strongest and most passionate appeal for the power of the human spirit that I have found. I have tried to convey the same message in this book—you control your life, your surroundings, your decisions, everything. If this message appeals to you, Anthony Robbins has created an incredible system for you to fulfill that ideal in your life. His approach is a little too "rah-rah" for some people, but if you can get past the infomercial hype, there is some helpful material.

5. **Begin to establish your reputation.** Everything you do during your first week on the job will be noticed. As the new recruit, you are in the spotlight and people will be staring. Your reactions to challenges and the way you carry yourself will start to create your professional reputation. A single negative incident during this time can put a label on you for years.

For example, imagine that you oversleep for your first big meeting and show up an hour late. That may be the first time that has happened to you in your life and you might be the most punctual person in the world, but from that point on you will be tagged as a flake who misses important meetings. Decide what message you want to send to the people around you. If you consider yourself to be a leader, be outspoken during meetings and volunteer for responsibility when it is offered.

A good reputation often can be a self-fulfilling prophecy. If people expect a certain type of behavior from you, you are more likely to behave that way. For example, if you have the reputation as a great public speaker, then you are more likely to volunteer for speaking responsibilities. If your reputation is that you are always organized and prepared, you will probably go to great lengths to be that way.

Your first few weeks in your new professional role are a great opportunity to showcase your best attributes and create a positive reputation. If you can create a reputation for excellence, hard work, and determination, then your future mistakes (and we all make them) will be easier to swallow. For example, when Michael Jordan was in his prime, he could lose a game because of a missed free throw in the final seconds and basketball fans around the country would still describe him as one of the greatest players in the game. If a rookie steps up and misses the same shot, the fans think he stinks and that he chokes under pressure. Right now you are the rookie, but you have the opportunity to create a superstar reputation.

Remember, no effort that we make to attain something beautiful is ever lost.

—HELEN KELLER

The Last Word

■ Rejection is part of any career search, but you don't have to accept it so easily. A "no" simply means that you have your work cut out for you to get the position.

■ A job offer creates a shift in the balance of power between you and the company. Once it's on the table that you are the company's choice to fill the position, you hold a few more cards in your hand.

■ Most job offers, even entry-level positions, are open to negotiation. If you handle it professionally, you can increase the quality of the offer while increasing the respect your boss has for you.

■ A job offer should be analyzed based on salary, benefits, and long-term opportunity. Sometimes the best offer will be the one that initially pays you the least.

■ Once you accept a position, work hard to ensure that you are prepared to excel from day one.

Section Six:
Unconventional Options

Twelve:
Entrepreneurs Have More Fun

Only those who dare to fail greatly can ever achieve greatly.
—ROBERT F. KENNEDY

If you look out into the world of jobs and see nothing that excites you, perhaps you need to create your own opportunity. After all, you need to do *something*. It would be nice if someone would pay you a six-figure income to sit on the beach and drink Margaritas, but that may be hard to find.

Most of the applicants I interview claim that they would like to run their own business eventually. In fact, most Americans make the same claim. The U.S. Bureau of Labor Statistics predicts that there will over a million new entrepreneurs by the year 2005. It sounds great to run a business and be your own boss. You're beholden to no one, free to do whatever you want, master of your own time.

All this is true, but there are trade-offs. Entrepreneurs are the first to tell you it is a great lifestyle but also the first to say that it is harder than you might think. The rewards can be great, but the rewards come because you bear the burden of risk on your shoulders. The success stories are well known, but there are other stories as well. Take this statistic, for example:

- **10 percent of Americans will try to start their own business at some time in their life.**
- **90 percent of those businesses fail within the first two years of operation.**
- **Therefore, 1 percent of Americans are able to run a successful business.**

People react to this statement in two different ways. Some hear this statistic, give a low whistle, a slow nod of the head, and start to second-guess the wisdom of their entrepreneurial leaning. They do not like the odds of success, and suddenly the security of a paycheck looks pretty good. Other people get excited because there is a 1 percent chance that they will run a successful business. It can be done, and they are the ones to do it. It's not too hard to see which people should become entrepreneurs. How did you react?

Being an entrepreneur is definitely not for everyone. No magic questionnaire or single personality description can tell you whether being an entrepreneur is for you, but entrepreneurs do tend to have four characteristics in common.

1. **Risk tolerant.** Entrepreneurs are capitalism's risk takers. Often they take incredible risks in order to

make their businesses successful. When my business was going through the first years of 100 percent annual growth, my partners and I financed the expansion through credit cards and loans that we personally guaranteed. Had the business failed, we would have lost our houses, cars, savings accounts, everything. Entrepreneurs need to take on risk like this and still be able to get a good night's sleep.

2.   **Handle stress well.** The risk associated with running your own business can lead to a lot of stress in your life. Most entrepreneurs I know can be facing five different direct threats to their business that could completely wipe them out but still play a round of golf and not think about it. If you are easily stressed out, entrepreneurship might not be for you.

3.   **Passionate.** Entrepreneurs tend to be almost evangelical about their business and about their ability to lead their business to success. Unless you are passionate about what you do, stay away.

4.   **Whatever-it-takes attitude.** Running a business is hard. In order to pull it off, you need to be willing to do the impossible. Here are some examples:

   ■ A friend of mine started a business in the hazardous materials field that required a special certification. Most people in this field study for two years and take test prep courses to prepare for a two-day certification exam. To make the business work, he needed that certification right away, but he didn't have the money to spend on the prep course. Instead, he bought the books and taught himself the material every evening for three months. He passed the exam on the first try. It was the equivalent of cramming an AA degree into three months while working full time. Whatever it takes.

■ Another friend bought a failing twenty-hour dough-nut store. He moved into the back of the store and lived there for three months while he turned it around. He now owns a chain of stores. Whatever it takes.

■ Another friend has run his Internet business for two years without taking a single penny out of it in salary. He works sixty to seventy hours a week on that business and then runs a DJ business on the weekends to pay his living expenses and to pay his employees' salaries. Whatever it takes.

"Whatever it takes" is the mantra of successful entrepreneurs. And trust me, it often takes a lot. The old saying about business owners is that they work only half days, either the first twelve hours or the second!

Don't get me wrong. I'm not trying to scare you away from being an entrepreneur. I can think of no better way to spend your career . . . if it fits your personality. To find out, I recommend that you interview some successful entrepreneurs in your area and ask them some tough questions about the drawbacks to running a business. If you find out that entrepreneurship is something that interests you, here are some reasons why I think it is a great way to spend a life.

God doesn't make orange juice, God makes oranges.
—JESSE JACKSON

Eleven Reasons to Become an Entrepreneur

1. **Control your own destiny.** If you succeed or fail, you have no one to point to but yourself. This is great if you have confidence in your abilities but a downer if you tend to scapegoat others for your shortcomings. As an entrepreneur, you are naked in front of a very harsh light. There are a lot of excuses you can use if your business fails, but none that work.

2. **Love your job.** It really doesn't matter what you do, but it just seems sweeter when you do it for yourself. The pride of ownership is very strong. When you buy your first house, you actually look forward to mowing the yard because it is *your* yard. It's the same with your own business. Activities that would drive you crazy as an employee get you excited as a business owner.

3. **Get paid to do your hobby.** You decide what kind of business you want to start. Often the most successful businesses are an extension of a hobby or a passionate interest. You already love to do it, so find a way to get paid for it. If you love the outdoors, start a guide service. If you collect coins, start an Internet coin dealership.

4. **Control your time.** As a business owner, you do have ultimate control over your time. However, realize that successful entrepreneurs are usually workaholics who spend more time on their businesses than on anything else. You never leave business at the office because you are always thinking about how to improve and grow. A business can run you, instead of you running it, so be careful what kind of monster you create. If you value

your time, don't start a business that will never let you leave.

5. **Hire people.** This is my favorite part of business ownership. It is a great feeling to hand people a paycheck that they earned working in a business that you started from the ground up. It is gratifying to see people buy a new car, a house, or things for their family because you created an opportunity for them to earn that check.

6. **Be creative.** There is no one to hold you back, so you can let your creativity flow. Open the floodgates and try everything. Remember all those times when you thought you could do things better than your boss? Be bold and try everything.

7. **Create wealth.** When you work in a job, you are paid for that year and that's it. Some sales jobs include a residual on future sales, but for the most part you're done. When you grow a business, you create an asset that can be sold in the future. However, some small businesses do not fit the mold. It will be hard to sell your fly-fishing shop that you run out of your parents' garage. But if you grow it into a chain of a few stores, you have an asset that you can sell in the future.

8. **Earn respect.** People respect entrepreneurs because they recognize that it is difficult to be one. Also, they often have ambitions of running their own business one day and are eager to get some advice on how to make it work.

9. **Challenge yourself.** You can find challenge in any career that your pursue, but as an entrepreneur, challenge comes to you. Financing, cash flow, marketing,

managing employees, production management, customer relations, sales: Everything you can think of is hefted on your shoulders. You learn quickly to delegate, but it is always your ultimate responsibility to get things done correctly.

10. **Empowerment.** People in conventional jobs often complain that they are constrained and do not have enough freedom. Actually, you are always empowered to do or say whatever you want in any job you have. The restriction is that you can lose your job for saying and doing the wrong things. The great thing about running a business is that unless you have a split personality, you can't fire yourself. You can lose customers and lose business if you make bad decisions, but there is no oppressive boss to tell you what you can and cannot do.

11. **It's fun.** Being an entrepreneur is a blast. If you have the ability and the desire, there is no better option.

> *The more original the discovery, the more obvious it seems afterward.*
> —ARTHUR KOESTLER

The Right Idea

There are more great business ideas than there are competent people. Find something that meets your criteria.

■ **Something you know about.** Don't try to start a computer company if your technology learning curve stopped with the Apple IIe. Pick something that you feel comfortable with and that is a showcase for your skills. If you are adamant about an industry about which you have little knowledge, take a year to educate yourself.

■ **Something you can afford.** If you have no money, no assets, and no rich relatives, do not spend three months making plans to build a eighteen-hole championship golf course. It might be a great idea, but stay grounded in reality. Create a plan to get yourself to a point where the golf course idea is feasible.

■ **Something that fills a need.** Be sure that there is a market for your product or service. This is hard to quantify. Who could have predicted the success of the Pet Rock or the hula hoop? Keep your ears open when people complain about not being able to find something. You might be able to provide it.

■ **Something with potential.** Everything has some kind of potential, but choose something that can explode. Do something original and bold. Entrepreneurs thrive best outside of boundaries and conditions.

Some Popular Home-Based Businesses

Computer programming	Public relations and advertising
Internet consulting and web design	Journalism and freelance
Financial and business consulting	Interior design
Healthcare services	Graphic arts
Computer consulting	Hobby businesses

> *Life is worth being lived, but not worth being discussed all the time.*
>
> —ISABELLE ADFANI

Now What?

After you choose the type of business you want to start, it's time to get educated. Learn everything you can about your industry and the market for your product or service. Identify who your competitors will be, and decide how you will compete against them. Estimate the money you will need to start your business and the amount of sales you expect to make.

The best way to organize all of these ideas is to write a formal business plan. The purpose of a business plan is two-fold. First, it organizes your ideas and your vision for your business. While most people think big decisions through in a systematic way, the typical entrepreneur is more than willing to leap without looking. Normal people think Ready, Aim, Fire. The entrepreneur's credo is Ready, Fire, Aim. Unfortunately for most entrepreneurs, having better aim in the form of preparation would save them a lot of money. Besides organizing the business idea, the business plan is also essential to raise money for your venture. Even if you plan on milking family members for the start-up capital, they will want to see that you have a well thought out plan.

There are several excellent books on business plans. Writing an effective plan is a big project that will require a lot of work. However, I cannot emphasize how important it is to your success. If you cannot maintain your focus and do the work necessary to write a coherent business plan, then you should save your money and not start a business. Entrepreneurs require an incredible amount of commitment and dedication. Make the business plan a symbol of that dedication.

Several computer programs can help you to write an excellent business plan. Of the various products on the market, my favorite is BizPlan Builder Interactive by JIAN. The program asks you a series of questions about your business and then plugs the answers into a well-formatted business plan. Writing the plan is still a lot of work, and you don't get out of all the soul-searching, but the end result is a business plan that will amaze investors. It can also provide you with all of the answers you need to legal, financial, and tax questions. The price is reasonable and the value is exceptional.

If you need additional help, try some of these sources.

Home Office Association of America
909 Third Avenue, Suite 990
New York, NY 10022
(212) 809-4622
Web: www.hoa.com

International Directory of Young Entrepreneurs (IDYE)
376 Boylston Street, Suite 304
Boston, MA 02117
(617) 867-4690
Web: www.idye.com

National Score Office (Service Corp of Retired Professionals)
409 3rd Street SW
Washington, D.C. 20024
(800) 634-0245
Web: www.score.org.

U.S. Small Business Administration
409 3rd Street SW
Washington, D.C. 20416
(202) 205-6600
Web: www.sbaonline.com

If you can talk brilliantly about a problem, it can create the consoling illusion that it has been mastered

—STANLEY KUBRICK

How to Raise Money

The biggest lesson you will learn early in your entrepreneurial adventure is that it costs a lot of money to start a business. The number-one reason businesses fail is because they are undercapitalized and run out of money. Here is the rule to predict how much money you will need.

1. Predict your first year costs and revenue.

2. Now, for a more accurate prediction, double your costs and divide your revenue in half.

3. Assume these are accurate predictions. Does your business still make sense?

A new business always takes more money than you predict, sometimes a lot more. The main reason is that every mistake you make will cost you money. As a first-time entrepreneur, you will make more mistakes that you could ever imagine. Make sure that you have the money to make a good run at success.

Unless you already have a successful track record in your field, it will be very difficult to get financing outside of your friends and family. You can try venture capitalists (also known as vulture capitalists); sometimes they are willing to finance an incredible idea in exchange for a majority position in the company. But as a novice entrepreneur, your chances of attracting outside financing are pretty slim. Family members and personal savings are the best sources for first-time entrepreneurs.

> *To get something done, a committee should consist of no more than three people, two of whom are absent.*
>
> **—ROBERT COPELAND**

Good Partner /Bad Partner

A partner in a business is the most involved relationship two people can have outside of marriage. It is a long-term commitment where you have to implicitly trust your partner as you would trust yourself. I have four partners, and they are the four people I respect and trust most, besides my immediate family. They are incredibly talented individuals, and we have a strong common purpose to grow our company. We have clearly defined roles in our partnership and a systematic process to resolve disputes among the partners.

> *The reputation of a thousand years may be determined by the conduct of an hour.*
>
> **—JAPANESE PROVERB**

The Business Plan

1. **Write a partnership agreement.** This is true especially if you are close friends with your new partner. Leave nothing uncovered and try to anticipate every possibility. This way there are no misunderstandings down the line and you can be sure that your visions

match. Some things to include in the agreement are: What happens if one partner wants to leave the business, does not share the financial risk, dies, gets lazy, or steals.

2. **Share the risk and the work evenly.** If one partner puts up all the money to start the business, she may feel bitter being equal partners with someone not taking any risk. If only one partner has access to money, the other partner needs to take more of the workload to compensate, adding sweat equity instead of cash to the partnership. Try to distribute the responsibilities equally and have a clear agreement before you start.

3. **Have a senior partner.** If one partner is more outspoken and charismatic than the others, elect him to be the CEO, president, team captain, whatever. This is the person your customers can contact and who can field public relations questions. If you can't decide on a captain, don't push the issue. My company has four general partners, each with an ego too large to choose a captain. It works well only because we have been effective in implementing the other four criteria listed here. However, it is unusual for this relationship to work so well. If the partners can agree on a team captain, definitely choose one.

4. **Give everyone a title.** Titles make your customers and employees more comfortable. Every partner can have the same title if you want.

5. **Have an easy way to settle the little stuff.** In my business there have been hundreds of small issues on which the partners disagree. Most of these issues have been resolved with a quick game of rock,

paper, scissors. The big stuff is debated for hours, even days, but the small stuff is decided on quickly. Many partnerships have broken down over small decisions that are more about ego and prestige than about what is best for the business. Keep the small stuff out of the way.

An acre of performance is worth a whole world of promise.
—W. D. HOWELLS

How to Train Your Entrepreneurial Muscles

If you do not feel like you are ready to jump into an entrepreneurial adventure, you may be right. Unless you have already had some serious work experience, you might want to get some training first. One option is to get a job in the industry in which you would like to open a business. Find a small business that is similar to the one you envision and go through the learning curve on someone else's dime.

A warning comes with this strategy. Even though you have the best intentions to get a few years of experience, and then start your own business, it seldom happens this way. After you are in your job for a few years, an amazing sense of comfort will start to surround your existence. You know exactly how to do your job with the minimum amount of effort; your steady paycheck is nicely divided among rent, car, food, fun, and credit cards; your boss has promised you a "big" promotion; and your life has found its own rhythm, a rhythm that you suddenly find yourself unwilling to disturb.

Every profession is full of people who intended to run

their own business some day. They are bound to their conventional jobs by golden handcuffs, unable to give up the sure thing for the risky unknown. There is nothing wrong with this, but if you are serious about setting off on your own, there are some things you need to do:

- **Give yourself a deadline.** Figure out the date in the future when you will start your own business. Write it down and tell people. Review the DBA philosophy in step six of the Six Steps on Purpose (Chapter 3). Especially read the section on Foolproof Goal Achievement. Monitor your progress and stick to your deadline.

- **Make a plan.** Write down the short-term deadlines of things that need to be done to organize your business before you quit your job. This list includes what you need to learn, the money you need to raise, and the paperwork you need to file.

- **Keep your overhead low.** Don't lease that sports car or the sport utility vehicle. Don't run up huge credit card debt. Keep your spending in check. If you don't, you will be beholden to your bills and you will not have the freedom you need to pursue your goals.

- **Be responsible for your goal every day.** When you deviate from your plan, take a long look in the mirror and ask the tough questions. Be hard on yourself. Every successful entrepreneur goes through periods of self-doubt, so don't be surprised if you start to second-guess yourself. Don't rationalize why you can't meet your deadline. Entrepreneurs do not make excuses, they create results. Accept nothing but success.

Do the thing you fear, and the death of fear is certain.

—RALPH WALDO EMERSON

Multilevel Marketing

There has been an explosion in multilevel marketing (MLM) organizations recently, and I get questions from students all the time about them. You probably have a handful of friends who approach you every third day to attend a meeting or buy some kind of product. These are the friends you now avoid because they will not accept no as an answer.

Multilevel marketing is a valid business, with some companies posting over $1 billion in annual sales. Basically, MLMs create a grass-roots distribution network by which to move products directly to consumers. This is accomplished by recruiting people not only to sell their product but also to recruit other people to sell their product and to recruit other people, and so on. The incentive for Joe and Betty Homeowner to convince their friends to enroll in the program is that they would receive a small percentage of whatever their friends sell. Then, when these friends convince other friends to enroll, Joe and Betty continue to receive a percentage of everyone's sales. The big draw is that once you create a huge network of people underneath you who are selling products and recruiting more and more people, you can just sit back and watch the money pour in. It very rarely works this way, but it sure sounds good, doesn't it?

Several different products are sold through MLMs, from makeup, vitamins, and toiletries, to financial planning, pepper spray, and long-distance telephone service. While I do have some friends who have been marginally successful MLM people, there are some things to watch out for.

- **Work ethic.** The only way to be successful at a business is to work at it with superhuman intensity. "Make 100k a year and work only 10 hours a week" is a gimmick, and you should be embarrassed if you fall for it. MLMs attract people who want to "get rich quick." When they don't, they quit.

- **Starting fees.** Many MLMs live off of the fees they charge for people to join. Ninety percent of people never do anything, and the MLM marketers keep the fees. Don't get involved with something unless you have done thorough research and are passionate about it.

- **Relationships.** MLM people usually go through a phase where they become overly evangelical about their new business. As an MLM, you may find that suddenly people forget to invite you to parties and everyone seems busy when you call. If you do jump into an MLM, be careful not to let it hurt the relationships that you value.

Multilevel marketing can be a good opportunity, and it is a legitimate and growth business. However, do not be fooled by promises of easy money and low effort. Watch out for high "initial fees." Remember that a fool and his money are easily separated. If you do decide to become involved in MLM, be aware that you have to apply yourself to it as you would any business and work your tail off. Excellence is rewarded in any industry.

So what do we do? Anything. Something. So long as we don't sit there. If we screw it up, start over. Try something else. If we wait until we've satisfied all the uncertainties, it may be too late.

—LEE IACOCCA

The Last Word

- Entrepreneurs are capitalism's risk takers. While being a business-owner is an exciting, fast-paced lifestyle, it is not for everyone. Before you think about starting your own business, decide if your personality matches the rigors of being an entrepreneur.

- There are more great ideas for new businesses than there are people willing to try them. As you choose the type of business you want to start, try to find a niche that reflects your passions.

- Before you run out and lease office space in a high-rise, write out your business plan and ask for feedback from successful entrepreneurs. You may be the next Bill Gates, or you may be the guy that loses his parents' retirement money in a half-baked Internet business. Don't be afraid to take risks, but get help along the way.

Thirteen:
Save the World

A diploma is not a certificate of right to special favor and profit in the world but rather a commission of service.
—WARREN G. HARDING

If being your own boss does not excite you, and you can't find your true calling in the conventional job market, try to save the world! Several programs give you the opportunity to make an impact. A word of warning: These programs are not designed to give you a chance to dabble in some charities just to make you feel good about yourself. These are strenuous, challenging opportunities that will test the limits of your abilities. They can be incredibly enlightening and life-changing experiences, but they are not for the faint of heart.

*Obstacles are those frightful things you see
when you take your eyes off the goal.*

—HANNAH MORE

Peace Corps

Billed as "the toughest job you will ever love," the Peace
Corps is not for wimps. Volunteers embark on a two-
year expedition to the most remote parts of the world to
assist developing countries is a variety of areas. You might
teach hygiene, work with irrigation and farming, teach
math in a local school, or build affordable homes. It is not
a vacation.

Assignments last for two years, with an additional
three months of preparatory training before you go. The
Peace Corps is active in over ninety developing countries,
and you can request where you would like to be placed. The
more flexible you are on your application, the better chance
you have of being placed.

You are provided with a monthly allowance to cover
food, housing, and basic expenses, and you have full dental
and medical coverage. After your assignment is complete,
you receive a readjustment allowance of $225 (rate as of Jan-
uary 2000) for each month of service. If you complete a full
term, this would amount to $6,075. This allowance is
designed to help bridge the gap between your return and
finding a new job.

While the Peace Corps is an incredibly difficult program, thousands of past volunteers have described it as *the*
formative experience in their lives. You may work in places
more remote than you can ever imagine or in the center of a
major city. In either case, you will be changing people's lives
with the work that you do. The impact you make is well
worth your investment.

How to Apply: Apply at least one year prior to when you want to start your assignment. Try to be flexible when choosing your country preferences. This will improve your chances of being selected. As most training takes place in the summers, the best time to apply is between September and March for the following year.

Call or write to:

PEACE CORPS
Room 8500
1990 K Street, NW
Washington, D.C. 20526
Phone: (800) 424-8580
Web:www.peacecorps.gov.

The Peace Corps is open only to citizens of the United States. Canadian citizens have a similar opportunity for service with a program called World University Service of Canada. Information about this program can be found online at www.wusc.ca

> ***Success is not built on what we accomplish for ourselves. Its foundation lies in what we do for others.***
> **—DANNY THOMAS**

Americorps USA

Americorps is a domestic version of the Peace Corps. Instead of traveling to a developing country, Americorps volunteers focus on helping communities in the United States. The goal is to produce a lasting change in the communities where projects are undertaken. These projects often are worked on in conjunction with local community groups and other national organizations. They include tutoring, environmental clean-ups, neighborhood renovations, building affordable housing, and working with youths at risk.

Volunteers receive an allowance to cover living expenses as well as full health coverage. After you serve for a full year, you will also receive an educational voucher for $4,725, which can be used to pay off an old student loan or be applied to future tuition fees.

Americorps has several offshoot programs like VISTA and Green Corps, which are listed below.

For more information about other programs or about Americorps in general, call or write to:

AMERICORPS USA
1111 Lincoln Street
Washington, D.C. 20888
Phone: (800) 942-2677.
Web: www.cns.gov

Americorps Vista

This Americorps program brings volunteers to impoverished communities to create innovative, long-term solutions to community problems. Actions are oriented toward helping people to help themselves and designing programs that can be easily administered by the community members themselves.

VISTA participants use the one-year program to set up local programs and work with community members on long-range problem-solving strategies. You may be involved in applying for a government grant, designing an after-school program, or implementing an adult literacy program. The most valuable service you provide is to recruit members of the community to take leadership roles in these programs so that they will continue after your program ends.

Volunteers receive a monthly allowance to cover living expenses as well as full health insurance. They also receive either a stipend of about $1,000 or a $4,725 education voucher at the end of the year. VISTA pays all travel and training expenses.

How to Apply: You can apply either for a local assignment, if you have a community in mind where you want to work, or a national assignment, anywhere that VISTA places volunteers. If you want to pursue a local assignment, look up the Corporation for National Service for a list of approved VISTA sponsors located in your state. You can apply to these directly.

For national assignments, call or write to:

AMERICORPS VISTA
1201 New York Avenue, NW
Washington, D.C. 20525
Phone: (800) 942-2677

Our deeds determine us as much as we determine our deeds.
—GEORGE ELIOT

Green Corps

This volunteer organization is committed to bringing environmental solutions and awareness to urban areas. Volunteers work with community leaders and organizations to ensure that the programs continue after volunteers leave. Projects include reversing the effects of lead poisoning, monitoring pollution levels, conducting clean-up programs, and creating awareness programs in local schools. You may work as an individual or as a team leader organizing other volunteers on projects with other non-profit organizations.

The ten-month program provides an allowance of $7,945. You also receive an educational voucher for $4,725 once you complete the program.

How to Apply: Contact the national office for information on how to become involved. Opportunities change annually as the organization grows and responds to new environmental challenges that arise.

Call or write to:

NEIGHBORHOOD GREEN CORPS
218 D Street, SE
Washington, D.C. 20003
Phone: (202) 547-9178

Doing nothing for others is the undoing of ourselves.

—HORACE MANN

Teach for America

This national organization gives highly skilled recent college graduates the opportunity to make an impact in communities throughout America by teaching. Volunteers are placed in rural or inner-city schools for two years to provide good teachers to the schools that need them most. As a participant, you would be an active part of the community and would attempt to introduce fresh and innovative ideas for volunteering and community programs.

You are paid the regular starting salary for the school district where you will teach. Teach for America is a very competitive program; only one in six applicants is accepted. It is a two-year program with a six-week preparatory period. Preparation includes introducing yourself to the community and the school where you will work.

How to Apply: The application process includes a written application, interview, group discussion, and a monitored teaching session. Letters of reference are also required. All majors are eligible, but science, computer, math, and foreign language majors have an advantage. Applications are accepted up until early April for the following fall.

Call or write to:

TEACH FOR AMERICA
20 Exchange Place
8th Floor
New York, NY 10005
Phone: (800) 832-1230

The man who moves mountains begins by moving small stones.
—CHINESE PROVERB

World Teach

This a great program if you have the travel bug or if you want to go into a field like international business or international relations. World Teach volunteers teach for a full year in a foreign country. Depending on your experience, you might teach at a secondary, primary, or university level. Previous teaching experience is not a requirement, as all volunteers complete a three- to four-week orientation. The orientation covers intensive language instruction and teacher training. World Teach has programs in China, Costa Rica, Ecuador, Namibia, Poland, Thailand, and South Africa.

As a volunteer, you follow the school schedule. This allows you to take time off to explore your host country and completely immerse yourself in the culture. Participants who make the effort are likely to return from the program nearly fluent in the local language.

Only college graduates are eligible to participate. You are not required to know a foreign language, but you will have to attend twenty-five hours of teaching English as a foreign language. Compensation includes a small stipend to cover your living expenses, and housing is provided.

How to Apply: The application process includes three essays and an interview. You will need to supply letters of recommendation, a transcript, and a résumé. World Teach has rolling admissions so you can apply at any time prior to the deadline for the program dates you desire. Plan on applying approximately six months before the program start date. Call or write to:

WORLD TEACH
Harvard Institute for International Development
One Eliot Street
Cambridge, MA 02138-5705
Phone: (800) 4-TEACH-O

We can do anything we want to do if we stick to it long enough.
—HELEN KELLER

AEON

This is a similar experience to World Teach, although AEON sends teachers exclusively to Japan. Candidates are required to have a genuine interest in the culture and society of Japan. Japanese language skills are helpful but not required. Candidates include accredited teachers, business professionals, and recent college graduates. New teachers are given extensive paid training in Japan and use AEON's curriculum in either an adult school or in children's schools. Teachers follow the school schedule and have many opportunities to travel and experience Japanese culture.

AEON offers a one-year contract with the possibility for renewal after one year. Teachers receive a competitive salary and benefits package, health insurance, furnished apartment, paid vacations/holidays and training, and a five-day, thirty-six-hour workweek. AEON's teachers also receive a cash bonus and airfare back to their hometown

How to Apply: Applications should be made four to five months in advance of departure. Send your résumé and essay entitled "Why I would like to live and work in Japan" to one of the following recruitment offices for AEON.

9301 WILSHIRE BOULVARD, #202
Beverly Hills, CA 90210
(310) 550-0940

203 NORTH LA SALLE STREET, #2100
Chicago, IL 60601
(312) 251-0900

230 PARK AVENUE, #1000
New York, NY 10169
(212) 808-3080
Web: www.aeonet.com

The only ones among you who will be really happy are those who will have sought and found how to serve.

—ALBERT SCHWEITZER

Local Charities and Nonprofits

Everything that is good does not come out of Washington, D.C. Do some research and find a local program that interests you, and ask if it can afford a stipend for a one-year program. Some of the best and most important community work is done at this level, so don't overlook it.

> **We must be the change we wish to see in the world.**
>
> **—MOHANDAS GANDHI**

The Last Word

- The programs just listed give you an incredible amount of responsibility and put you in a position to change people's lives. But don't kid yourself about how hard these programs are on their participants. They are not for the faint of heart.

- Should you choose to embark on a world-saving crusade, be just as intense and goal-oriented as if you started your career. In fact, you should be *more* intense because there will be more than just your well-being on the line. In many cases, you will be one of the few positive role models a young person has to emulate.

- These programs are great opportunities to create strong personal skills and character traits while giving to a community. If you can take the hard work, you will not regret it.

Fourteen:
The One-in-a-Million Chance

**Fear not that your life shall come to an end,
but rather fear that it never has a beginning.**
—JOHN NEWMAN

One More Argument for Passion

Many of you reading this book know what you really want to do. For all the talk of following your passion, you probably have some secret goal that you are discounting because it's "too far-fetched." What is it? Do you want to write the great American novel? Do you want to live in the Rocky Mountains as a trail guide? Do you want to be an actor? What is that one thing you wish you could do?

We are a conflicted nation. On one side, there is so much pressure for success in our society that anything outside of the narrowly defined boxes of "normal" behavior is discounted. On the other side, the heroes in our society are the people who live outside the conventions that we all demand of each other. Dennis Rodman dresses like a woman, dyes his hair pink, and we go crazy. The hero in the movie tells his boss to shove it and we applaud. The next day we dress in our conservative clothes and go to work to face the boss we hate. This doesn't make sense.

A certain segment of society has escaped this trap. These people decided from an early age that they would follow their dreams, regardless of how impossible success seemed. They committed to action in the face of incredible odds and refused to let society dictate or define their futures.

Is it really that easy? Just decide that you want to be a movie star and it happens? Of course not. For every story of someone who made it, there are thousands of people who didn't, but at least they tried. If you had to decide between attempting your dream and not making it or living your life with the regret that you never even tried, what would you choose?

Well, guess what? You *do* get to choose.

You are at the best possible time in your life to take a chance on a long shot. You can get by on very little money, you have the freedom to move anywhere, and you have the energy of youth. Take advantage of all these factors to take a stab at that elusive dream. If you wait, you'll suddenly find yourself with a mortgage, a stack of credit card debt, and strong roots that will make risks . . . well, too risky.

Imagine that your family has a tradition that dates back as far as anyone can remember. The tradition applies to every family member who graduates from college. As a member of this family, you are forced to take one year off from whatever your plans are and try something completely off the wall. You are required to spend the entire year pursuing a completely impractical goal. Past family members have written novels, tried to break into the film industry, worked in politics, toured as musicians, and tried out for professional sports teams. Some have been successful and created a career for themselves, but most just tried their best for a year and then went back to their original career plans with no regrets. Complete the following exercise. You might be surprised to find where it leads you.

IF YOU WERE FORCED TO PURSUE YOUR DREAMS FOR ONE YEAR . . .

1. What goal would you pursue during your year?

2. What about your goal do you find appealing?

3. Describe your life if you were able to fully achieve this goal.

4. Give a detailed explanation why this is a completely impractical course of action for you to pursue.

5. Pretend that there was no option—you have to pursue this action. Describe in as much detail as possible what you need to do to get ready to start your journey.

6. If you don't try for your goal now, do you see yourself ever doing it in your life? If not, why not try it now?

Something interesting might happen as you think through these answers. Your far-fetched idea might start to sound a little less out there. You might start thinking "Why not roll the dice a little and try to make the impossible happen?" And you would be right to try it.

I do want to issue a warning, however. I have meet several people who have used this philosophy to justify doing nothing. They postpone entering corporate America to write a novel and end up playing a lot of golf, watching a lot of TV, and leeching off their parents. From their reclined position on a comfy couch they exclaim, "*Hey, look at me. I'm following my dream!*" Taking a chance requires a commitment to action. Be ready and willing to work hard to achieve your destination.

If you decide to take a risk and pursue a long shot, there are a few things to keep in mind.

■ **The same rules of achievement apply.** There are a lot of success stories in whatever field you decide to pursue. None of those stories begin "I just showed up and everything fell into place by itself." Take responsibility for your success and define yourself by your work ethic and your determination.

- **Create a plan with definite goals.** Just because you are chasing a dream, it doesn't mean that you can't be concrete with your goals. Find someone in your field and get some good advice. Map out a clear plan to get to your goals and get it done.

- **Work on your dream every day.** Henry Ford commented that "Successful people get ahead during the time that other people waste." This is especially true when you are pursuing a one-in-a-million opportunity. Whenever you find yourself with nothing to do, find a way to move closer to your goal. Be creative and find something that will attract attention. History seldom takes notice of the quiet person in the corner.

- **Don't forget to eat.** Please don't starve to death after taking this advice. Following your passions does not mean that you forget to take care of your basic needs. Maybe you quit a job you hate to write poetry, but remember to get a part-time job to make ends meet. I don't want to meet you when you're homeless and starving. "Hey, you're the guy who told me to quit my investment banking job and write bohemian poetry. Well, look at me now, buddy! Thanks for the advice!" However, how you define your basic needs is important. A convertible Mercedes for weekend romps to the Hamptons does not qualify as a basic necessity. Sacrifice some stuff in order to follow your dreams. You'll be able to buy stuff later once your passion propels you to success in your field.

If you have something that you are dying to do in your life, you need to get out there and do it. There is no better time, and life is too short to accept missed opportunities. Unless you make a decision to chase your dreams, you will never catch up to them. This decision has to be a serious one because you will need to put your life on hold to commit the effort necessary for success. It is a decision that could fundamentally change your life.

> *Life is a fatal adventure. It can only have one end. So why not make it as far-ranging and free as possible?*
> —ALEXANDER ELIOT

The Last Word

- Imagine if Muhammad Ali had been a shoe salesman.
- Imagine if John Steinbeck had been an accountant.

Section Seven:
Secrets

Fifteen:
The Secret Keys to Success

Secret #1: Create Your Own Lottery

No one ever gets very far unless he accomplishes the impossible at least once a day.

—ELBERT HUBBARD

There is only one difference between you and successful people:

Successful people are a success. You have the potential for success.

The distance between your potential and the realization of your potential is determined by the seriousness of your dedication to your goals. What do your goals represent to you? Are they a passing fancy? Something that you hope to accomplish but doubt you ever will? What is your level of commitment?

Every time I buy a lottery ticket, my goal is to win the lottery. Otherwise, I wouldn't buy the ticket. But when I set that goal, I doubt the goal will be reached and I'm not crushed when I find out that I didn't win. I am in the hands of fate, hoping that my lottery numbers will be drawn. But I spend the dollar because there is the one-in-a-million possibility that I will reach my goal and win the lottery.

If you set your life goals as if you are playing the lottery, then your chances of success are about that good.

It is easy to want things. Wanting does not require that you take any action. Most people go through life wanting but do very little to take the actions necessary to achieve or acquire the things they want. It comes back to how you perceive your goals. Some people set their goals just like the lottery goal. *If I don't achieve it, it's OK because I never really thought I would achieve it anyway.*

These same people are too willing to downgrade their goals once they face an obstacle. They downgrade to an easily achievable goal and then congratulate themselves for "making it." For example, my lottery goal is to win $1 million, I'm still excited if I win $5. At least I won something.

If you do not take your goals seriously, you will allow yourself to settle for achievement far below your personal expectations. You will downgrade your goals to meet your circumstances. *I don't have the challenging career I wanted, but at I least I have a job.*

Make your goals nonnegotiable. Believe you *will* achieve your goals, regardless of what setbacks or challenges you may have to overcome. Do not allow yourself to settle for anything less than your highest expectations.

You have no idea how close you are to being in the top 1 percent of achievers in this world. Most people do *nothing,* and the fact that they do nothing means that if you do anything you can be exceptional.

Sound a little hard? A recent study shows that in an eight-hour workday a typical employee works somewhere between four and five hours. The number one use of free time in this country is watching TV. People graduate from college with decent grades and still can't find the United States on a map. Is it the school's fault? It seems to me that history is full of examples of brilliant men and women who taught themselves. They actually took the responsibility to extract the information from the resources around them. For example, Abraham Lincoln had only a formal elementary education. Everything else he taught himself.

There are amazing opportunities available for people who simply act. Only through action directed toward results can you expect to achieve the goals you want. Do not set goals as if you are playing the lottery. Create serious goals and be prepared to do whatever it takes to achieve them.

> *Assume responsibility for the quality of your own life.*
>
> —NORMAN COUSINS

Secret #2: Go into Cloning

> *The person who says it cannot be done should not interrupt the person doing it.*
>
> —CHINESE PROVERB

Learn from people who have what you want. Success requires an incredible amount of painful trial and error, but there is no need to reinvent the proverbial wheel. The trick is to learn as much as you can from other people's errors so as to avoid the pain yourself. Clone the positive character traits you can learn from successful people and use them to create your own success.

The term "secret of success" implies there is some magical formula out there that will ensure your happiness. Unfortunately, there are no cure-all formulas, but there are some lessons learned from experience that can help you to speed through the learning curve. Success and happiness seem like elusive goals, but people do achieve them. These people have the "secrets" you need.

If you want to be wealthy, find wealthy people and find out what makes them tick. If you want to be a better communicator, find someone who impresses you and pick his brain for a while. Successful people are eager to help others (and usually eager to talk about themselves). It really is as simple as asking "How did you do that?"

Most people have to fail at something more than ten times before they figure it out. Each failure gives them new insight and instincts to prevent the next failure. Becoming excellent at something is a gradual process of constant readjustment and rethinking. The exciting thing about role models is that you have guides who have done the homework for you. They can guide you through the land mines and tell you war stories about the mistakes they made early in their careers.

One warning about role models. Listen carefully to the advice you receive and be aware that there may be some generation gaps, especially if you are talking to someone quite a bit older. I had a female friend who wanted to go into international business, so she found a man prominent in the field and met him for lunch to learn about his career. The conversation was full of advice and war stories from fifty years of business experience, but his general point was that women should not go into business because they would not be respected! This concept is obviously outdated and was more than a little insulting to my friend (who, by the way, is now a highly respected businesswoman).

Listen to advice from anyone and everyone you meet, but keep a clear head and use only the advice that makes sense to you. In my friend's case, she took a lot away from that conversation that helped her career. Also, she used the man's attitude about women in business to prepare herself for other people she would meet in her career with the same attitude. Use any advice that will help you get to your goal, but filter the advice through your values and your level of ambition.

For example, if you want to be an executive in the film industry, a conversation with an old industry veteran will give you incredible insights and advice. But if you are impatient for success, you also want to find the person who achieved success at a young age and find out how she did it. Find a role model who most closely resembles your circumstances and who has what you want.

Obviously, you have to learn certain skills and lessons on your own. There is no substitute for experience to learn intangible skills, such as leadership, good communication, empathy, and tenacity. Also, there is always advice you will not believe; sometimes you just have to find things out for yourself. However, a good role model can show you the best way to gain those skills in as short a time as possible.

Use role models in every part of your life: in your career, your personal life, everything. Be a dedicated life learner and find the best teachers. You have a limited amount of time to reach your destination, and a good guide always helps make a journey easier.

> *It's a very short trip. While alive, live.*
> —MALCOLM FORBES

Secret #3: Get Some Pain

> *On the human chessboard, all moves are possible.*
> —MIRIAM SCHIFF

One theory of human behavior states that all actions are a reflection of two basic motivations: (1) avoid pain and (2) acquire pleasure.

Every action can be traced back to one of these motivations. For example, you will take a sip of coffee because you anticipate the pleasure of the taste and warmth of the drink. If the coffee is too hot and you burn your tongue, you will not take another sip of coffee until it cools off. You want to avoid the pain so you wait until it can offer pleasure.

This is not a new concept. Motivational speakers like Anthony Robbins have created entire philosophies and self-help programs based on this simple premise. The tricky part is to identify sources of pain and pleasure and how we associate these with different parts of our lives. If you are overweight, you have a constant battle between pain and pleasure. Food represents immediate pleasure and gratification, while being overweight may create pain if you feel unhealthy or unhappy with your appearance.

As a rule, the battle between pain and pleasure goes to whichever is more immediate. Pleasure is not as exciting if you know you have to go through pain to get there, and pain does not seem as bad if we get some pleasure first. Negative consequences are never on our minds when we are having fun and experiencing pleasure. Allowing our actions to be dictated by the most immediate consequence is instinctual. Our instincts demand that we pursue pleasure and avoid pain.

The best way to create positive changes in your life and maintain your commitment to your goals is to change how you associate pain and pleasure with your actions. For example, if you read this book and skipped the written exercises, you associated some kind of pain with completing the item. It could have been the pain of self-reflection, the pain of spending time writing instead of doing something you really wanted to do, or even the pain of getting out of your chair to find a pen. Whatever the case, you were not convinced that the exercises would give you enough pleasure to make the effort/pain worthwhile.

Now imagine that you knew with 100 percent certainly that the exercises in this book would make an enormous positive influence on your life. Imagine that there was no doubt that they would help you define your future, prepare for it, and ultimately capture it. What pleasure you would feel if you could achieve your dreams and your goals. Imagine the tangible results—money, a nice house, recognition from your peers, satisfaction, whatever you covet. Now, take the tangible feeling of that pleasure and place it on top of the pain that the exercises might cause you. Doesn't the pain pale in comparison?

Next, take the mental image of your future success and throw it out the window. Imagine yourself unable to achieve your goals, stuck in an unrewarding job that you hate, unable to quit because you are in debt. How does this result make you feel? What pain do you associate with this outcome? How will you feel if none of your ambitions come true, even though you had the opportunity to make them happen? That is some very serious pain.

There is the challenge. You have to pick whatever are your hot-button issues that you know will make you act. You can convince yourself that the short-term pain is worth it for two reasons. First, the pleasure will be worth it, and, second, there is a greater pain for not doing the activity than the pain for doing the activity.

Working out to get in shape is a great example. If you are out of shape, exercise is the last thing in the world you want to do. When you exercise, you are forced to recognize how out of shape you really are. If you do not work out, wear baggy clothes, and avoid mirrors when you are naked, you never have to admit it. The short-term pain of exercise is enough to make most of us avoid working out altogether. But if we associate the pleasure of being in shape and the pain of being unhealthy with the act of exercise, it is easier to get into the gym.

But to do some foolproof association, you have to make it concrete and make it personal. For the working-out example, your associated pleasure might be a trip to the tropics in two months and the pleasure of wearing a new bathing suit, or the pain of being embarrassed to wear a bathing suit if you do not work out. Maybe you could mentally associate exercise with running a race for charity and the pleasure you would feel by helping your community. Or you could associate not going to the gym with the pain of failure to run the race after you told your family and friends about it. Choose whatever hot-button issue will motivate you to get into the gym. If it doesn't work, you have to find a more powerful association.

The challenge is to associate the possibility of future

pain with the behavior you are trying to modify. If you want to make yourself do the exercises in this book, then associate that activity with your level of commitment to your future. If you want to get in shape, then associate the activity with the pleasure of a future event. If you can't get up in the morning and the pleasure of sleeping in is too tempting to pass up, train yourself to think immediately of the consequences of your behavior.

I am the original hate-the-morning, hit-snooze-a-thousand-times late riser. I mean, I hate to get up. But when I do manage to get up early, I love the quiet of the morning and I feel good about my accomplishments. Once I decided to wake up every day at 5 A.M. to get a jump on the day and capture the pleasure I felt from being up early. The first few mornings were horrible, but I became used to it after a while and now am a habitual early riser.

I used pain association to break my sleeping habit. I convinced myself that sleeping in made me accomplish less and made it less likely that I would achieve my goals. If I couldn't even demonstrate my determination to get out of bed, how would I succeed at my life goals? Sleeping in now symbolizes to me a lack of determination and will, and I am not willing to accept that I do not possess those traits. Even today, I have an internal dialog as I sit on the edge of my bed every morning after I have turned off my alarm. All of the great reasons why I should lie back down and sleep come flooding to me. My best argument to myself is that if I lie back down, then I am a loser. Case closed. Up and off to the shower I go.

Add pain to your life by associating it with behavior you want to change. Also, be aware that short-term pain sometimes is necessary to avoid the long-term pain of unfulfilled ambition. For example, suppose you want to quit smoking. Obviously, there is short-term pain when you quit because of withdrawal from nicotine, but pain also results because you lose pleasure. But what if you fully felt the long-term pain your habit will cause you?

This works with any habit that you want to change. Write down the ambitions you have for your life and try to comprehend the pain of not accomplishing those things. Using the smoking example, imagine a day spent with your future grandchildren and think of the pleasure this would bring. Now develop the pain that would be created if you die before you can have that experience. Imagine your spouse as he or she ages alone and uncared for, and ask yourself if inflicting this pain is worth the pleasure of a cigarette. Associate the behavior with the pain. Every time you pick up a cigarette, force yourself to think of the different levels of pain that cigarette will cause. What character failure do you demonstrate if you are unable to control your behavior? Why is your short-term pleasure more important than the pain you will cause the people around you?

Next, associate pleasure with your behavior change. In the last example, cigarettes become the pain of loss and abandoning your family, but the action of not smoking represents a decision to have pleasure in your life. It is an empowering feeling. You are creating an action or behavior to give yourself long-term pleasure and fulfillment. The short-term pain can be difficult, but once you connect the behavior change with your future pleasure, you can start to welcome the pain because it brings you a step closer to fulfillment and pleasure. Every day of pain when you stop smoking is a day closer to losing the craving. Every morning of pain to wake up early puts you one step closer to achieving your goals.

If you acknowledge the source of your motivations,

controlling your behavior becomes easier. Ultimately, when you add pain and pleasure through association, you are more likely to be successful in creating the behaviors you expect from yourself. The decision is yours.

> *Make the most of yourself, for that is all there is to you.*
>
> **—RALPH WALDO EMERSON**

Secret #4: Dream Less

> *Sleep.*
> *Those little slices of death.*
> *How I loathe them.*
>
> **—EDGAR ALLAN POE**

"Dream less" seems like an odd statement. This entire book begs you to dream more and to take actions to fulfill your dreams in the face of the restrictions of "the real world." Don't worry, I'm not going to get practical, but I want to discuss the difference between dreams and action.

As I have mentioned before, I used to be an avid sleeper. I loved to sleep, and I would sneak a nap whenever I could. It felt so good to sleep, and I loved having dreams. Then I heard some great words of wisdom that have affected my life dramatically: "If you love to sleep, it probably means that you don't care much for your life."

That one statement hit me hard because there is so much truth in it. If you doubt it, think of this. How hard is it to get out of bed at 6 A.M. to take out the garbage? How hard is it to wake up on Christmas morning? Get the picture? When we are excited about something in our lives, we pop out of bed in the morning and we are ready to rock-

and-roll. If we face just a regular, monotonous day, then the snooze button gets a workout.

I used to love sleeping in because I had great dreams. I was buzzing around the world, meeting famous people, and living quite a life. When I woke up, I had to take the dog out, get the newspaper, and go to work. Which option would you choose?

The problem is I could never remember my dreams with any detail, but my daily life was constantly in the front of my mind. I realized I didn't care much for my life, but my life was not improving because I was sleeping all the time! I decided to give up the dreams in the morning snooze sessions and instead wake up and start working on my life. Every day I try to make my life something I want to wake up for.

Go back to the Christmas example. When I was growing up, I thought of Christmas Eve as an obstacle standing between me and the good stuff. When I went to bed that night, I couldn't wait for the morning to come so I could jump out of bed and wake up my parents. And I was up *early*. Obviously, every day of your life is not going to be Christmas Day, but imagine if you were even half that excited about your routine day.

The trick is to convince yourself that every day can be one of two things: an exciting day worth waking up early for or a step toward an overall improvement in your life. Create the life that will excite you and motivate you to get out of bed and live. Make sleep seem like an inconvenience, not a goal. Your life should be more exciting than the dreams you have when you sleep. If it is not, wake up and start working on it!

If a man wakes up famous he hasn't been sleeping.
—WES IZZARD

A man's greatest strength develops at the point where he overcomes his greatest weakness.

—ELMER LETTERMAN

It is very hard to take full responsibility for your actions and the outcomes your actions produce. Whatever the circumstance, there is always a convenient scapegoat that you can use to dodge responsibility. If you get bad grades, it's the teacher. If you hate your job, it's your boss. If you are unhappy, it's the circumstances that surround you—circumstances that are, of course, out of your control.

It is easy to *say* we should take personal responsibility for our actions, but it is a much easier *action* to assign blame to other people. Doing so avoids being self-critical, which can be a painful, ego-deflating process. When we push off the blame to someone else, we conveniently avoid any unnecessary pain. I want to show you that personal responsibility does not have to be a burden but actually creates a strong base for achievement. An ethic of personal responsibility takes ownership of your mistakes and failure but ultimately allows you to own your life.

Sometimes it is hard to take responsibility because there truly are external factors that affect the events in your life. You might be from a very impoverished neighborhood with terrible schools, or you might have some kind of physical condition that makes success in some areas harder for you than for others. Faced with incredible obstacles, people react in different ways. Some use adversity as a crutch for why they cannot be successful. Others simply work harder for success because they refuse to let their environment and condition dictate their lives.

I have met some incredible people in my life who have

decided not to bow down to circumstance. It helps me to remember these incredible people when I face personal obstacles. For example, when I struggled with grades in school and wanted to blame my teachers, I thought of my friend who put herself through college while working a night job and being an incredible single mother. When I get tired physically, I think of the people who come to the gym in a wheelchair and work out twice as hard. When I feel low about someone I know having success only because his parents helped him, I think of the great stories of people who have risen from incredibly humble beginnings through their dedication and hard work.

It is easy to blame others, but stories like these help to remind us that we have the power to make things happen or not. Even if you have a horrible teacher, you can make yourself learn. Some of the greatest minds in history taught themselves out of books. Some of the greatest leaders started as simply another face in the crowd.

To paraphrase Mark Twain, "Every person is given twenty-four hours a day. Some people just seem to accomplish more in that time than others." Whatever odds you are up against, there is an important fact to keep in mind: Someone before you has faced larger odds and bigger obstacles, but she made it. She persevered and defeated the odds. Knowing that, face down every obstacle with the knowledge that you can choose to overcome it. It has been done before, and there is no reason why you cannot do it again.

If we can agree on the following premise, then we agree that only you can be responsible for your success: If it has been done, it can be done.

Don't sell yourself short and blame your circumstances or other people. When you assign blame, you say that you are not as strong as the people who have beaten the odds. If you live in a high crime neighborhood where survival is a full-time occupation, think of the people who made it. If you face racism and bigotry, look at the people who have overcome those obstacles. If you have a physical disability, look at the people who still compete in sports and lead incredible lives.

Surprisingly, when you accept complete responsibility for your life, an incredible burden is lifted. The term "burden of responsibility" makes it sound as if you have to carry the weight of the world on your shoulders. The weight is actually lighter than you might think. The true weight comes whenever you blame someone or something for your failures because you are saying that the direction of your life is out of your hands, beyond your control. What a statement!

Imagine if I came to you with this option: I agree to relieve you of all personal responsibility for your happiness and success. In exchange, you agree not to choose the direction in your life and to allow your limits to be dictated to you. I will be the scapegoat for all your shortcomings; in return, your choices will be confined by the limits I place on you.

What a horrible existence! But that is exactly what you say when you blame your failures on anything other than yourself or give up on a dream because of some obstacle. We are too quick to give up on our dreams because "that is a male-dominated field," "I need to know someone in the industry," or "I had terrible teachers and my GPA is too low." When you acknowledge a barrier and allow it to defeat you, you acknowledge the barrier's power over you. The crazy thing is that people choose to accept this condition by acknowledging limitations.

An obstacle that you accept and do not fight against is an excuse. It is a way to shift responsibility away from your obligation to overcome the barrier. Condition yourself to always accept responsibility and look at every obstacle as a test on how much control you want in your life.

To take responsibility is to take control. When you take control, your life will never be confined by your circumstances or by the prejudices of those around you. This level of control happens only because you choose to make it happen. When obstacles impede your progress, you accept the responsibility to find a way around them. Maybe the path will be easier for someone else, someone with family connections or more natural ability. Who cares? You have your work to do and an obligation to yourself to persevere and realize your potential.

Personal responsibility is a statement that your life is controlled by the actions of one person: you. When you assign blame, you give power to whomever or whatever you blame. Be in charge of your life. Choose not to live as a reaction to the people and circumstances around you. Choose to take responsibility.

> *All of the darkness of the world cannot put out the light of one small candle.*
> —ANONYMOUS

Secret #6: Try Like a Baby

> *It's not whether you get knocked down, it's whether you get back up.*
> —VINCE LOMBARDI

Are you ready for the best advice you will ever get?

Late one night, I was driving through Arizona on my way to New Mexico and I was listening to an Anthony Robbins tape that a friend had given me. I have mentioned before that he is one of the few motivation coaches I recommend to people. Rather than a bunch of "rah-rah," or New Age psychobabble found in most books in this genre, Robbins has a straightforward, concrete approach that provides a powerful framework for achievement. That night he used an analogy that made a lot of sense. In talking about perseverance and the ability to bounce back from failures, he asked a simple question: "How many times would you let a baby fail at walking before you stopped it from trying any more?" That got me thinking. By the time I reached New Mexico, I couldn't wait to write this section and share this advice with you.

Approach every difficult goal that you set for yourself like a baby learning to walk.

If you have ever watched a baby trying to take his first steps, it looks painful. It's a lot of falling down, crying, bruises, wobbly legs, and frustration. If you watch the early attempts, it seems impossible that the baby will ever walk.

So, as Anthony Robbins asks, how many attempts to walk would you give a baby before you stopped him from trying? How many failures would it take before you decided that a perfectly healthy baby would never walk? How many times would he need to fall down until you decided that he should just crawl for the rest of his life?

You can look at a baby and know that no matter how many tries it takes, eventually he will learn how to walk. It makes perfect sense when we talk about a baby, but what about when it comes to your life? How many times are you willing to fail at your goals before you give up? If you started with the assumption that eventually you would make it, would you ever give up? If you give up too soon, are you willing to go through life as a "crawler"?

Think about that for a second. Imagine that you were fully developed intellectually when you learned to walk. After failing to walk a thousand times, you allow your frustration to overcome you and you decide that you will never be able to walk. You stop trying. You can see that other people are able to walk and that they had just as much trouble as you, but "they're just lucky," because they made it. Imagine your life as a "crawler." Think of the limitations you have placed on yourself and the experiences that you have thrown away. A "crawler" will never run a race, hike through the mountains, or jump in excitement. You gave up on a difficult task and your life changed completely because of it.

Obviously, I draw a parallel from this to the decisions you make in your career and your life. Each time you fail at something, you have the power to decide whether you call the failure a defeat or another step toward success. Think of the dreams and goals you want to achieve and imagine that there are two possible worlds: one where you achieve your dreams and one where you lower your expectations to meet "reality." Basically, imagine one world where you crawl and one where you can run.

Do you feel the tragedy in that? To have the ability for greatness, but to stop short simply because of frustration. All you need is the concrete belief that you will reach your goal. You will walk eventually. It's just a matter of when.

A few more "baby" points:

■ **Success follows success.** After a few days of wobbly steps, confidence grows and you try to walk more often. With enough practice, you can literally walk in your sleep. If you want to be brilliant at something, do it over and over again. The best professional athletes are those who practice and train the most.

- **Success allows greater success.** As confidence grows, a simple walk becomes a run, a dance, or a jump. Be great at whatever you do because this gives you the confidence to stretch yourself in new ways and create more success.

- **Rewards encourage success.** A baby walks to get something. She walks to her parents, walks to food, or walks to satisfy a curiosity. What reward drives you? Make the reward so strong that you are driven to your success.

- **Learn from people who have experience.** It helps when you are a baby to be surrounded by people who already know how to walk. It shows you that it is possible, and you have good role models to follow. Surround yourself with people who are successful in their lives for these same reasons.

> *Nobody can make you feel inferior without your consent.*
> —ELEANOR ROOSEVELT

Secret #7: Practice Vivid Intensity

> *The unexamined life is not worth living.*
> —SOCRATES

Life is short and far too important to spend casually. Take advantage of the great opportunity you have to capture all of the adventure that life presents. There is a saying that youth is wasted on the young, because it is not until later that you appreciate the special circumstances of this age. You are young, full of energy, and faced with more options than you can start to imagine. With limited commitments and obligations, you are free. What are you doing with your opportunity?

We all have dual personalities. On one side, we are creatures of habit. We fall into a routine and stay there until something forces a change. When we go somewhere new, we say, "Give me few days to get into the swing of things," which is code for "Let me find a monotonous routine so I can feel comfortable."

On the other hand, we are escapists who dream about adventure and excitement. We go to the movies and watch television to see people live the lives we want. We see exotic locations, live incredible romances, and go on wild adventures. All this while we lounge on the couch with a bag of chips and a soda.

Imagine if you used just half of your "escape time" to ensure that you lived an exciting life, instead of watching one. Again, life is short, and in the end, all we have are our experiences and the impact we made on the people around us. Of course, there is the daily grind—laundry, walking the dog, washing dishes—but don't force yourself into a continual grind.

The next time you choose to watch TV or sleep instead of living, ask yourself this question: Five years from now, will I remember this day?

This is a powerful question. If you do not remember the day, and no one around you does either, what purpose did it serve? I'm not saying that you have to spend every day fighting crime or working for a cure for cancer, but live to create memories that you will remember. A day of leisure can be a memorable day, if you make it so. It's hard to remember what happened on a sitcom.

Find the things in life that drive your imagination, stretch your limits, and create a positive influence on your environment. Create many memories for yourself that you will actually remember. Live life with intensity, with full vividness. A great bumper sticker says, "Turn off TV. Turn on life." Escape into a better life for yourself. Practice vivid intensity.

> **The moment of victory is much too short to live for that and nothing else.**
> —MARTINA NAVRATILOVA

Secret #8: Knowledge is not Power

> **What counts is not the size of the dog in the fight, but the size of the fight in the dog.**
> —DWIGHT D. EISENHOWER

You probably know something you could do right now to improve your life. You could take actions today to accomplish something you "have been meaning to do" for a long time. Whether it is to finally send your résumé to a company you want to work for, to call an executive for an informational interview, or even to ask someone you've had a crush on for a date, you know there are things you could do right now to make a change in your life.

You know the things you should or could do to make a positive impact on your life, but knowing is never enough. There is no power in knowledge. True power is found only in action.

It is amazing that we have the power to change our

lives immediately and absolutely with a single action. You could this second decide to quit your job, move to a cabin in the woods, and try to write the great American novel. The knowledge that you want to do that or that you plan to quit your job does not create any change in your life. Your knowledge is internal, but the actions you take create external reactions that can change your life dramatically.

I always wonder if people think about their dreams as much as I do about mine. I love talking to my wife about the future we want together and for our family. It's fun to dream about things we want to do and see together in our lives and how we want to achieve them. I remember doing the same thing before I graduated from college, always wondering and imagining what I could create with my life.

I believe (I hope) that people carry incredible aspirations with them throughout their lives. We humans are creative and romantic creatures, especially in our youth, when nothing is out of reach and everything is not only possible but probable. The greatest tragedy of human existence is that most dreams are beaten back by the coarseness of reality. Adult life can be a rough sandpaper that wears down the sharp clarity of youth. Early visions of achievement and grandeur are pushed down and beaten back by newly accepted definitions of "reasonable," and "practical." The everything-is-possible mentality of youth is replaced by the it's-not-that-easy mentality of maturity.

When we are young, it seems completely logical to quit a job you hate and take a year off to travel the world, work for world peace, live in poverty and write a book, or start a new business on a shoestring and a prayer. As we get older, these types of options seem more and more unreasonable. Think about that. Subjected to reason, sudden change from a state where we are unhappy to a state where we are happy seems like a bad idea because of the risk of failure.

The pressures of society to be a "producer" and to fit into a nice box with a job title makes sudden and dramatic change wrong. People who quit a job or school to pursue a dream are thought of as flaky. Their friends sit back and think to themselves, *I wonder what happened to him.*

Try this exercise. Imagine you are having dinner with a group of friends. Someone tells the story about Dave, a guy that you've met once or twice through mutual friends. Dave quit his job last week at a prestigious stock brokerage and enrolled in a culinary school to become a chef. What's your reaction to the story? Is it disdain: "That guy just couldn't hack it in the big leagues"? Or sympathy: "Wow, he had a great career going"? Or respect: "That guy has guts to do what he wants"? Your reaction will tell you a lot about your attitude about change and pursuing your dreams.

The ability to create sudden and dramatic change in our lives is an incredible power. The only thing more amazing about this ability is our unwillingness to use it. I love being accused of having a naïve view of the world because of my faith in achievement and the limitless capacity of the human spirit. I think the naïve ones are those who bury their heads in the sand, lost in a desert of mediocrity, and feel they have reached their capacity for greatness.

Look at the great figures of history. Doesn't it seem impossible that single individuals would be remembered by the world hundreds, even thousands of years after they died? How could they have been so different that they stand out among the billions of humans who have existed? What was so different about these people that makes them different from you? If anything, look at the amazing advantages you have in comparison to those people. The advances in technology, education, and health alone make your life an amazing opportunity compared to what past generations have encountered. Knowledge is more available now than at any other point in the history of humankind, but still only those individuals with the courage and brashness to act will achieve greatness. Power arises from action: the power to create, the power to revolt, the power to change, the power to transform. It all stems from action.

I'm not saying you need to fly off to the Amazon to explore the rain forest or start a political revolution, but I want to challenge you to explore the limits of your own environment. Make a decision to act. Create actions that reflect your ethics and your dedication to fulfilling your capacity. Too many people accept mediocrity because they fear the actions necessary to pursue their goals. Decide not to be one of those people. Do not be afraid to fail miserably. Every effort toward your dreams is a success, regardless of the outcome. The only true misery in life is regret for a lack of action. Make a list of actions you have postponed due to fear of change. Procrastination is simply a form of fear: fear of failure, fear of success, fear of rejection. Use your potential for action to create and impact the world around you. Don't wait. Act now and always.

> *One man with courage makes a majority.*
> —ANDREW JACKSON

Secret #9: The Importance of the Big "O"

> *And as we let our light shine we unconsciously give other people permission to do the same. As we are liberated from our fear, our presence automatically liberates others.*
> —NELSON MANDELA

A central theme throughout *No Parachute Required* is control: control over decisions, control over actions, and control over eventual outcomes. We are all responsible for the life we create for ourselves and for what we give back to the world around us as we move through it. We face choices every day, and our reaction to these choices determines the impact our passage through time creates. Our minds allow us to be instantly creative or destructive, positive or negative, wonderful or terrible.

You walk down a sidewalk and see a homeless person begging for money. As you pass by, you dig into your pockets and give him the change you find there. As you pass by, you laugh at him and shove him off the road. As you pass by, you stop to talk and convince him to find help at a shelter nearby and promise to stop by tomorrow to see how he's doing. As you pass by, you look at him across the street because you crossed over to avoid the encounter.

These scenarios show the best and worst of us. We are all capable of each reaction, and each reaction is a decision about how we view and interact with the world.

> *In the long run, the pessimist may be proved to be right, but the optimist has a better time on the trip.*
> **—DANIEL REARDON**

Optimism

I remember a conversation from many years ago with a friend of mine. It's one of those strange, unlikely memories that insists on staying with me, improbably surviving through the years when more important events should have replaced it. My friend Sharon was the classic overachiever type—valedictorian, athlete, and so on—who attended Pepperdine University while I was at the University of California at Santa Barbara. It was during a late-night car ride between these schools that the conversation turned strangely philosophical.

Sharon was talking about how she couldn't do everything she did without a strong religious background to act as her support system. She couldn't understand how I, who was very nonreligious at the time, could sustain myself without the comfort of a faith structure. I replied that my support was a faith in the basic goodness of people, the idea that people want to improve, they want to help, and they want to make the world better.

She could barely contain herself. "Oh my God, you are so naïve" was her not-too-subtle reply. She went on to describe her own view of people, her voice and body language betraying the hurt behind her words. "People are back-stabbers, willing to step over you to reach their own goals, eager to see you fall so that they can stand taller. They are purely self-motivated, and you have to be the same way just to stay even with them."

Maybe this conversation stays with me because I remember feeling so profoundly sad for her. As she described her views, all I saw was the cage holding in the potential she had to appreciate the best in people and to share in the finest aspect of our humanity. It's the old saying, "Look for the worst in people and you will find it. Look for the best in people and you will find it. Your prejudices will not disappoint you."

There is a fundamental truth in that. We can find whatever we look for in people's behavior. That being the case, why not look for the best? Why not expect and perceive the best intentions in behavior? Why not assume people are good and start there? Why not be prejudiced *for* people instead of being prejudiced against them?

Optimism does not have to be naïve. It is not being Voltaire's Pangloss and looking through rose-colored glasses, writing every disaster off as a great adventure. Optimism can simply be giving each person and situation the benefit of the doubt. Optimism is confidence in your ability to impact any situation to create a positive result. Finding the best in people is a demanding hobby, but it can fill you with energy. The opposite can drag you downward, sap your strength of purpose, and tear away at your capacities. Decide what prejudice you will use to view the world. You will find that the more good you look for, the more you will find, both in others and in yourself. It sure beats being angry at the world. By the way, if you see my friend Sharon, let her know.

> **Your prejudices will never disappoint you. Anything you look for in humanity, you will find.**

Secret #10: Get Lucky

> **It's hard to detect good luck—it looks so much like something you've earned.**
> —FRED CLARK

One of my hobbies is to collect information from very successful people to determine what made them a success. I use autobiographies, secondhand accounts, and personal interviews to try to get down to the elemental ingredients for success. One of my favorite conversations was with my own grandfather, a retired two-star general and World War II veteran.

General May had a successful military career and rose through the ranks by placing first or second in every officer training class he attended. He spent his career also trying to learn how successful men designed their lives and carried themselves. His exposure to successful individuals was broader than my own, as he was able to speak with major military leaders, governors, and several U.S. presidents.

I sat down with him as I entered my own prelife crisis and asked him for advice. I wanted to know what made success. What were the secrets he had learned through those years of development and exposure to major personalities? He was quiet for a while, eyes squinting slightly as he formulated his answer. I waited for what I knew would be life-changing advice.

"Every person I know who was truly successful, all possessed the same fundamental quality."

Now I'm dying. What is this one quality? What is the secret?

"Every person who is successful is that way because they are extremely lucky."

Lucky! This is the great advice I get to steer me on my future! What a rip-off!

"But, you have to define luck in a very specific way. Luck is when opportunity meets preparation. Luck = Opportunity + Preparation."

If we look at this as a mathematical equation, there are two constants and one variable. Luck, which can also be termed "the result" or "success," is a constant because we determine how it is defined. Everyone perceives success in different ways. If you get a big promotion at work, one of your friends might congratulate you, while the other sympathizes with you because you will now have more responsibility and less free time.

Opportunity is also a constant. I often get an argument on this point because there is privilege in the world and not all opportunity is equal. However, I have met people from extremely privileged backgrounds who have done nothing with their lives, and I have met people who have risen from abject poverty to accomplish amazing tasks. Is it more difficult to rise from poverty than to slide into the family business? Absolutely. But opportunity exists, and it can be captured.

That leaves only one variable: preparation. People can define success, and opportunity exists for everyone, but preparation is usually where the equation breaks down. What are you willing to do so that you can take advantage of opportunity and create the luck you want?

For example, I interview people all the time who want to go into international business. This is an exciting and high-growth field with incredible opportunity. I ask them what languages they are willing to learn to be successes in this field. Nine times out of ten, candidates say they do not like languages and are going to work with English-speaking countries. Obviously, someone who is not willing to prepare for a career in international business by learning a language will not be very "lucky" when the time comes to enter the job market.

Preparation never stops because:

■   **You can always improve.** The greatest athletes always practice the most. They are the first on the field and always work hard to improve.

■ **Opportunity is unpredictable.** You never know when new options will present themselves. The key is to be prepared to take advantage of any opportunity that serves as a vehicle for your skills. Suppose you meet someone who owns a business who has to hire a new director of sales and they have to hire someone right away. If you have created a strong background built on concrete results, you just got "lucky."

Pursue luck/success through preparation. If the preparation is difficult, then you have to gauge your level of commitment to your goals. Decide how serious you are about your goals and make a decision either to pursue them or to change them.

It is important to understand that it is OK to change your goals. In fact, I was one of the people who wanted to be in international business until I took my first college-level foreign language class. I decided that I was not passionate enough about the field to learn the languages, so I changed direction. However, call your decision for what it is and change your focus to a new goal. Do not continue toward your goal and ignore the fact that your commitment to it is not strong enough to make you prepare. Move to a new direction that does excite you and prepare strongly for that future.

Luck is when opportunity meets preparation. Good luck.

Secret #11: Be Uncomfortable

You must do the thing you think you cannot do.

—ELEANOR ROOSEVELT

It is human nature to acclimate to the environment. We adapt quickly to change, but we prefer the status quo because it is comfortable and known. People love to complain about their circumstances—their jobs, their bosses; their relationships—but they seldom do much to change. Regardless of how much you like or dislike something, the fact that you are used to it places it in your comfort zone. The comfort zone includes everything that you are used to, anything that you can do without thinking twice about it, anything that you know you can count on.

A comfort zone can be a good thing. Your family and friends are part of your comfort zone. Possibly your religious faith is in your comfort zone. These are the things that give us a foundation and support throughout our lives. However, sometimes too much comfort can derail your goals for your future.

Stress is inherent whenever you try something new. Stress comes from the unknown, and change usually involves the unknown. Therefore, change tends to bring stress while the status quo, even if it is not what you want, is comfortable. For example, have you ever stayed in a relationship longer than you knew you should? Most people have at some point in their lives. They are not happy with the person they are with, but the unknown of being alone or trying to find someone else keeps them in the relationship.

You will have to face very difficult choices throughout your life. When these decisions come up, it is always easiest to choose the path that is most comfortable; that is the decision that produces the least stress and uncertainty. But do you think that staying in your comfort zone will lead you to the achievement you want?

The challenge is to be conscious of your comfort zone

and actively pursue outrageous goals in spite of it. This is difficult to do. If you maintain the status quo in your life, you will not have stress, you won't be nervous about tackling something new, you will have less fear of failure. However, accomplishment begins with an attempt. If you never attempt the things you fear, they will hold you and your ambition captive.

Complacency due to comfort will slow you down and allow your aspirations to move farther and farther away. Choose action over comfort and challenge yourself to do what you fear. It's the only way to truly find out what you can accomplish.

If you never attempt the things you fear, they will hold you and your ambition captive.

Secret #12: Foolproof Stress Reduction

If you want to test your memory, try to remember what you were worrying about one year ago today.

—E. JOSEPH COSSMAN

Stress has become a fixture in the working world. All people are stressed for what they feel are very good reasons, and they carry that stress with them like so much baggage. Life doesn't need to be this way.

The starting point to control the stress in your life is to understand its source. Doing this is the easy part, because there is only one source: the unknown. If you absolutely know something for a fact, you don't stress about it. Your boss calls you in for an unscheduled meeting—stress. Someone tells you the meeting is about a promotion—no stress. Someone tells you the meeting is about your poor performance—stress, not due to the meeting but because of the uncertainty of the results of the meeting.

I know people who will stress for days because they have a big unknown. They get a speeding ticket and agonize for days whether they are going to lose their license or not. They work through every possible scenario of how their life will change if they lose their license. Finally, after days of stress, they call the courthouse and their license is fine. No more stress, but what a waste of energy!

Another manifestation of the unknown is stress from "too many things going on." Sometimes the world seems too crazy to handle, and everything is spiraling out of control. Small issues can become enormous when they are pushed into such a cluttered background. You find yourself feeling an overwhelming amount of stress, but it is hard to put your finger on its cause. Here are a few tactics you can use for stress control.

■ **Write down what is stressing you.** Have you ever told someone your "big" problem and halfway through the story you started to feel petty because the problem sounded dumb? Things we stress about often are dumb, but they get built up in our minds to be bigger than they actually are. Write down your problems in language as simple as possible. You may find yourself laughing at them.

■ **Write down a question whose answer would alleviate the stress.** Once you write down your problems, analyze the root issues and determine what unknown fact is stressing you out. If you are concerned about your future with your company, why not ask your boss that question specifically. If you are stressed about someone in the office whom you think has a problem with you, simply ask him. Once you know the answer, then you can decide on an action.

- **Weigh the pros and cons.** Every decision has give and take. Write down all of the pros and cons to every decision. Doing so will help you to organize your thoughts and make a clear decision.

- **Prioritize your stress.** Think of the most stressful week you had in a past job or in school. Pretty bad, right? Now imagine something truly important happened during that week—your parent was diagnosed with a major illness, a sibling was in a car accident, whatever. Do you think that any of the things you stressed about in school or in work would have even entered your mind if you were faced with a true crisis?

I'm not telling you to be apathetic regarding your life and not care when small things go badly, but don't let the small things paralyze you and keep you from enjoying life. Our time is way too short to lose sleep because someone gave us a dirty look or because we dent the car. Big deal. You will not remember these things years from now, so why worry about them today?

Stress will always be part of your life. It's a sign that you care about what happens to yourself and those around you. It is easy to allow these concerns to fester in our minds and poison our outlook on all of the good in our lives. One small issue blown out of proportion can impact everything you do. I mean, don't you find it hard to appreciate a sunset when you are mad at the world? Use stress to wake up your instincts for action and apply yourself to solve problems and uncover the unknown. You'll be much more easygoing, and you'll enjoy more sunsets.

Sixteen:
The End of the Beginning

Go confidently in the direction of your dreams.
—HENRY DAVID THOREAU

I hope that you have enjoyed *No Parachute Required* and that you have found a few useful insights and tools along the way. When I sat down to write this book, I started by typing a list of the central points and themes that I wanted my readers to walk away with. It was a very basic list at first, but it evolved as I wrote the main text and new ideas and concepts crept into the book. I started to remember the complex emotions that make up the prelife crisis, the excitement of entering the real world, the frustrations of choosing a path, the anxiety of making the wrong choices.

The list also changed because I got older. It sounds strange, but two years in your mid-twenties can bring about a lot of changes. When I started the book, I was single; now I'm married. When I started the book, I ran a small $2 million business in two states; now I run a $10 million business in sixteen states. The last two years of working on this book and asking people to help me understand their experiences and emotions has led to some insights that I did not possess when I started. Here is the list of insights in its final form and serves as my parting thoughts for you.

The Last Word

Throughout the entire process, I kept adding and deleting from my list of what my philosophical goals were for this book. Here is its final form.

- You will spend half of your waking hours on your career, so do the hard work necessary to make smart career choices. Life's too precious to waste time doing something you are ambivalent about.

- You only go around once, so make the term "my life's work" mean something.

- You will be most successful at what you are most passionate about. Use passion in all your career decisions.

- Nothing is more tragic than regret. Attempt all of your dreams and prioritize your life. No one on her deathbed says, "I wish I had spent more time at the office."

- Character traits are habit forming, so tackle every part of your life with vivid intensity.

- Remember that success is when opportunity meets preparation. The opportunities will come, so prepare well.

- The only way to impress people is to be an impressive person. Create a track record of success and carefully guard your reputation.

- Other people have accomplished what you want to do and had more against them than you. If they can do it, so can you.

- Success is a journey, not a destination.

While the last bullet point may be a cliché, it contains a fundamental truth about life that can't be disregarded. The point of this book is not for you to get a great job and then say, "Phew, I made it." Nor is it for you to be the youngest person in the company to get a corner office and think "All right, now I've made it."

"Success is a journey, not a destination" means that you can't expect there to be a mythical finish line in your career or personal life where everything is perfect. And that's not a bad thing. Think about it. How incredibly boring would life be if we did have a finish line in our lives and we reached a point where we no longer felt the need to strive to improve ourselves or the world around us? The key is not to worry so much about a destination but to enjoy the journey along the way. I believe the preceding points are some pretty decent guidelines of how to do just that.

This chapter is titled "The End of the Beginning." This book, the advice in it, the exercises for you to uncover your direction in life, the tools designed to open the right doors for you—all are just the beginning of your journey. As you finish this book, you have completed the first small step toward your future. Knowing what you should do and actually doing it are very different things. This book is the map for the first few miles on a journey that is thousands of miles long. But beginnings are important because they often determine what the end will look like. Let me use one last analogy.

Imagine that you are an airline pilot flying directly from Los Angeles to London. You're not that concerned about reaching London, but you are excited by all the things you would be able to see if you stayed on course. You start your journey, but your navigation equipment is off by one degree. If you maintained this slightly wrong heading, you would not only miss London, you'd miss England entirely. More important, you would be so off course that you would not see and experience all the things you wanted to see on the journey.

Life is a little like flying that airplane. You now have the tools to take off and start your journey, but slight miscalculations and navigation errors can create long-term consequences. By the end of your journey, you might have missed out on the things you wanted to do and accomplish because you started out on the wrong course. From time to time your life will need some course corrections in order to head in the right direction. This is where most people miss great opportunities to create a happier, more fulfilling life. It's easy to get so caught up in the day to day that we forget to ask "Am I heading in the right direction? Is the path I'm on going to give me the experiences I wanted to have on this journey?" If so, great. If not, it's time to muster the courage to make a change.

I hope that you will hold on to this book in the years ahead and refer back to the exercises occasionally to see how you fare. Shakespeare said, "This above all: to thine own self be true." I implore you to follow that advice but to make certain that you continue to ask yourself the tough questions and to take the difficult actions when they are necessary. Life is short. Live it well.

My best wishes go with you.